DANNY BOYLE

LUST
FOR LIFE

DANNY BOYLE

LUST
FOR LIFE

MARK BROWNING

CHAPLIN BOOKS

First published in 2011 by Chaplin Books

Copyright © Mark Browning

ISBN 978-0-9565595-1-7

A CIP catalogue record for this book is available from The British Library.

Design by Helen Taylor

Printed in the UK by Ashford Colour Press

Chaplin Books
1 Eliza Place
Gosport PO12 4UN
Tel: 023 9252 9020
www.chaplinbooks.co.uk

Contents

· INTRODUCTION ·

'I want people to leave the cinema feeling that
something's been confirmed for them about life'

Danny Boyle[1]

The genesis for this book was the moment Danny Boyle came
bouncing, in his words 'in the manner of Tigger,' onto the stage to collect
his Oscar for Best Director in 2009. *Slumdog Millionaire* had been in
competition with David Fincher's *The Curious Case of Benjamin Button*
in a number of categories, and proceeded to win every single one. On
the one hand, Fincher's movie had a $150 million budget, state-of-the-
art special effects, and a cast headed by Brad Pitt and Cate Blanchett; on
the other, Boyle's movie had only $20 million behind it, no special effects
to speak of, dialogue that was partly in Hindi and a cast of minor actors
and non-professionals. In fact, before Fox Searchlight picked up the film
for a theatrical release, it was destined to go straight to DVD. Could
Fincher, a perfectionist famous for demanding extended re-shoots and
with a highly technical approach to filmmaking, have even been capable
of making *Slumdog Millionaire*? It would be hard to imagine a greater
juxtaposition of styles and it made me think about Boyle's career and
how he had reached that point.

Boyle was born on 20 October 1956 into a working-class family (his
mother a hairdresser and dinner lady; his father a farm labourer) and was
imbued with a strong work ethic from an early age, underlined by an all-
encompassing sense of Catholic sin and redemption. He had a place at a
seminary in Upholland in Wigan until persuaded by a priest, Father
Conway, that perhaps this was not his true vocation, and instead went to
Bangor University to study English and Drama.

His career began in the theatre, as an usher for the Joint Stock Theatre
Company, known for their cutting-edge productions, and eventually as a
director. In 1982 was appointed artistic director at the Royal Court
Theatre Upstairs, where he was responsible for a number of small-scale
productions including Howard Brenton's 'The Genius' and Edward Bond's
'Saved', the latter winning a *Time Out* award. In 1985, he graduated to the
main stage, directing several further successful projects, including 'The Last
Days of Don Juan' for the Royal Shakespeare Company.

---

1 Page 2009 p.3.

1

When he moved into television, he went first to the BBC in Northern Ireland to produce the powerful drama *Elephant* (dir. Alan Clarke 1989) about the sectarian killings, before moving back to the mainland to direct an historical drama about a religious sect, *Mr Wroe's Virgins* (1993), and two early episodes of *Inspector Morse*, one on Masonic ritual and one on rave culture. While his work on *Morse* shows little obvious cinematic flair, his direction of these episodes did help to create, in collaboration with actor John Thaw, one of Britain's best-loved TV detectives. It was this experience at the BBC that taught Boyle the basics of media production, working with modest budgets but within an organisation committed to high-quality drama and with a reputation for social realism.

Boyle began his filmmaking career in 1994 with *Shallow Grave*, the first of three films made with producer Andrew Macdonald and writer John Hodge (*Trainspotting* was to follow in 1996 and *A Life Less Ordinary* in 1997). The first two of these, produced in collaboration with Channel Four Films, helped revive the British film industry, although the portrayal of drug-taking in *Trainspotting* provoked criticism and Boyle became characterised as a director interested only in gritty, working-class pictures. *A Life Less Ordinary* was an attempt to break away from this and to connect more directly with an American market. This brought its own problems: Boyle found that larger budgets and crews entailed creative compromises, something that was also to affect the follow-up film, *The Beach*, released in 2000. Both films were met coolly by critics and neither met the commercial expectations of Twentieth Century-Fox, now Boyle's financial backer.

In 2001, Boyle took a step back from feature films, returning to the small screen to direct two small-scale, gritty dramas for the BBC: *Strumpet* and *Vacuuming Completely Nude in Paradise*. The break gave him the chance to re-group creatively and to experiment with lightweight digital cameras in collaboration with cinematographer Anthony Dod Mantle, an experience which directly contributed to the success of his next feature, the horror film *28 Days Later*. Released in 2002, and backed by Fox Searchlight, Twentieth Century's distribution arm dealing with more experimental and innovative filmmaking, it was a commercial and critical success. It also marked Boyle's ability to move between a variety of genres with equal success, a tendency continued with *Millions* in 2004 and *Sunshine* in 2007. *Millions* failed to find its audience on general release, partly due to its ambition and partly due to the sad fact that an intelligent children's film is something of a generic rarity. The science fiction of *Sunshine* was more successful but took a long time to bring to the screen – the creation of a complete fictional universe was an experience which Boyle found exhausting and probably not one which he would want to repeat any time soon.

Still with Fox Searchlight, Boyle teamed up with writer Simon Beaufoy, whose work he admired, particularly on *The Full Monty* (dir. Peter Cattaneo 1997), to create *Slumdog Millionaire* in 2008. Vikas Swarup's 2006 novel *Q&A* had been a bestseller and Boyle leapt at the challenge, intrigued not so much by a narrative based on a TV show as the idea of filming a Bollywood-style love story in India. The film was a huge success and led to eight Oscars in 2009, including Boyle as Best Director.

After much industry and media speculation, Boyle followed this up with *127 Hours* in 2010, based on the true story of Aron Ralston, a climber and thrill-seeker who was partly trapped under a boulder for several days in the Utah mountains, and who had to face the dilemma of dying a slow death or cutting off his own arm.

There is little existing critical literature about Boyle's work. Only one of his films to date, *Trainspotting*, has received individual book-length consideration. Martin Stollery (2001) and Murray Smith (2008) both write interestingly about the film, but their studies are fairly brief and do not use intertextuality as a critical tool. There is growing interest in Boyle himself, with two books of interviews published in 2011 (by Amy Raphael and Brent Dunham), but in a sense these act as something of a distraction from the raw material of the films themselves. Before this book, the only attempt to open out the field of studies into Boyle's work has been Edwin Page's *Ordinary Heroes: the Films of Danny Boyle* (2009). Page takes an auteurist position and looks at the films for evidence of what he identifies at the beginning as the director's favoured themes and stylistic devices. The difficulty with this approach is that it assumes these themes are present in all his films and are readily transparent to every viewer, whereas I would argue that meanings in any visual medium are by no means undisputed or universal. It is important to remember that Boyle is telling stories, not delivering themes, and that seeing characters as 'carriers' of messages can lead to reductionist assertions about 'the ultimate message' of a film, such as Page's contention that 'money does bring happiness' is the message of *Shallow Grave* and that *Slumdog Millionaire* is 'part of the university of life for all who watch it'.[2] Page also overlooks an opportunity for more insightful contextual analysis by trying to assign single meanings to particular stylistic devices, so that

2 Page 2009 p.29 and p.220.

voice-overs are categorised as being used to denote main characters, multiple screens to show more than one setting, and shots through glass and water to 'add texture'.[3]

Rather than seeking to impose a reading across all Boyle's work, this book looks at each film and considers what makes it effective, through a close analysis of style, narrative structure and performance. It views Boyle not as an auteur but as part of a collaborative team that consists of actors, writers and cinematographers with whom he has a close and trusting relationship. In watching Boyle's films, I was struck by their celebratory, life-affirming tone – the way he seems always to opt for the positive over the negative – and how he continues to make brave choices in terms of genre, narrative, character and directorial style, subverting the expectations of the industry and of the viewing public. This book is written for discerning film viewers who are familiar with, or curious about, Boyle's work: hopefully, it should make readers reconsider films they think they already know and seek out some they might have missed.

3   Page 2009 p.15.

CHAPTER ONE

· ADAPTATION ·

'It is written'

> one of four options from the opening
> gameshow-style credits in *Slumdog Millionaire*

Writing on Danny Boyle has routinely overlooked one important fact – that a number of his best-known films are adaptations. *Trainspotting*, *The Beach* and *Slumdog Millionaire* are all based on novels, and *127 Hours* is taken from Aron Ralston's book about his own experiences, *Between a Rock and a Hard Place* (2004). Even Boyle's early TV work including episodes for *Inspector Morse* (ITV 1990 and 1992) and the drama *Mr Wroe's Virgins* (BBC 1993) had a pre-existing literary framework. The Morse episodes 'Masonic Mysteries' and 'Cherubim and Seraphim' were scripted by Julian Mitchell but based on characters created in Colin Dexter's novels; and *Mr Wroe's Virgins* was scripted by Jane Rogers from her own book. As well as favouring established literary sources for his films, Boyle prefers to work – where possible – with the original writers who, by implication, know the material best. For his first four features Boyle worked with John Hodge, who produced original scripts for *Shallow Grave* and *A Life Less Ordinary* and adaptations of *Trainspotting* and *The Beach*, then with Alex Garland on *28 Days Later* and *Sunshine*, and more recently with Simon Beaufoy on *Slumdog Millionaire* and *127 Hours*. The film *Millions* was a one-off project with writer Frank Cottrell Boyce. Beaufoy, though not a novelist, had proven his ability, with films like *The Full Monty* (dir. Peter Cattaneo 1997), to craft involving, human-centred dramas with which audiences can connect.

Commentary in the mainstream media about film adaptation is often dominated by a strain of adaptation theory known as fidelity criticism, which – as Brian McFarlane explains – assumes that an author's intention is transparent and that the further a film version diverges from what the author intends, the weaker the adaptation.[1] This stance is underlined by studio marketing campaigns, which routinely emphasise a film's connection to a book or author in order to underline the closeness of

---

1 McFarlane 1996.

the bond between source and adaptation, thus implicitly stressing its cultural credentials.

The cultural dominance of the fidelity discourse means that films based on texts are routinely scrutinised for how 'faithful' they are to their literary source, with all the moral failings implicit in such a term when it is felt that the adaptation 'strays' from the original. This is perhaps felt even more powerfully when the source text is based on a real event. Some negative on-line reactions to material added by Boyle to *127 Hours*, such as the scene in which the three main characters drop into a large pool and which does not appear in Ralston's book, are exacerbated by the sense of departure from the 'truth'.

This chapter considers what happens when Boyle translates texts from novel to screen: what he keeps, what he changes, how and why. Discussion will include analysis of why some adaptations are more successful than others and why faithfulness to a source text does not necessarily produce a more effective film. The chapter will focus less on issues of fidelity than on the effect of changes and perhaps, more interestingly, where residual elements of a source text persist.

One possible way to break out of the critical cul-de-sac of adaptation theory, a relatively new area of debate and one which seems to be hamstrung by the use of similar, repetitive case-studies, is to look at the ideas of Gérard Genette. A literary theorist, Genette seeks to separate the process of adaptation into distinct but related elements. More recently, Robert Stam has refined Genette's work to talk of 'transtextuality', which Stam takes to mean 'all that which puts one in relation, whether manifest or secret, with other texts.'[2] This broader, more flexible approach helpfully starts to move analysis away from a straightforward one-to-one relationship with a written text (what a specific scene does with a specific extract of text). I have discussed the theory underlying Genette's ideas in my book on the films of David Cronenberg, but a basic summary would be helpful here.[3] Genette identifies five types of transtextuality: inter-textuality, paratext, metatextuality, architextuality and hypertextuality.

The first, 'interxtextuality,' refers to the ways in which other texts are directly referenced in 'quotation, plagiarism and illusion' both in the form of words and in aspects specific to particular media, such as a recognisable camera movement.[4] This use of referencing is of particular relevance to Boyle's use of multigeneric elements, discussed in Chapter Two.

---

2   Stam in Stam and Raengo (eds), 2005 p.27.
3   Browning 2007 pp.26-32.
4   Stam 2005 p.28.

Genette's second type, 'paratext', refers to 'the relation, within the totality of a literary work, between the text proper and its 'paratexts'-titles, prefaces, postfaces, epigraphs, dedications, illustrations…in short all the accessory messages and commentaries which surround the text.'[5] Actual text on screen is rare in Boyle's work, usually only appearing as self-aware, tongue-in-cheek references like the 'Yin and Yang' in *A Life Less Ordinary* or the delusional sequences in *The Beach*, during which the colours and movement on screen become redolent of a primitive video game with the words 'game over' appearing in flashing lettering. An exception to this is *Slumdog Millionaire*, where text-on-screen is an implicit part of the gameshow that is at the centre of the narrative: the words 'it is written' can legitimately appear in the opening sequence, thus linking the narrative to Swarup's novel, to a sense of destiny and to conventions of Bollywood love stories. Stam extends Genette's term beyond texts to include 'posters, trailers, reviews, interviews' and even DVD commentaries. Boyle's commentaries, compared to many of his contemporaries, are particularly energetic and enthusiastic and he seems happy to embrace this means of connecting with his audience.

That said, Boyle seems to avoid what he would see as 'unnecessary' comments about his work, unless specifically related to the promotion of a new film. He is quite content to be interviewed by the media and usually appears helpful, even charming, to journalists but does not court publicity beyond this. He has little presence as a celebrity in the mass media and his private life remains just that. The controversies surrounding the treatment of the location for *The Beach*, or the question of exploitation of the young cast in *Slumdog Millionaire*, both discussed in Chapter Five, were in neither case sought by him and indeed had been actively anticipated. His plans for the restoration of Maya Beach on the island of Kho Phi Phi Leh in Thailand and the setting up of trust funds that would activate when the *Slumdog Millionaire* child actors reached a certain age, were in place before the topic was picked up by the international press.

Genette's third and fourth categories further articulate a sense of relationship between texts. The third group, 'metatextuality', describes the process by which one text comments upon another critically, explicitly or implicitly. This can include 'readings or "critiques" of the source novel.'[6] Unlike filmmakers such as Wes Anderson, whose work is full of such interlinked references, each film of Boyle's is discrete, with

5   Stam 2005 p.28.
6   Stam 2005 p.28.

only occasional exceptions, such as the character of Hugo (Keith Allen), the enigmatic and short-lived flatmate in *Shallow Grave*, who also appears as a drug dealer in *Trainspotting*, thus underlining the fact that the money, discovered in *Shallow Grave* after Hugo is found dead, is likely to have come from drugs.

Genette's fourth group, 'architextuality', refers to the titles or subtitles of films. There are both issues of legality and marketing here. Boyle generally works with his writers throughout the filmmaking process rather than trying to remove them at the earliest opportunity and thus far legality has not been an issue: Boyle has been able to re-use titles wherever he thinks appropriate. There is a tension, however, between retaining close links with the source material and the importance of being able to 'sell' a title, leading to the novel *Q&A* being renamed *Slumdog Millionaire* for the film and *Between a Rock and a Hard Place* being re-titled, more succinctly and dramatically, *127 Hours*. The term 'Q & A' has connotations as a cliché of office/management-speak, a software program and even a talk-show in both America and Australia. It also lacks precise relevance to the story Boyle is trying to tell. In the UK 'trainspotting' is a well-known sign of cultural 'loserdom' but as a title, it proved mystifying to other markets, particularly the US, where subtitles were also needed to decipher unfamiliar Scottish accents.

Stam defines Genette's fifth term, 'hypertextuality,' as referring to 'the relation between one text…to an anterior text or "hypotext" which the former transforms, modifies, elaborates, or extends'.[7] For Genette, the hypertext 'speaks' to and of its hypotext, and would be unable to exist without it.[8] Hypertextuality then represents 'the ongoing whirl of intertexual reference and transformation, of texts generating other texts in an endless process of recycling, transformation, and transmutation, with no clear point of origin'.[9] Therefore one might speak not only of the link between a hypotext and its derivative hypertexts, but of relationships between different hypertexts. This has particular relevance for filmmakers closely associated with specific genres, such as John Carpenter's work in horror, or for a particular series or franchise, such as George Lucas' *Star Wars* films. As yet, Boyle has not produced a sequel (although he has an ongoing interest in a follow-up to *Trainspotting*) and all his feature films have been based on modern texts with contemporary settings, giving slightly less opportunity for hypertextual interweaving.

7   Stam 2005 p.31.
8   Genette 1997 p.5.
9   Stam 2005 p.31.

Lust For Life: Trainspotting (1996)

The adaptation of *Trainspotting*, written by John Hodge and based on Irvine Welsh's 1993 novel, is discussed further in Chapter Four on national identity, but some comment here is appropriate. The film's appeal is both related to and different from that of Welsh's narrative. Early editions of the novel, published by Norton, feature front-cover illustrations of a large grinning skull or two figures wearing skull masks. Boyle takes this narrative of death and decay, and turns it into a celebration of youthful energy against the background of heroin addiction that warps everything with which it comes into contact. Welsh's use of non-Standard English, and particularly the ranges of different dialect forms for different speakers, is an overt challenge to the literary mainstream. Boyle retains a flavour of this but the main narrator, Mark Renton (Ewan McGregor) is changed from a red-headed, spotty youth with a working-class Leith accent to a young man with boyish good looks and a more socially prestigious Edinburgh accent.

The film focuses primarily on Renton's point of view delivered via voice-over from the outset. Whereas novelists like James Kelman are not prepared to compromise on the regional nature of the language in their novels – Kelman has resisted having his works, including the Booker Prize winner *How Late It Was, How Late* (1994) adapted for the screen at all – many of Welsh's more unusual dialect terms and phonetically transcribed speech (as well as ubiquitous swearing) were not translated directly from novel to film. Even then, some dialogue had to be re-recorded at a slower pace for American audiences. The linguistic assault of the novel, in which there is no speech punctuation and most of Renton's internal monologue is delivered in the manner of random thoughts, is moderated into conventional on-screen dialogue, clearly attributed to specific speakers. In the novel, Welsh indicates the obsession of Sick Boy (Jonny Lee Miller) with Sean Connery by transcribing all his thoughts with the 's' sounds shifted to the distinctive 'sh' (as in 'Mish Moneypenny'). This is fully appropriated by Boyle, particularly in the scene in the park which features close-ups of Sick Boy's face, as he delivers his Connery impression while taking aim with an air-rifle at an annoying dog and its owner. Welsh, who himself has fostered something of the status of a counter-cultural icon, appears in the film as Mikey Forester, a dealer who provides Renton with suppositories. This suggests that the film has Welsh's tacit approval, although he had no input in the script.

The power of Boyle's film primarily derives from the pace and exuberance of its storytelling and from its driving soundtrack. The editing is ruthless in cutting between action which might be simultaneous but which also features little eddying sections, such as when we see both the myth and reality of the fight involving Francis Begbie (Robert Carlyle) in a sequence that mixes past and present at will. To reach a more mainstream, transatlantic audience, more transgressive elements were stripped out of the novel, such as the casual sexual violence of Begbie who openly and repeatedly punches his 'girlfriend'.[10] The film also subverts the politics of the novel so that Renton becomes less a left-wing rebel and more a model Thatcherite. Indeed, there is almost a political misanthropy at work in the novel, which Boyle and Hodge removed. For example, in the novel Renton describes tourists and shoppers on Princes Street as 'the twin curses of capitalism,'[11] a sentiment which does not appear in the film. In the novel, the first day of the Edinburgh Festival is significant, foregrounded as the point at which Renton begins (and abandons) his self-imposed detox programme, but in the film the Festival is merely made into a gag about the group's embracing of random violence and rejection of (stereotypical) loud Americans. The death of the baby, a truly horrific climactic scene in the film, occurs much earlier in the novel, underlining the lack of hope in Welsh's narrative. Moving the death of the baby to later in the film allows Boyle to build viewer engagement with Renton so that, by the time this horrific event does occur, Renton does not forfeit viewer empathy completely. The novel's passing references to Lou Reed and Iggy Pop, in the internal monologues of Renton and Tommy, are moved into the soundtrack of the film, most obviously in the sequence when Renton overdoses (Lou Reed's 'Perfect Day') and in the opening chase (Iggy Pop's 'Lust For Life').[12]

Not only is the narrative reconfigured around Renton, but episodes which occurred at some distance from one another in the novel (such as Spud and Renton's sexual experiences) are brought together so that the film can intercut between them. The novel's tangential episodes, especially those which showed Renton in a less sympathetic light – throwing stones at squirrels, having sex with a partner of a supposed friend, and fleecing the benefit system – are not present in the film. A scene of Renton with a psychiatrist, who attempts to coax him into considering why he is drawn to heroin, is also not used except for the 'Choose Life' speech, Renton's sarcastic list of the lifestyles and symbols of consumer capitalism,

---

10   Welsh 2004 p.58.
11   Welsh 2004 p.228.
12   Welsh 2004 p.8, 71.

all of which he rejects. This speech is expanded and delivered as the opening mantra for the film and all versions of the theatrical trailer. The choice not to use a scene with the psychiatrist may have been for reasons of length or to remove a slightly static situation, but without it the film does not really attempt to explain why Renton takes drugs, apart from the obvious pleasure it provides. Episodes in the novel featuring Renton in London frequenting seedy pornographic cinemas, and an unpleasant sexual incident in which he is the object of a predatory Italian, remained unused for similar reasons, as they would cast him in an unflattering light and make it hard for the audience to accept that his character is developing in a positive direction. Other scenes in the novel would have presented difficulties to visualise, such as the funeral of Matty, another minor character, where Welsh juxtaposes a number of different characters' thoughts. Contrasting voice-overs would be possible but, late in the narrative, this would just distract from our empathy with Renton, who Boyle and Hodge offer to us as a source of hope.

Even quite explicit scenes in the film, such as the glimpse of the amputated leg of drug-dealer Swanney, better known as Mother Superior (Peter Mullan), or its tasteless consequence as he sets up a sign on Market Street claiming to be a Falklands veteran, are dealt with much more swiftly and with less overtly repulsive imagery than in the novel.[13] Two of the novel's characters, Davie and Venters, are absent entirely from the film. In Davie, Welsh has a character close to that of Patrick Bateman in Brett Easton Ellis' novel *American Psycho* (1991), in the way he plays tricks on Venters who is dying from AIDS, telling lies and faking photographs about torturing and killing his son. It is a small but deeply disturbing part of the novel: Boyle modulates the savagery of Davie into Begbie's aggression, and the concept of Ventners as a victim of forces beyond his control is transposed into the sympathetic portrayal of Tommy, his tragic death a result of his falling prey to the addictive power of heroin just as Renton is getting himself clean.

The character of Diane (Kelly Macdonald), present in the novel only as a minor, peripheral figure, becomes in the film a conflation of several peripheral female characters but still feels rather contrived, appearing only for Renton's seduction and then being summarily expelled to the margins of the narrative once more. As a representative of an independent-minded, sexually liberated, hard-drinking 'ladette', she is not really given enough space (or dialogue) to breathe. Diane's appearance in her school uniform, and Renton's realisation that he has just slept with a schoolgirl, is a great visual joke but it also removes her from an active role in the adult narrative – there is nowhere for the story to go after that but an embarrassed walk back to school, if we are not to cast Renton in a much more morally dubious light. When Renton shares with her Sick Boy's plan to buy drugs cheaply in Scotland and then sell them for an inflated profit in London, her question ('so why have you told me about it?') sounds perfectly reasonable – at this point she is just a narrative device. The choice to place her alongside the male protagonists on the main film poster gives her a status that she does not really possess in the film and suggests an anxiety on the part of the studio that the film needs a more balanced gender approach.

Paul McGuigan's *The Acid House* (1998), the only other Irvine Welsh film adaptation to date, shows us how the film *Trainspotting* might have been. It retains a fractured structure (dramatising three separate short stories), but arguably with a consequent difficulty in reaching a large audience. Like *Trainspotting*, the first section, 'The Granton Star Cause', features grubby scenes of domestic unpleasantness and a football game with subtitles to identify characters, plus a surreal episode in which God appears as an old man at a bar and turns an immoral character into a fly. In the second section, 'The Soft Touch', Kevin McKidd, who plays Tommy in *Trainspotting*, appears as Johnny, a similarly passive character who is a victim of the manipulations of Alec (Tam Dean Burn), a poor man's Begbie. 'The Soft Touch' is, perhaps, truer to the gritty side of Welsh (who again appears himself in an opening cameo as a drug dealer) with broader accents, fewer sympathetic characters and a smaller, domestic setting, dominated by poverty rather than drugs. The final section, 'The Acid House', features an animatronic baby, a tab as a communion wafer and Ewen Bremner as Coco, in scenes that are shot with a distorting wide-angle lens to convey a drug trip (as Boyle does in his job-interview scene with Spud), so that even small movements of Bremner's head close to the camera are exaggerated for comic effect.

Paradise Lost: The Beach (2000)

Xan Brooks asserts that Alex Garland, author of the 1996 novel *The Beach*, upon which Boyle's film is based, 'writes the sort of zesty, dialogue-driven prose that converts easily into a screenplay format,' a view of the adaptation process that suggests that all you have to do is strip out the dialogue to convert a bestselling novel to a successful script.[14] It is true that there is a strongly cinematic dynamic to Garland's prose style: for example, when the protagonist Richard dreams, Garland writes, 'it was more like a movie. Or news footage, swaying on a hand-held camera'.[15] Standing in the dope-field on the island, Richard says 'I can only see our backs, and the image is slightly elevated, as if I'm standing further up the slope'.[16] However, such a strong visual element does not make the adaptation process a simple one and, indeed, Boyle said (on the DVD commentary) that he did not want the film to look like a literary adaptation.

Boyle's film changed Richard (Leonardo DiCaprio) from an Englishman into an American. At one level, this seems a small change, a nod to the commercial realities of a big-budget film requiring a recognisable star from the major source of finance. However, there is a strong sense that the film becomes a juggernaut for DiCaprio's star status which, post-*Titanic*, was immense. As Brooks puts it, 'DiCaprio spreads his towel all over *The Beach*' and 'Boyle's film has allowed itself to be rebranded as a Hollywood star vehicle'.[17] This change, and making the group of backpackers to whom he gives the map of the island also American, results in the finished film feeling like Harry Hook's 1990 remake of *Lord of the Flies*, an essentially English story remade with American actors. The shift does help to create greater historical resonance with the American experience in Vietnam: by placing an American at the centre of the story, effectively 'colonising' the narrative, we are invited to see the situation of the characters as a microcosm of the war itself, especially given Richard's fixation with *Apocalypse Now*. With the casting of DiCaprio, the film loses the distinctly English 'voice' of Richard, though Boyle's original choice of star was Ewan McGregor – a Scot. There is a compensatory move of Sal, the leader of the group, from American to English (played by Tilda Swinton), and the use of British actors in minor roles (such as Patterson Joseph as Keaty) but this introduces overtones of a British colonial past to the island community, something that is reinforced by scenes of them playing cricket on the beach. Arguably retaining Richard's character as English would also have pointed to colonial Britain, but the key here is that the thematic coherence of the film is compromised by the commercial pressures of casting.

On the DVD commentary, Boyle calls Richard 'an aggrandiser', but his status as a strong hero, a man of action, is not necessarily convincing. In the novel, it is Richard who is first to jump over the waterfall (later

14   Brooks in *Sight and Sound* 10:3, March 2000, p.40.
15   Garland 1996 p.61.
16   Garland 1996 p.82.
17   Brooks in *Sight and Sound* 10:3, March 2000, p.40.

revealed as the hidden gateway to the beach), though less out of bravery than out of frustration that they seem to have reached a dead-end on the trail. In the film, Boyle presents Étienne (Guillaume Canet) and Richard as bickering cowards, shamed by Françoise (Virginie Ledoyen) who pushes between them and jumps first. Also, whereas in the novel, Garland focuses on what is happening in the community when Richard is away on sentry-duty at the waterfall – observing the next group of Americans as they plan to cross – Boyle stays with Richard, so we can observe his increasingly fragile hold on reality. Richard's disappearance in the novel is a source of mystery and conjecture because Sal keeps the island community ignorant of what he is doing.

In terms of the adaptation process, characters or incidents that are troubling or likely to play out over time, are marginalised or omitted in the film. One key motivation for slimming the narrative down in this way is to appeal to a mass audience, who might expect DiCaprio to play a central heroic role rather than be just one part of an ensemble piece, such as Robert Altman's *Short Cuts* (1993). It was Boyle's original intention to include more coverage of peripheral characters, and a number of such scenes were filmed, but Boyle talks about such a film being 'indulgent' and the hypothetical three-hour film that might have resulted as 'dangerously exclusive'. The brutal nature of commercial cinema, which can barely afford digressions from the narrative thread, might well, for example, have cut the scene in which the maid mops down the wet floor in the hostel around a fizzing box of wires, but Boyle confesses he kept this in because he liked it. A number of minor characters – Yugoslavian girls, the so-called 'weather-girl', a pair of Australians who speak in an impenetrable dialect, and a survivor from the shark attack who then undergoes some form of mental collapse – all of these were sacrificed in the final cut. As a prime medium of film is light, the panic and drama of the pitch-dark underwater dive to reach the boat used by Sal and Richard (strongly evocative of Doris Lessing's short story 'Through the Tunnel') was impossible to film effectively. In addition, the 'Stomp' sequence in which, one by one, characters join in a communal sing-song with improvised percussion instruments, carefully choreographed to introduce a range of characters, was shot but cut for reasons of length and digression from the main plot. This is a pity because we could have seen the loss of self in communal rhythm, rather like the dance that leads to the death of Simon in *Lord of the Flies*, as well as indulging Boyle's delight in non-naturalistic musical numbers (like the song and dance routine in *A Life Less Ordinary*).

The figure of Jed, who in the novel is a precursor of the isolated, deluded fantasist that Richard rapidly becomes, apparently being given 'missions' by Sal, keeping watch away from the main community, is absent from the film. In the novel, Jed and Richard use slang military terms derived from Vietnam movies, such as 'FNG' for 'Fucking New Guy' and Richard admits 'I knew what to do because I'd seen Tour of Duty.' Garland also has Jed rather than Sal accompany Richard on the rice run, focusing on the obsessive fantasist element in the plot rather than the film's shift towards romantic entanglements and a climactic episode for Richard's sexual betrayal of Françoise. In the novel, Richard and Jed watch *Schindler's List* at a café before they reach the island and Richard measures the time he has to wait to see Françoise again by the appearance of the little girl in the red coat. Hence, Schindler's symbol of fragility and beauty snuffed out by hatred is appropriated by Richard as a marker of his lust for someone else's girlfriend. In the film, Richard continually lies to Françoise and Sal in front of the whole group, saying that he has not shown the map of the island to others, whereas in the novel he admits to Jed that he has. The novel thus gives Richard the semblance of a conscience which is absent from the film.

John Hodge's script opens with Richard's passport being stamped, establishing that the film is in large part about Richard's search for an identity, but the film as released only manages to convey this in part. The back-story of Richard's last failed relationship (and by implication, others before that) only surfaces in the stoned ramblings of Sammy, a minor character with whom Richard shares some drugs at the beginning, and in Keaty's dismissive comments on the island about Richard's chances with Françoise.

In Garland's novel and Hodge's script, the notion of Richard's experience and view of life as being mediated through screens is more coherent – as well as the *Schindler's List* scene, there are brief mentions of Richard playing with his Game Boy in the restaurant near the beginning, which would have featured the 'Game over' motif that recurs in his deluded run through the jungle later in the film, giving the sequence additional resonance. With this early scene missing, Boyle's coda, which places Richard in an Internet café, is not enough to explain the nature of his mental breakdown. Similarly Richard's fascination with Vietnam, his 'fanboy-style' immaturity and his nerdish fixation with game-playing, all of which lead him to see himself as a cross between James Bond and Rambo, is largely lost in adaptation.

There is a step-by-step dilution of this characterisation from Garland's novel, to Hodge's screenplay, to what we have on screen, leaving the finished film oddly unsatisfying and making Richard's behaviour odd, and at times inexplicable, to film audiences. Hodge's script originally included lines for Richard such as: 'Vietnam: the defining event of history for my generation. That is to say, it defined us because we didn't know the first fucking thing about it...but, hey, at least we'd seen the movie'.[18] The inclusion of such material would have made both his obsession and his naivety more coherent. His craving for a heightened sense of reality is expressed ironically in Hodge's script as a search for greater cinematic reality ('more visceral. More real. Like IMAX, maybe') but again this is cut from the finished film.[19] Similarly, Hodge's script includes lines where Richard rehearses heroic dialogue, casting himself as a dynamic leader able to act in the midst of battle.[20] These moments of self-dramatisation are cut from the film and without this, his insistence in continuing to search for the hidden beach seems to be more about impatience or making the logical choice than a demonstration of initiative. In the book there is a bizarre scene in which several individuals mutilate the bodies of the murdered backpackers. As a symbolic scene of disavowal, this might be justifiable but in filmic terms but it would have caused Boyle real problems with a film certificate and would have changed the nature of the preceding narrative. Other, more explicit, episodes from Garland's novel are also absent, including an outbreak of food poisoning and the discovery, by Richard, of a dead body.

On the DVD commentary, Boyle talks about how he prefers to avoid back-stories and keep film narratives 'in the present or future tense,' in other words constantly moving forward. However, the problem with Richard's character is that in both script and performance, it is paper-thin. Seeing him sitting alone does not make him a strong loner; seeing him press on past the dope-fields in the search for the elusive beach, does not make him a conqueror and a leader; spending a few idle hours with a Game Boy does not justify Keaty's comment about Richard's prominent prehensile thumbs, as if he has evolved into a different species. The idea of him as a mythic restless soul, who is looking for ever more extreme experiences, does not become true for viewers by his simply stating that he is looking for 'something more beautiful, exciting and dangerous'. Although we hear his voice-over tell us 'I just kept telling them we'd get there. Trust me,' all we see is a rather gangly youth who is

18 Hodge 2000 p.13.
19 Hodge 2000 p.20.
20 Hodge 2000 p.38 and pp.44-45.

selfish in his pursuit of pleasure rather than showing himself as a charismatic leader. He is Françoise's lover, but his exact attraction for her (beyond his physical appearance) is problematic. Bugs (Lars Arentz-Hansen) later asks him 'can you do anything? Can you make anything?' to which the answer seems a strong negative.

Despite his opening line ('my name is Richard. What else do you need to know?'), the fact is we *do* need more — a lot more substance before we can empathise with him as a character. The *Moby-Dick* allusion might remind us that Melville's first-person introduction to his central character ('call me Ishmael...') begins an epic voyage of discovery of several hundred pages.[21] By contrast, the first sight of Richard only serves to emphasise that he is a blank, one of thousands pursuing literally the same travel cliché. He thinks of himself as different and exceptional, but everything we see about him proves otherwise. He is provoked into drinking snake's blood when stung by the accusation he is just like all the other Americans, unwittingly proving the point exactly. The film seems to assume he has some special powers of oratory or charisma but, though Étienne and Françoise do accompany him to the island, we do not see him persuading them. Even the deleted scenes at breakfast or leaving the hostel make no attempt to bridge this narrative jump and all three characters are the poorer for it. It is hard to see the French couple as mature, or Étienne as somehow morally dignified, when they act so irresponsibly and irrationally from the outset, agreeing to travel to a mystery island with a complete stranger simply on the grounds of a childishly drawn map. They seem exactly what they are — pawns in the plot, which needs to move the narrative to the island as soon as possible. The contrast between Richard's rehearsed lines, asking Françoise and Étienne to come to the island with him, shown in a series of jump-cuts, with the actual stumbled and less polished delivery, make this attempt at persuasion even less likely. The messing-up of rehearsed lines is played for laughs in Robert's kidnap demands in *A Life Less Ordinary*, but here the lack of narrative logic weakens the film.

Similarly, Daffy (Robert Carlyle), the source of the island myth and the one who gives Richard the map, is afforded only minimal screen-time to introduce the concept of the island and hint at a bond between himself and Richard. Yet if we are to believe in Richard as his spiritual heir, we need to see why. Daffy's loss of sanity and subsequent suicide is not really explained: the contradictions in the beach community do not seem sufficient to motivate it and if they are, why do they only affect Daffy? A deleted scene with Sal and Richard on the boat to Ko Pha Ngan on a trip away from the island to buy supplies, raises this plot problem explicitly in dialogue, only to shelve it with a dismissive comment from Sal that Daffy was 'fucking crazy'. It clearly bothers Richard who thinks increasingly of Daffy but again, exactly why is unclear. It should be said, however, that such ambiguity permeates both Hodge's script and Garland's novel as well as the finished film.

In *Trainspotting*, Carlyle's character, the psychotic Begbie, acts as a representative of an aggressive, male, homophobic, drinking culture. Here, Daffy is a joke character treated seriously. His eccentric appearance does briefly inject some life into the film, his head twice suddenly appearing above Richard, through the mesh at the top of the flimsy walls between the rooms, once from a long shot and then, in a pseudo-horror trope, in a closer shot, making Richard (and the viewer perhaps) jump a little. Daffy's dialogue talks of 'too much input…too much sensation,' but actually when we reach the island, we are confronted by a continual lethargy and a distinct lack of sensation.

During Daffy's description of the beach, Boyle cuts via dissolves to a helicopter-shot of the island chain and the first glimpse of its beauty. It is a vision of paradise on earth, but it is also simultaneously interwoven with contradictions. At the same time as telling Richard about the island and giving him the map, he also warns 'nobody can ever go there'. It would be reading too much into his brief appearance as constituting a Mephistopheles to Richard's Dr Faustus but Daffy is nevertheless a figure of temptation, knowing that the hints he gives will be enough to fire Richard's curiosity. He asks Richard to believe in a mythical place and it is as if, by having faith, it will make it true.

The discovery of Daffy's body the next day is also contradictory. On the one hand, Richard's dialogue via voice-over tells us how disappointed he is with the scene, which does not match up to his cinematic expectations ('you never believe that something's gonna happen for you. Not like it does in the movies. And when it actually does, you want it to feel different'). On the other hand, Boyle uses conventional means of creating suspense (slow, cropped, point-of-view shots of the central horrific image, which only gradually become visible as Richard walks round Daffy's bed). Either we are expected to take such images as horrific or not – we cannot oscillate between disappointment and fear. Later, Richard's supposed breakdown is partly motivated by recurring nightmares and visions of Daffy, which need the initial experience to be cast as frightening for these scenes to work. Richard's mental instability is clearer in the novel in which, as soon as he reaches the camp, he has a series of cartoonish nightmares of Daffy.

Richard tells lies at several points in the film, which may humanise his character but does not make it particularly admirable. He does not tell the police, who are investigating Daffy's suicide, about the map; lies to Étienne, Françoise and Sal that he has told anyone else about the map; tells the backpackers that the map he gave them was 'fake', and denies to Françoise that he has slept with Sal. In his denials, there is the nominal notion of the 'cock crowing three times' but there is really not enough in the plot to sustain a religious reading of this – Richard is just a moral coward, who lies (like many of us do) because it is often easier than telling the truth. Exactly why he gives a copy of the map to some anonymous backpackers is unconvincing. Perhaps it is gratitude for the beer and dope they have given him, as lip-service to some hippy ideal of togetherness, or just simple fear that he wants someone to know where he is going.

Richard's motivation is not something that the film dwells upon. However, without a back-story or a rationale for his actions, we need these deficits to be filled with something else – narrative speed, action, or charismatic acting performances – all of which are equally lacking. Apart from a kiss, the novel leaves the relationship between Richard and Françoise at the level of his infatuation. Boyle, possibly again under studio pressure, pushes the sexual content a step further, introducing a second sexual relationship, between Richard and Sal. There is no substance to the relationship between Richard and Françoise, other than the camera lingering voyeuristically on her from his point of view as she emerges like a Bond-girl from the sea; later as she sits looking across at him in the communal hut, and as she turns over, sitting with him on the beach. Richard's voiceover only serves to give his so-called 'infatuation' the status of a schoolboy crush with some adult lust thrown in. When Keaty lists the reasons why Françoise would not be interested in him (including 'you're a bit weird'), we may tend to agree, finding the bringing of the two together little more than a contrived plot device. Her invitation to him to walk with her on the beach is a fairly obvious seduction ploy and motivates the subsequent slow-motion underwater kiss and love scene. The unreality of the emotional subtext is reflected in its method of production, shot day-for-night and with the CG necessary to make the phosphorescent plankton visible.

Richard's mental degeneration while on patrol alone needs greater on-screen time and substance to be convincing. The notion of the elitism of the community being taken one stage further makes sense with him as a form of hermit, imagining himself superior to the main group (particularly when, from a God-like position up on the cliffs, he views a group fishing), but this cannot happen overnight. His dreams of Daffy suggest that he is following the same trajectory of mental breakdown but the scene of discovering his body, which had been shown initially as something that Richard found fascinating, now shifts into supposed horror, with the body sitting up and grabbing hold of him. However, Carlyle's all-too-brief appearance does not give us enough substance to invest him with the status of an Ancient Mariner figure.

Almost immediately after Richard begins his regime of patrols, he starts to adopt the persona of a secret agent/Rambo figure, hiding behind logs and wielding a stick as an imaginary gun. The lack of clear motivation for his rapid degeneration, its blatantly childish manifestation and its equally swift disappearance when he rushes to warn the others about a new raft of backpackers, all make this the weakest part of the film. Hodge's script includes self-aware references to his sentry duty being a cross between a video game and a Vietnam movie.[22] This loss of touch with reality is made clear in a sequence in which DiCaprio adopts an exaggerated running style, captions and a game-score appear on screen, colours become lurid (contrasting with jungle sequences drained of colour) and animated tigers and birds are present as adversaries. Richard taunts the gun-toting dope-farmers, refers to them on his voiceover as 'players' and imagines his victory over all those around him with a flashing 'game over' sign. The design of the 'game' is evocative of Nintendo's puzzle-solving Banjo-Kazooie, which suggests Boyle does not want the overt violence of a shoot-em-up game, although this would actually be more suitable for Richard's macho delusions. The novel does describe Richard playing 'a private game,' creeping around the jungle in the style of a video game, giving himself three lives and pretending that any noise he made would be a life lost, but the novel is full of such references to delusional fantasies, whereas this episode seems oddly out of place in the film.[23] Boyle shows him parading bare-chested and uses a close-up to show him eating a caterpillar. The inherent elitism of the group is taken a step further in Richard's claims of God-like omniscience: 'I was the only one who saw how it all fitted together', he says.

22 Hodge 2000 p.110.
23 Garland 1996 p.256.

His hallucinogenic dreams reach a climax in a vision of Daffy's room, now riddled with bullet holes and with the added drama of a wind machine effect, where Daffy merrily fires a heavy machine gun from an open window, by implication at the rest of the island's inhabitants. Richard's whooping, together with his easy embrace of armed aggression-as-adventure, attempts to expose the height of his fantasy (military domination and destruction). Games and movies may be the mainstay of his imagination, but there is little sense that Richard has sufficient depth as a character to possess a tragic soul. When he says at the end of the film that he fears being unable to recover 'the person I used to be,' the viewer may feel this is no great loss. Discovered in a darkened hut by Keaty, Richard starts burbling about admiring Daffy and then steps back into shadow, in a thinly veiled homage to Captain Willard (Martin Sheen) in *Apocalypse Now*. Daffy, however, is no representative of elemental evil like Kurtz (Marlon Brando) and Richard's attempt to weave around him a cult of personality ('he had a certain style') just seem ridiculous.

The magic mushrooms, which Daffy offers Richard in a dream, play a stronger role in the novel and would at least motivate some of the visions that Richard has. In the film, the dissolve from Daffy to Richard does suggest that he is becoming Daffy's spiritual heir, a feeling strengthened by the repetition of the earlier line, now delivered by Daffy, that it is Richard who is 'fucked in the head'. The game-playing extends to the arrival of another group of wannabe paradise-seekers who are shot by the panicked gunmen: one girl dies because Richard deliberately jumps out and scares her, revealing her position. The spray of her blood is enough to miraculously bring Richard to his senses. He runs, pursued by the gunman, and the chase ends with the pursuer falling into a trap Richard has made and with Richard leaping from the waterfall once more.

The novel includes two ending scenes: one in which the survivors are picked up and one in which Richard, sometime later, is sitting in front of a computer, telling the narrative that we have just experienced. The film opts for the latter, though the former appears as an alternative ending on the DVD. This alternative ending includes a close-up of Richard which indicates his reluctance to be rescued by the beings he has come to despise, something that echoes Gulliver in Jonathan Swift's *Gulliver's Travels* (1726) and Ralph in *Lord of the Flies*.

In the book, the final section acts almost like an epilogue in a Victorian novel, updating us about the various characters' post-fictional lives – the finished film opts for a more optimistic tone of global interconnectivity, glossing over the delusional character of Richard and the essentially hollow nature of the island community. But the film provides little sense of satisfying closure. The last image we see of the group shows them disconsolately sailing away on a raft. Unkle's song 'Lonely Soul', which accompanies this sequence, is both epic and melancholic in tone, suggesting an emptiness to this act of apparent liberation as if we are witnessing a failed experiment, or a rejection of/ejection from paradise. Hodge's original script had ended with Sal's suicide, but Boyle rejected this on the grounds that the ending we see was, as he puts it, 'a way of offering something in the film'. This is important as it suggests a need, as much aesthetic and even religious, as commercial, to offer some hope to the audience at the end.

In the coda of the film, we see Richard in an Internet café, seeming just as self-absorbed as he ever was. When he states 'of course you can never forget what you've done, but you carry on', this implies he has endured martyr-like suffering, which is something we really have not seen in the preceding film. He has lied repeatedly, enjoyed the sensual pleasure of the island and caused the deaths of two people, but has hardly undergone any privation beyond what he has inflicted upon himself as part of a deluded fantasy. If the film does raise the question of what constitutes paradise, it does not really explore it in any depth or come to any grand conclusions. His claim that he was 'a part of something' still begs the question, of what? The group was so devoid of meaning that his allegiance to it makes his own character seem weaker still. The action of Richard looking at the others in the café could be said to underline the interconnectedness of people and a willingness and curiosity to reach out beyond the self. However, they are all doing this via the comfort of technology rather than interpersonal communication. The final snapshot of the island dwellers, posing in a group shot, looks more like a cast picture at the end of a shoot. The picture may not represent a 'parallel universe' as much as the actual universe that characters like Richard inhabit – a limited universe that they attempt to invest with metaphorical meaning but which literally, like the beach, is empty.

Q&A: Slumdog Millionaire (2008)

It is written', one of the possible answers to a question asked of the protagonist, Jamal (Dev Patel), on *Who Wants to be a Millionaire* carries not only the sense of destiny which pervades the narrative of *Slumdog Millionaire*, but also a literal truth, as the film was based on a novel, *Q&A* by Vikas Swarup (2006). The concept of the book is an original premise that taps into the global franchise of a TV programme and the dreams it represents; it allows the back-story to be told as part of a mystery narrative, in which the hero demonstrates through his life-experiences how he knows the answer to every question. Film theorist Noel Carroll developed the Socratic idea that it is the posing of questions that makes a narrative engaging, and although he was writing in the context of horror films, the way in which *Slumdog Millionaire* is structured, following the question-and-answer format of the novel, effectively gives life to this theory.[24]

As with most adaptations from a lengthy novel to a 120-minute screenplay, many elements had to be cut, leaving only those parts that had a direct bearing on the spine of the story – the central romantic pairing between Jamal and Latika (Freida Pinto). There are, therefore, no references to the India–Pakistan war of 1971, no voodoo murder, no murder on a train, no examination of organised betting on cricket, and only veiled allusions to contract killing. We do not see the workings of the Catholic Church, either in its benevolent form as shown in the novel by Father Timothy, or in its corruption in the juvenile home in Delhi. Swarup's hero has brief periods of relative wealth (money fortuitously falls in his lap twice through the death of an employer), allowing him to explore a wider range of social classes, whereas the film keeps a strict focus on just one. Swarup's panoramic view of the full social spectrum includes prostitutes and glue-sniffers, life in the lower-middle-class cramped tenements of the 'chawl,' as well as life as in diplomatic circles, through the portrayal of an Australian family who have dozens of servants and all the trappings of colonial wealth. Inevitably this spectrum is pared down. Those in the upper-middle class and those in abject poverty and misery right at the very bottom do not figure in the film. It may surprise viewers but the children depicted in Boyle's film do not represent the very lowest strata of society revealed in Swarup's novel: there is a further group of individuals who have literally nothing – no shelter, no family and no hope.

Boyle and scriptwriter Simon Beaufoy changed the protagonist's name from Ram Mohammad Thomas to Jamal Malik, to make it simpler and to avoid the religious balancing act described in the book that results in such a long, unwieldy name. They thereby lose Swarup's notion that his hero would be an Indian Everyman, a foundling who sounded as though he was a Hindu-Muslim-Christian, and instead make Jamal a

24 Carroll 1990 pp.130-136.

Muslim whose mother is killed by a Hindu mob. As Swarup himself commented on the name change, 'it's more dramatically focused as a result, perhaps more politically correct.'[25]

Prem, the TV quizmaster of *Who Wants to be a Millionaire*, is a more negative character in the novel than the film, involved in the sexual exploitation and abuse of girls. He is also devious: during a break in the show, he tips off the hero about what he says is a forthcoming question and answer, but only in order to trick him into agreeing to play in a higher level of the quiz, from which he cannot back out. He expects the 'slumdog' to fail. When the final question is due to be delivered, its choice is decided on the toss of a coin, an image also used in the film at the end and revealed as two-headed – symbolic of making one's own luck in life. In the novel, Prem delivers the final question, only to claim it was part of a commercial, replacing it with another final question. After the hero threatens him at gunpoint, Prem tells him the correct final answer and then he follows the advice to win the prize. The novel stretches the reader's credibility in the way Prem constantly switches back and forth between friend and foe. Film very rarely copes with such 'flip-flopping' in terms of motivation, so Boyle portrays him as a charming rogue who tries to trick Jamal by telling him the wrong answer to a question, but when Jamal wins, Prem dances and appears to celebrate with him.

In the novel, an epilogue wraps up all narrative loose ends so that the slum children are freed from an exploitative camp, Ram's friend Salim (Boyle makes him Jamal's brother) survives to become a film star, with projects funded (unknown to him) by Ram's money, and Prem is found dead in suspicious circumstances. Swarup has his hero ultimately live in a large house, in the same area where Prem previously lived. There is no direct equivalent of the novel's epilogue in the film, which closes with a non-naturalistic dance routine at the railway station. It is a way of seeing the main characters again (and perhaps more importantly, the actors), so that we see different incarnations of Jamal and Latika in a blend of conventions from Bollywood (the closing number), and western theatre (the curtain call).

In terms of the starting point of the narrative, Swarup begins his novel with the quiz having been filmed but not yet screened. Simon Beaufoy's script moves the opening of the narrative slightly so that Jamal is arrested before the final question, so that the whole film deals with the process of interrogating Jamal on the eve of the climactic show, thus adding another

25 Swarup in *The Guardian*, 16 January 2009.

level of suspense to the narrative and motivating the telling of his life-story. We might assume the opening shot of a bath full of money is a flashback, as that seems to be the general structure of the scenes shown outside the confines of the TV studio. It is only when we reach the end of the film that we realise this is a rare example of a flash-forward and the money we have seen scattered at the outset is not the winnings on the show but the fruits of the criminal lifestyle which Salim is now forsaking. By shifting the arrest to the point of the penultimate question, the film narrative uses the huge TV audience to create greater suspense, underlining the mythic nature of the story and the interconnectedness of the global and the personal.

The novel is written in the first person but Beaufoy and Boyle chose not to transpose that into a voice-over. If viewers heard Jamal's voice as narrator, we would know that he had survived the events we are witnessing, thus removing an element of suspense: it would also have made him seem more in control of events than he actually is.

In the novel, Salim is only a fellow orphan, whereas the film makes him Jamal's brother, thereby adding intensity to their parallel fates. Rather than Swarup's decision to make his protagonist a foundling who suffers a series of abusive foster-parents, the film's hero suffers a series of personal losses. First he experiences the death of his mother in a religious riot, then separation from his childhood friend Latika, when Salim lets her fall from his grasp as she is trying to join the boys aboard a moving train, and ultimately he endures alienation from his brother who gives himself up to a life of crime. However, whereas Swarup's hero seems hardened by repeated disappointments, Jamal learns from his experiences, something we see as he answers seemingly impossible questions in the quiz. In the novel, the main characters occupy a slightly more affluent position than in the film, with the hero working for an ageing film star and Salim delivering food.

Swarup also includes a much wider range of settings. In the novel, the slum is largely tangential, rather than absolutely central as it is in the film. Swarup describes the boys waving from a train at half-naked slum children but the film removes this distance – Jamal, Salim and Latika (Rubina Ali as the young Latika) are all children from the slum, just as the youngest set of actors were recruited from the slum. When Swarup's hero does finally descend to the Dharavi slum, there is no sense of euphoria, as there is in the film with the opening chase-scene. Perhaps without cultural and linguistic knowledge, the country's poverty might seem ennobling but clearly for Swarup this is not so. A diplomat by profession, who admits that he has never visited the Dharavi slum, Swarup is more concerned with slums as a generic idea than a specific location. 'They consist,' he says, 'of the same cluster of corrugated-iron sheets masquerading as roof; the same naked children with pot bellies frolic in the mud with pigs while their mothers wash utensils in sewer water'.[26]

The film, not surprisingly, foregrounds the more visual elements of the novel. For example, in the book, the boys only overhear talk about children being deliberately blinded and manage to slip quietly away from Maman's camp. The film shows us the actual blinding of a boy in unflinching detail, creating suspense by showing Jamal being led towards the same fate, before he struggles free. In this way, Swarup's description of child exploitation and mutilation is elevated dramatically by Boyle, climaxing in an escape and a chase.

The presentation of authority is altered in the film adaptation too. The novel names the police inspector 'Godbole' in a conscious and ironic reference to E.M. Forster's *A Passage to India* (1924), where a professor of that name accepts cultural differences with sensitivity. Here, Godbole instigates torture on the grounds of unsubstantiated prejudice. In the film, by using a sergeant as his underling, the inspector (Irrfan Khan) is slightly distanced from the act itself, and the allusion to Forster is lost as the name Godbole is heard only fleetingly. Swarup has the torture interrupted by the intervention of a lawyer so that the subsequent narrative becomes the hero's explanation to his defence counsel, rather than to the police, and takes place in her home rather than in the police station. By making the inspector the audience of the tale, the film allows him to be gradually convinced of Jamal's innocence, and thereby humanised.

The central romantic plotline in the novel is less straightforward than in the film. Swarup's hero falls in love first with Gudiya, who he rescues from a fire, and then with a prostitute called Nita who has been tortured with cigarette burns. He swears revenge on the perpetrator, ultimately revealed to be Prem, the quiz-show host. For the film, Beaufoy makes the film more accessible for the viewer by linearising the flashbacks, making Prem (Anil Kapoor) more of a charming rogue than a sadistic abuser and turning Gudiya and Nita into the character of Latika who is present right from the start of the narrative. A key difference from the book is the way that the love-story in the film runs through every life-experience that

26 Swarup 2006 p.370, pp. 275-6.

Jamal recalls as he answers the questions on the show. Whereas in the novel, the hero uses his phone-a-friend lifeline to call an English teacher, whose son he had helped earlier, the film seizes this opportunity to reunite Jamal with Latika on live television in front of millions of viewers. Boyle achieves a powerful coalescence of narrative threads with a romantic climax, the winning of the money, and the removal of evil as Salim shoots the gangster Javed (Mahesh Manjrekar).

There are a number of residual linguistic echoes of the book in the film script. Beaufoy claims the term 'slumdog' is original and not in the novel, but 'stray dogs' are mentioned from the third line of the novel and the hero later talks about living 'like a dog'.[27] 'I begin to think of myself as a mongrel', he says, 'peeping through a barred window into an exotic world which does not belong to me'.[28] Boyle's shot of a dog in the slum chase sequence literalises the idea of a being who is theoretically the lowest of the low, but in fact is highly alert, watching everything and just waiting for a chance. The shot of the dog, only momentarily interested by the spectacle, also ameliorates the apathy that Swarup attributes to the slum-dwellers themselves.[29] Other linguistic echoes include A.R. Rahman's score for the final dance number, 'Jai Ho!', meaning 'Victory!', which might have been inspired by a scene in the novel where war veteran Balwant Singh tells a lengthy war story, finishing his tale with a final battle cry, 'Jai Hind' ('Victory to India!').[30]

Actions from the novel are often present in the film but are shifted slightly in terms of tone and function. For example, a film idol arrives by helicopter in the novel, but it is only in a movie the boys are watching. They do meet a film idol, but it is in the darker context of an old man trying to grope Salim. Boyle translates this grubby scene of sexual exploitation into one of the more memorable comic set-pieces of the film, in which the young Jamal, like Renton in *Trainspotting*, must dive down into human effluent in order to achieve something transcendent: in this case, the autograph of his hero. Swarup's narrative also features a hero besotted with the sight of a beautiful girl in a street, as part of the mythology surrounding the Taj Mahal,[31] and Boyle translates this into Jamal's glimpse of Latika at the railway station, an iconic vision that sustains him emotionally through the course of the film. Even sequences in the film that seem explicitly 'cinematic', such as the vision that Jamal

---

27   Swarup 2006 p.11, 29.
28   Swarup 2006 p.131.
29   Swarup 2006 pp.11-12.
30   Swarup 2006 p.216.

has of pushing Salim off a tall building, derive directly from the novel, where the hero pushes Gudiya's abusive father from a roof, killing him.[32] Boyle keeps the murderous action purely imaginary, however, thereby not morally compromising Jamal and risking a consequent forfeiting of viewer sympathy for him.

Given that the structure of the film necessitates persistent cutting from Jamal's memories back to the TV studio and police station, it is a great achievement to maintain audience engagement with the emotional core of the film. The structure could have become repetitive or, perhaps worse still, dominated by the small-scale TV studio rather than the epic tale (one of Boyle's initial misgivings about the premise) but the pace and engaging nature of the back-story does not allow that to happen.

As usual with Boyle, there is little deviation from the filmscript, which for him represents a core reality to hold onto in the maelstrom of filmmaking. The notion of serving the narrative is a key one for Boyle. Jamal's answers to the quiz questions motivate not only the flashbacks of his life but key elements in his search for Latika. The explanation of how he knows the answers to the quiz questions therefore becomes a demonstration of his love and a means of them being reunited.

Conclusion

In Boyle's 2001 TV film *Strumpet* (discussed in Chapter Three), the poet Strayman (Christopher Eccleston) boasts: 'I don't rewrite, re-edit, copy down. They (the words) go where they go'. This suggests a process of laissez-faire romanticism towards creativity and the written word. Boyle's own approach is much more tough-minded than this. The fact that he generally keeps writers attached to projects is the exception rather than the rule in contemporary filmmaking. Scriptwriter John Hodge even appears in a cameo as a detective in *Shallow Grave* and as a security guard in *Trainspotting*, while writer Frank Cottrell Boyce plays a teacher directing a nativity play in *Millions*. However, there may be something Machiavellian in Boyle's methods, keeping friends close and enemies closer, to paraphrase Michael Corleone (Al Pacino) in *The Godfather, Part II* (dir. Francis Ford Coppola 1974). In this way, they are less likely to criticise Boyle in the press and are also available for re-writes. Their presence reflects Boyle's respect for the written word and those for whom it is their prime medium. With *127 Hours*, for the first time in his

31   Swarup 2006 p.278.
32   Swarup 2006 pp.85-86.

career, Boyle named himself as co-writer (with Simon Beaufoy) on the credits, which suggests the depth of his personal commitment to that particular film as well as his growing interest and active involvement in the writing/adaptation process. He adopts both a strictness about the sanctity of the text and a flexibility about its delivery – a combination that can be traced to his theatrical background. This is all a far cry from the fictional scene in Robert Altman's *The Player* (1988), where Hollywood producer Griffin Mill (Tim Robbins) has the temerity to suggest that writers could be eliminated from the filmmaking process altogether. Boyle appreciates that while there are hundreds of individuals working on a production, without writers there could be no film.

CHAPTER TWO

· A TALE OF SEVERAL GENRES ·

Danny Boyle has worked in a number of different genres and so far has resisted commercial pressure to specialise in any one in particular. In most forms of mass entertainment (fiction, pop music, TV/film), this is relatively rare, with pressure coming from studios to stay with what is successful at the box office. His unpredictable choices (such as *127 Hours* after the success of *Slumdog Millionaire*) might make him critically popular but arguably this makes it harder for distribution companies to promote his work and has meant that certain films, such as *Sunshine*, have failed to find their audience on theatrical release. However, it means that he can remain free to make choices based on a greater sense of artistic integrity, resulting in films like *Trainspotting*, *Millions* and *Slumdog Millionaire*. It also signals that he sees each film as a distinct entity: so far, though tempted to make a sequel to *Trainspotting*, he has not been able to find a script of sufficient quality to match his aspirations – and perhaps he is waiting for his original cast to age appropriately (to match Irvine Welsh's sequel, *Porno* from 2002).

Boyle has made films that are clearly capable of categorisation by genre, such as low-budget horror (*28 Days Later*) or science fiction (*Sunshine*). Elsewhere, however, he is drawn to stories precisely because they defy easy categorisation, such as *Slumdog Millionaire*, which features no stars, is partly in Hindi and set in a culture at polar opposites to Hollywood. It seems that what fires his interest is not a 'star vehicle', but the presence of an engaging set of characters involved in a conflict which tests their natures, and which requires high-quality acting talent to portray. Where he has compromised on this (such as casting Leonardo DiCaprio as the lead in *The Beach*), there been consequent compromises in areas of characterisation, and Boyle has stated himself that he is better at working with more modest budgets, smaller crews and possibly less imposing egos in his leading actors.

Genre is one of the most important elements in selecting whether to pay to see a film in the cinema, rent/buy a DVD or even watch a movie on television. If a film comes up in casual conversation, 'what's it about?' or 'who's in it?' are questions that might be asked, but the underlying question is 'what kind of film is it?' Questions about a film narrative, or the presence of certain stars, inevitably produce assumptions or perhaps further questions about what genre best describes it. Basically, genre is a convenient way to manage expectations. It helps viewers make sense of new experiences and process them as part of what they have already been seen before. As theorist Steve Neale states, the pleasures of genre derive from a creative tension between 'instances of repetition and difference'.[1] If a film contains too few genre markers, audiences may feel confusion and possibly even anger that they cannot 'place' a narrative. If it is too repetitive, it becomes predictable and forgettable. Boyle's films in this chapter are comprehensible without having seen many screwball comedies, viral horror films or science fiction epics, but if we have, our understanding and appreciation of these films can be greatly deepened.

How genre operates is a complex issue. Some theorists, such as Will Wright, have listed narrative features, whose combined presence he suggests constitutes the existence of a particular genre.[2] This is relatively simple with genres like the western, where the iconography of saloons, horses and the location of untamed territory at a certain point in the history of America, play a fairly central part. There may be some hybridisation into subgenres, such as the comic-western of *Blazing Saddles* (dir. Mel Brooks 1974) or *Wild Wild West* (dir. Barry Sonnenfeld 1999) but there is a core identity based primarily around location. Science fiction is a broad and contentious term but the film discussed in this chapter, *Sunshine*, would generally fall into this category, again primarily due to its setting. Once a narrative is set in outer space, involves space walks and a cast full of astronauts, apart from some horror hybrids like *Alien* (dir. Ridley Scott 1979) or parodies like *Dark Star* (dir. John Carpenter 1974), science fiction seems its natural generic home. Similarly, fan-driven debate over *28 Days Later* lies primarily in what kind of horror film it is, more specifically its frequent and inaccurate description as a zombie film, rather than whether it is a horror film at all. Here, the generic categorisation is not dominated by setting (indeed the use of a British location is perhaps an unexpected element) but by the response expected in the audience – it is a film attempting to provoke a visceral reaction.

Boyle's creative restlessness embraces a range of distinct genres. I have chosen to discuss *A Life Less Ordinary*, *28 Days Later* and *Sunshine* specifically because all three are closely associated with a particular genre, (romantic comedy, horror and science fiction respectively) yet it is the

1 Neale 1980 p.48.
2 Wright 1977.

ways in which they subvert generic expectations that make them interesting. All three films are openly derivative but at the same time extend, with varying degrees of success, the boundaries of what their specific genre might encompass. Of these, the most slippery genre is undoubtedly the screwball comedy, which is almost as much a mode of thought as a specific genre.

Modern Screwball: A Life Less Ordinary (1997)

Audience reaction to *A Life Less Ordinary* tends to polarise between those who love it and those who hate it. Generically, it is a romantic comedy but it – bravely or foolishly, depending on your point of view – tries to stretch audience expectations by drawing on a key subgenre of this group – the so-called 'screwball comedy'. Pitcher Carl Hubbell (who played for the New York Giants, 1928-1943) developed a kind of baseball pitch in which the ball moved in unexpected ways, and screwball comedy has similar unpredictable twists and turns. Inversion is a key principle – of class, gender and setting. From its background in The Motion Picture Production Code of 1930, or the Hays Code as it was more commonly termed, setting out a censorious list of what was and was not allowed to be depicted on screen, Hollywood screwball comedies of the 1930s and 1940s sublimated their sexual content into the dialogue and iconography of the setting: characters, especially men, seem unable to express their romantic feelings, except through barbed insults.

Features of this subgenre might include unexpected juxtapositions with characters thrown together by fate, typically as the bringing together of a rich, pampered woman with a working-class man. There is ever-present conflict between the two leads until they, and sometimes the plot, are exhausted. The main character is usually removed from a life of ease, the value of which is questioned through a series of obstacles including brushes with the law. Narratives often involve a literal journey, encountering minor eccentric characters along the way. Rapid-pace dialogue (relatively innovative in the early sound era) is central to screwball comedy, sometimes with dialogue even overlapping the female lead's snappier one-liners and putdowns. As in Shakespearean comedy, characters play roles to test each other and, like Shakespeare, the ending is signalled as harmonious by conflict-resolution, and often marriage.

The centrality of dialogue means that the scriptwriter's role is important here. *A Life Less Ordinary* was John Hodge's third collaboration with Boyle so it was a well-established relationship, and certainly there are individual witty lines, such as in the phone-booth scene when Robert (Ewan McGregor) is fumbling his ransom-demand lines. Hodge seems less comfortable, however, with moving beyond the social realism of *Shallow Grave* (1994) and *Trainspotting* (1996) and beyond the shores of Britain.

Critical approaches to screwball generally fall into two general categories – that favoured by Stanley Cavell, which emphasises the narrative as a spiritual journey, leading to a gaining of wisdom and a sense of elevation above prosaic everyday life; and that put forward by theorists like Wes Gehring, who see the narratives working in the opposite direction, highlighting social pretentiousness and eventually reconciling the characters to the everyday.[3] The problem with *A Life Less Ordinary* is that we do not see the romantic female lead, Celine (Cameron Diaz), brought low to learn the errors of her ways. On the contrary, she seems as spoilt at the end of the film as she is at the beginning. One convention of screwball is that the hero and heroine seem to display instant antipathy to one another, but during the course of the plot the intensity of their animosity is really a kind of displacement theory, a sign of the depth of their passion for one another. The problem is that modern audiences do not 'buy' this. The sudden conversion of hatred into love seems implausible.

As opposites do not easily meet in everyday life, possibly because of class divisions, plots have to be contrived to bring such meetings about, for example via kidnaps as in *Ruthless People* (dir. Jim Abrahams, David and Jerry Zucker 1986), in which a rich heiress, Barbara Stone (Bette Midler) is kidnapped, but when the squeamish kidnappers (Judge Reinhold and Helen Slater) deliver their demands, they find her husband Sam (Danny De Vito) is quite happy for them to kill her. There may be brief screwball interludes in other genres, such as Alfred Hitchcock's *The 39 Steps* (1939), in the sequence where a couple, who barely known each other, are handcuffed together and who eventually fall in love. There has also been some sideways movement of screwball into the caper movie (such as Steven Soderbergh's *Oceans* franchise from 2001, 2004 and 2007) but in general terms, screwball had only stuttering success after its heyday in the 1930s and 40s. To postwar audiences the eccentricities of screwball seemed irrelevant: they were interested in more violent, brutal storylines. The central male character, usually an ineffectual anti-hero, did not seem to offer postwar audiences the kind of reassuring on-screen presence they were looking for. Screwball offers a light escape from the world,

---

3 Cavell 1981; Gehring 1983.

rather than interaction with it, and after the horrors of a global conflict, perhaps such lightness seemed misplaced.

In recent years, separate elements of the subgenre have resurfaced, such as the witty, barbed exchanges that highlight the sexual chemistry between Han Solo (Harrison Ford) and Princess Leia (Carrie Fisher) in *Star Wars* (dir. George Lucas 1977), between David (Bruce Willis) and Maddie (Cybill Shepherd) in *Moonlighting* (1985-1989), or even in *The Gilmore Girls* (2000-2007) but as a whole, the generic ingredients now find their natural home as a subgenre of romantic comedy. There have been major box office successes such as *When Harry Met Sally* (dir. Rob Reiner 1989), *Sleepless in Seattle* (dir. Nora Ephron 1993), Notting Hill (dir. Roger Michell 1999) and *Bridget Jones' Diary* (dir. Sharon Maguire 2001) but it seems that adding a zany element to romantic comedy is too alienating for many modern audiences, especially for a lower demographic, who might be expecting an *American Pie*-mixture of gross-out and sexual content. In either case, gross-out pleasures or more decorous romantic narratives only work through clear generic signaling – something screwball has always challenged.

The Madonna vehicle *Who's That Girl?* (dir. James Foley 1987) attempted to update Howard Hawks' *Bringing Up Baby* (1938) but without commercial or critical success. Screwball does not seem to work unless given a period setting (such as George Clooney's 2008 *Leatherheads*, set in the 1920s) or unless associated with particular directors who seem to have some of the same kooky characteristics as the subgenre itself, such as the Coen Brothers (known as 'the two-headed directors' as they share responsibility and credit for all the major decisions on their films). In *Intolerable Cruelty* (2003) or *O Brother Where Art Thou?* (2000), there are elements of screwball in plot and character types, but what makes these films distinctive – and perhaps is the key to their success – is the presence of a credible screwball hero. It is telling that the examples here involve Clooney, possibly the last of a dying breed of hero who can be seen as romantic and sassy, but also ridiculous and weak at times (something that Ewan McGregor struggles to achieve in the film in question here).

Perhaps an additional factor is that most heroes of classic screwball were older than leading men now (such as Cary Grant, who made *Bringing Up Baby* at 34 and Clark Gable, who starred in *It Happened One Night* at 33), meaning that they had more experience of acting – and perhaps life – to bring to these roles. McGregor is known for his charm but it is of a distinctly youthful variety (he is 26 here). Perhaps Clooney is credible in such roles because of the maturity he can bring – he is exactly 10 years older than McGregor.

After a confrontation with his tyrannical boss Mr Naville (Ian Holm), cleaner Robert Lewis (Ewan McGregor) finds himself kidnapping the boss' daughter, Celine (Cameron Diaz), almost by accident and holing up in a remote log cabin. Celine is unimpressed with Robert's prowess as a kidnapper and has to instruct him in what to do. Gradually, in their pursuit of a ransom, the pair form a romantic bond. Screwball narratives are dominated by farcical plot twists, often based on mistaken identity and here we have Robert taken for a kidnapper, when really his 'victim' is driving the situation. The whole narrative has a 'frame story' as an inquisition about true love by some very worldly angels, who are under strict instructions from God to make a romantic situation work for once (this aspect is discussed more fully in Chapter Six).

This was the third collaboration between Boyle and Ewan McGregor, after *Trainspotting* and *Shallow Grave*, and his presence on posters and promotional material which suggests witty, fast-paced dialogue, is balanced by that of Diaz, who had established her status as a prominent player in romantic comedies with *She's the One* (dir. Edward Burns 1996) and *My Best Friend's Wedding* (dir. P.J. Hogan 1997), and was on the verge of global stardom with *There's Something about Mary* (dir. Bobby and Peter Farrelly 1998), which made her an icon of adolescent male lust. The trailers featured fast editing, suggestive of pace and action, and highlighted key moments like the telephone-booth ransom demand, accompanied (as all Boyle films were up to this point) by a cutting-edge soundtrack of ambient and alternative/indie dance music. Thus audiences were expecting a romantic comedy, perhaps including some dark humour, but definitely a feel-good experience.
　　The opening sequence of *A Life Less Ordinary* introduces the lifestyle of Celine Naville, a spoilt, upper-class screwball heroine. In a long shot, shown from above, she appears to swim through the film title itself, in an image of languid control. We hear British trip-hop band Sneaker Pimps' 'Velvet Divorce,' whose lyrical phrases like 'I can walk on water' and 'perfect world' appear to complement Celine's life. In terms of the melody, however, the song is quite dark and may seem at odds with audience expectations of both the film's comedic content and Diaz's star persona. Almost like a TV commercial, in a stylised image of perfection,

a low angle catches a Rottweiler running through the shot at the pool's edge, framed against a cloudless sky. The iconography of decadence is reinforced with a long, low-angle shot of a large house, a butler bringing drinks and an overhead shot, taking in the poolside table as well as the water. As Celine emerges from the pool, she is framed with the sun behind her and, in a sleek black swimsuit, is linked to the dog shown earlier – she is slim, beautiful and rich. She tosses an apple to her butler and then shoots it from his head with a pistol. The casual toss, and his calm reaction, tell us not just that she is a good marksman and that this is a habitual 'game', but speaks eloquently of Celine's empty life which she fills with unnecessary danger. The stylised action and shot composition as she stops, turns and raises her gun, make the scene feel close to a Bond credits sequence.

On the soundtrack we hear a voice, subsequently identified as that of Robert (Ewan McGregor) saying 'she's the secret daughter of Marilyn Monroe and John F. Kennedy,' and describing a character using adjectives that might apply at this stage of the film to Celine – 'beautiful,' 'smart' and 'successful'. Boyle's camera slowly descends from a bird's-eye shot to Robert at a small table in a store-room: from the uniforms and half-eaten lunch on the table, we realise the dramatic story is nothing more than Robert pitching an idea for a trashy novel to his co-workers. However, his listeners are not impressed, judging that it is 'kinda obvious'. From the outset, Boyle is treading a problematic line between challenging some generic conventions (the ability of the hero to express himself) and still expecting audiences to accept others (that the hero and heroine are worthy and suitable romantically for each other).

Inter-cutting between the store-room and the poolside mansion suggests that the two leads (and their social worlds) will connect, although as yet we do not know how. Celine's suitor Elliot (Stanley Tucci) attempts a reconciliation but she rejects his overtures, reminding him that he is a 'cheat,' which suggests that fidelity is important to her (later, she is to reveal herself to be completely amoral). Trying out the William Tell stunt again, this time on Elliot, she accidentally wounds him as he flinches: her lack of emotional reaction, asking her butler 'would you call a doctor?' and the stereotypical English understatement of his reply ('It would be a pleasure madam'), suggest that they do not care, or that they live such lives of luxury that they do not need to worry about such trifles. Conventionally, the callous nature of a spoilt heroine might soften by interaction with a lower-class hero, but Celine's character retains this element of this coldness right through to the end of the film, undermining the potential viewing pleasure of a romantic resolution.

Boyle departs from conventional screwball by introducing fantasy elements, which (as in the toilet-diving scene in *Trainspotting*) are partly motivated from within the scene. After being dumped by his girlfriend Lilly (K.K. Dodds), Robert becomes drunk and is in a state of emotional despair. Boyle uses overt stylisation to suggest that Robert's world is literally out of kilter (upon waking, he is framed at 45 degrees and it takes a while for him to hear a knocking at the door). In his dream state, his room is bathed in red from a tinted lens and, after an aural montage of the rejections he has faced that day, the screen fades to red and we see an animated pumping heart, shot by a bullet (linking him with Celine as shooter and potential breaker of hearts, and his own status as heart-broken lover).

The pursuit of an eligible husband underlies Celine's meeting at her father's office in the following scene. The father–daughter relationship is clearly not close, as we hear about her mother, described as as 'scuttling along the bottom' of society, and how the father worries that Celine's romantic fussiness (as he sees it) will cut her off from socially eligible husbands. Typical of a screwball heroine, Celine is articulate in her antagonism to him and her principled stand against such a match – 'her only mistake was marrying a man like you,' she says, referring to her mother, 'a mistake I've taken great care to avoid'. Naville speaks down to Celine, and this is made visual by shots of him standing at the window while she sits in a chair. This, together with the threatened punishment of being sent to work, implies that Celine has led a sheltered and pampered life thus far. This is picked up later when she reveals she never learned to drive a car 'because I didn't need to'.

Robert interrupts the meeting to protest at his sacking (he is to be replaced by a robot cleaner) and attempts a spectacular gesture, picking up the robot to throw it through Naville's window. The action backfires: not only does the window not break, but the machine continues to work despite falling to the floor – a clear vindication of Naville's faith in the machine's superiority over human labour, and a small nod to parables like Chaplin's *Modern Times* (1936), which blend light-touch politics with comic absurdity. Like the typical screwball hero, Robert is continually and comically humiliated, but Boyle interweaves this with taboo language and violence. The kind of screwball slapstick seen in Charles' repeated falls (bravely performed by Henry Fonda) in *The Lady Eve* (dir. Preston Sturges 1941) is reflected in Robert disappearing under a scrum of security guards who are seeking to have him thrown out of the building, but here Boyle momentarily reasserts a more modern, brutal aesthetic as Robert manages to grab a gun and deliver the command 'nobody fucking move'. For a second or two, he is control before being pummeled to the floor once more.

In a surprising first encounter between the two leads, unseen by her father, Celine (dressed in anachronistic, Hepburn-like blue mid-length coat and distinctive zebra-coloured gloves – associating her with the look of a classical screwball heroine) kicks the gun back to Robert, thereby subverting the roles of accomplice and victim. The whole sequence from the failed throw onwards, with Robert wriggling free from the security guards, is cartoonish rather than realistic (continuing the sense of Chaplinesque humour). Guns and threats to kill are not sources of genuine dread here and the situation edges towards the absurd as Robert demands at gunpoint that Naville give him his low-grade cleaning job back. It is during Robert's deadline of counting to five that we have a greater sense of why Celine might be attracted to him – he too is a rebel and is ordering her dictatorial father around. Her empathy with him is suddenly so strong that she completes the count, which startles him and he shoots Naville in the leg by mistake.

The quick-fire dialogue in which she tries to help him to count to five, assuring him it is no shame if he had an inadequate education, is also typical of screwball comedy, particularly where the woman is given some of the best lines and drives the exchange. It is Celine who suggests that he kidnap her so she can escape the clutches of her father. Her sudden miraculous ability (however inexpertly) to drive their getaway car is hardly remarked upon beyond Robert's unhelpful 'mirror, signal, manoeuvre'. They have been thrown together by circumstances and, in the confined space of the car, the exchanges are more comedic and witty than openly discordant. In many screwball comedies the narrative follows a literal journey, often that of a couple on the run from the authorities, during which they learn something about themselves and question assumptions about their previous lives. In *It Happened One Night,* for example, Ellie Andrews (Claudette Colbert), like Celine, is a spoilt heiress on the run from her father's control, and falls into the company of Peter Warne (Clark Gable) who, like Robert, is a lowly unemployed man.

Rather than being abducted, Celine is indulging in some consensual role-playing and the two are fugitives from Celine's father rather than from the police. The pair commit their first crime by breaking into an isolated cabin. Robert ties her to a chair, during which she recounts being kidnapped when she was 12 years old, prompting a genuine expression of horror from Robert. There is also some role reversal as she appears to have more knowledge about kidnapping than he does, with him constantly seeking approval ('how am I doing?'). He even asks, clearly in need of guidance, 'so what did they do next?'. There is some sexual tension in the proximity of the two, the tying up (with Robert momentarily framed from above, between her legs) and Celine's outspoken frankness ('are you going to try and have sex with me?'). When he hesitates, unsure if this is a question or a challenge, she starts asking if he has a problem, implying it would be dysfunctional not to do so. Although probably intended to be funny, there is a darker edge to the actions and dialogue here, which undermines both the humour and any sense of romantic identification we might have with the couple. This exchange is relatively coy compared to the sexual chemistry and suggestiveness of *Out of Sight* (dir. Steven Soderbergh 1998), where convict Jack Foley (George Clooney) and US Marshall Karen Sisco (Jennifer Lopez) are forced to share an intimate ride in the boot of a car. Robert claims 'there are no sexual motives for my actions,' but unfortunately compared to the frisson between Lopez/Clooney, this couple seem in need of a spark between them, cinematically speaking.

The next morning, Robert finds her chair empty and is momentarily crestfallen before we pan, via his point of view, to another chair where Celine is sitting. This clarifies her role – she is not a victim but a willing accomplice. The film treads an awkward line at times between scenes that are witty and that update the notion of gender reversal, and references to a darker world of flesh and blood in which the reality of armed robbery (in a later scene at the bank) means threatening to shoot children and running the risk of being shot oneself. There are glimpses of a darker generic territory occupied more comfortably by David Lynch or Quentin Tarantino, which do not always gel well here. Lynch and Tarantino, in *Blue Velvet* (1983) and *Reservoir Dogs* (1992) respectively, establish from the outset the graphically violent consequences of criminal acts. This awkwardness of tone here is reflected in the title of the romantic novel which Celine later finds in the cabin, 'Perfect Love' – she dismisses it as 'bullshit' yet keeps reading.

Traditional roles continue to be reversed – Celine is splitting logs and it is Robert who is engrossed in the romantic novel. We may not have the cross-dressing of *I Was a Male War Bride* (dir. Howard Hawks 1949) but we do have Robert in an apron at the stove preparing a meal. The notion of a romantic dinner, however, is undercut by her ingratitude: she lets him spend time preparing the food before declaring that she does not eat meat. The film seems to want to satirise conventions of romantic narratives at the same time as expecting audiences to be receptive to them. This is what traditional screwball does, but with characters who are consistent, empathetic and who operate within a playful environment: like Shakespearean comedy, screwball is not a world where truly awful things are allowed to happen. Introducing swearing and threats of real violence might seem like an attempt at updating the genre but they remove this sense of a 'safe' context. A different set of narrative imperatives start to apply if characters really can shoot and kill each other and, in situations of genuine jeopardy, banter seems self-indulgent and irrelevant.

The ransom demand scene in the phone-booth is a comic highlight of the film and therefore a natural choice for inclusion in the theatrical trailer. We do not hear any of the dialogue from the recipients of these calls, condensing Robert's ransom attempts via a series of jump-cuts. Robert is stereotypically British in his telephone manner, allowing himself to be interrupted and constantly apologising. Celine grabs the receiver and demonstrates the correct register before instantly dropping back into a calmer, polite mode in speaking to him. Like Sally's faked orgasm in *When Harry Met Sally* (dir. Rob Reiner 1989), it is that sudden switchback which provides the humour, especially when juxtaposed with Robert's subsequent montage of bungled attempts: being too friendly, embellishing his delivery too much, or getting parts of the threat the wrong way round ('right daughter, I've got your arsehole here'). Eventually he gets his patter right but delivers it to the wrong number.

Later, Robert carefully constructs a ransom demand by cutting letters from a newspaper, but his efforts are immediately deflated by Celine's observation that there is no need for anonymity, as Naville already knows who he is. In *Bringing Up Baby*, we also have a similarly mismatched couple, Huxley (Cary Grant) and Susan Vance (Katharine Hepburn) whose initial enmity is partly based on the gulf between their relative social positions and a hero who, like Robert, is weak and emasculated. Robert claims that Celine views a kidnapper as just another 'lifestyle accessory' and his voice rises hysterically when he says 'I'm trying to do my best under really difficult circumstances'. However, she is genuinely offended that he only asks half a million dollars, as a poor indication of her social worth. She begins to speak using the first person plural, overtly linking them as more active accomplices: 'we have the chance to make millions of dollars', she tells him. Later, after the failed pick-up, at which Robert loses the car and gains no money, she gives Robert a pep talk as a failed kidnapper.

There are some direct allusions to previous screwball comedies, such as the swapping of places to gain a ride from a passing car (Robert ignored, Celine prompting a slamming of brakes), which is taken directly from *It Happened One Night*. These are juxtaposed with an updating of screwball conventions in terms of camera placement and sexual politics. At the second attempted ransom drop, Robert and Celine are first shown from behind, via a handheld tracking shot, passing the time by recounting their sexual histories, (in a similar way to Andie MacDowell in Mike Newell's 1994 *Four Weddings and a Funeral*). When Celine agrees to go on a date, this shifts the film more firmly onto romantic comedy ground, but Robert's status as hero continues to be diminished: he tries to tell her about his idea for a novel, but she guesses the likely course of his story straight away. It appears that the film is not going to follow the cliché of the hero becoming a bestselling novelist after facing several hardships – the plain fact is that he is not a great writer (or even a very good one). Like Marion Ravenwood (Karen Black) in *Raiders of the Lost Ark* (dir. Steven Spielberg 1981), Celine challenges the passivity of a classical heroine by adopting/parodying its opposite, excessive masculinity. She lines up glasses of tequila like chess pieces and challenges Robert to a drinking game, the prize being her freedom. At this point, Robert clarifies the obvious in that 'the kidnap's over', but Celine wishes to be indulged, evoking her image as a spoilt rich girl.

Boyle blends fantastical sequences into the 'reality' of his films, such as the subsequent bar-room scene in which Robert and Celine suddenly break into a song and dance routine, jumping on the bar and performing choreographed moves – all without the clear markers, such as a wobbly screen effect, that would tell the audience that the scene has shifted to fantasy. In some ways, the introduction of fantasy elements can add to the potential depth of characterisation, but in genres dependent upon a certain cartoonishness such as screwball, this can make audiences more uncertain still about the validity of what they are viewing and thereby what kind of response is expected of them. Andrew Sarris once described the screwball comedy as 'a sex comedy without the sex' and that is what we have here.[4] We cut to a scene of Robert waking and a dissolve of Celine dressing in a coy evasion of whether any sexual contact has taken place. Although now socially acceptable, inclusion of sexual scenes are not always necessary (think again of *Four Weddings*) – audiences are able to read cues relating to sexual activity, but these cues must be clear. If the

---

4　Sarris in *American Film*, 3:5 1978 p.13.

camera pans away and the following scene opens in a bedroom, the implication is clear, both in the 1930s and now, but here it is the non-committal reaction of Celine, showing no emotion towards Robert, neither affection nor enmity, which makes it ambiguous as to whether this is a post-coital scene or not.

Linda Williams' analysis of the narrative structures in pornography uses a comparison with musicals in which the various sexual permutations equate closely with different kinds of dance numbers.[5] Ewan McGregor says that the song and dance routine 'kind of replaced the love scene,' as it effectively signals a pause in the forward momentum of the narrative but is also a comment upon it, implying that the couple is sexually compatible without having to show it.[6] Perhaps Boyle's intention was to prevent the film sliding into other generic areas such as the erotic thriller, but Celine's enduring frostiness is an ongoing problem for the viewer. As a glacial screwball heroine with whom the hero might indulge in some playful banter, this might work, but for viewers to believe that the couple are involved romantically we need to see some show of genuine emotion from her character.

The bank robbery scene itself is very uneven in terms of tone. Robert and Celine are hardly Pumpkin (Tim Roth) and Honey Bunny (Amanda Plummer) from Tarantino's *Pulp Fiction* (1994). Although Celine produces a gun, the threats she makes to bank staff feel more of a childish test for Robert. She talks of having 'a great time' but viewers might well feel more sympathy with Robert in angrily walking away from her. The timing of their first on-screen kiss (which may happen after they have actually slept together, depending on how you read the symbolism of the song-and-dance routine in the bar) seems wholly contrived. Boyle's use of slow-motion attempts to invest the moment with significance, but as there is little sense of development of either individuals or their relationship.

After the robbery, Celine and Robert, standing next to their getaway car, are held at gunpoint by a security guard outside the bank. We then cut to a strange shot of Celine, lying on the back seat of the car, apparently suffering from a gunshot wound (an action unexplained at that precise moment), in an explicit reference to Mr Orange (Tim Roth) in *Reservoir Dogs*. Then we return to the two of them once again standing by the car. Celine kisses Robert but crucially, we then cut to a shot of Celine wounded on the backseat and *at the same time* her arm appears in

5 Williams 1989 pp.132-134.
6 Page 2009 p.75.

the right side of the frame as she stands next to Robert: in other words, she is literally in two places at once.

We then realise this is an impossible snapshot, a flash-forward glimpse of one possible future, a psychic vision granted to us. Presumably Robert averts this potential future by throwing himself heroically in front of her when a security guard shoots at them, taking the bullet that was destined for her. It all happens very quickly and could be seen either as ambitious on Boyle's part or unnecessarily complicated. The first kiss we see between the pair is an important shot (one used on trailers and posters) and to place it within a sequence that disrupts the chronology of the narrative, albeit briefly, threatens to confuse and/or alienate viewers.

Rather than take him to a hospital, Celine drives Robert to Elliot, at his dental practice. In another example of the uneven tone of the film, the potentially comic effect of a kooky dentist, sporting an obvious head bandage from Celine's William Tell stunt in the opening scene, is undercut by the overtly gory shot of his making an incision in Robert's leg without anaesthetic (possibly an in-joke, related to scriptwriter Hodge's parallel profession as a doctor). Celine, who is unmoved by Robert's clear agony, then agrees to pose in a nurse's uniform for Elliot's Polaroid in a Lynchian scene of perversity.

The final scene in which Celine mistakenly shoots Robert in seeking to rescue him from Naville represents another 'impossible' action. She shoots Naville's hired killer, Mayhew the butler, through Robert's body. We see the path of the bullet, slowed down, passing through Robert's back and apparently bursting his heart. Miraculously, however, his heart heals and he survives. The course of the bullet is a parallel for the myth of Cupid's arrow and the subsequent healing reflects the idealistic concept of suddenly falling in love.

 The resolution of the narrative is unsatisfyingly messy. The two-shot of Robert and Celine addressing the audience directly to deliver platitudes about love and destiny seems extremely heavy-handed and although there is a romantic scene shot in extreme high-angle as the pair leave a bar, having just got married, the knife that Robert spins, turning between the yin and yang signs of 'Beginning' and 'End,' reflects the stuttering nature of the narrative.

The animated sequence over the closing credits implies the preceding film has been a romantic comedy of logical progression, culminating in an apparent happy ending, but that is not so. It has not been a slapstick, light-hearted romp at all. Not all elements of the screwball subgenre are present and those that are, simply create confusion. Screwball does not take itself seriously: sentimentality and clichéd romantic situations are usually subject to rebuke and satirical undercutting, but in *A Life Less Ordinary,* this lack of seriousness is undermined by the assertive, authorial final pieces to camera.

It is a film full of false starts, with an uneven tone, inconsistent character development, and dialogue that sometimes tips over into the purely sententious and pretentious. There is no real consideration of the role of work (a significant part of classic screwball, like Hildy in Howard Hawks' 1940 *His Girl Friday*, who sees work as key to being independent). Celine does not have to work and is not really brought round to understanding the value of it. In general, the bringing together of the lovers in *A Life Less Ordinary* is too easily achieved. They undergo physical jeopardy, being chased and shot at, but there is no significant change in their characters by the end. In *It Happened One Night*, Peter Warne teaches Ellie about 'real' life on the road, but here Robert does not have anything to teach Celine and she shows no inclination to learn.

There is little inverted class snobbery typical of screwball because, while Boyle's film is critical of Celine's character, Robert's is not really much more admirable. He tries to do what is right (not wanting to swear or be rude on the phone, for example), but cinematically that does not make him interesting: indeed, he is quite dull, limited by a clichéd view of the world, which is reflected in his writing. We do not have the scheming to find a suitable man from the outset (such as with Susan in *Bringing Up Baby*); the element of remarriage, such as with Dexter Haven (James Stewart) and Tracy Lord (Katharine Hepburn) in *The Philadelphia Story* (George Cukor, 1940); and, though the banter may be fast at times it does not reach the point of the overlapping dialogue of Hildy and Walter (Rosalind Russell and Cary Grant) in *His Girl Friday*.

In conventional screwball comedies, characters act eccentrically (think of Carole Lombard as Irene, faking a fainting spell in Gregory La Cava's *My Man Godfrey*, 1936). The key problem in *A Life Less Ordinary* is that Celine's Willian Tell routine is not quirky and endearing, but suggests a bored callousness. Screwball can be a very self-aware genre, something that is usually achieved through the agency of the woman. In *The Lady Eve*, for example, Jean (Barbara Stanwyck) observes the appearance of Charles (Henry Fonda) in a make-up mirror and provides us with commentary upon him, in the guise of a proxy director. Thomas Sobchack and Vivian C. Sobchack refer to 'the predatory female who stalks the protagonist', but that level of narrative drive never comes from Celine.[7] Problematically for

---

7   T. Sobchack and V. Sobchack 1980 p.208.

A Life Less Ordinary, although Celine may be literally driving the car and providing knowledge about the mechanics of kidnapping, we do not really have the sense of an on-screen courtship going on.

The decision to attempt to breathe life into a moribund, anachronistic genre is perhaps a brave one, but the reason for its decline may lie outside the ability of a filmmaker to influence. Screwball is centrally concerned with sexual politics: making generalisations about what is, or is not, appropriate behaviour is much less clear in today than at the highpoint of the genre in the 1930s and 40s. The social mobility and upheaval caused by the Depression provided a motivated backdrop for the extremes of society to meet, and particularly to question the moral value of the feckless rich. Prurient fantasies about high society, easy-living and bringing social betters down a peg or two, all popular in the Depression, may still be shared by viewers today. What is different now, perhaps, is a greater focus on celebrity rather than wealth, and the ability to meet this demand via tabloid magazines and reality shows such as *The Simple Life* on MTV.

A Life Less Ordinary needs more sophistication in the writing, but also quite possibly in the audience too, to be able to process the generic cues on offer. Jacques Derrida once proposed 'there is no genreless text.'[8] That may be so, but the problem is that audiences may no longer have the 'reading tools' to be able to place texts that largely refer to the sexual politics of a bygone age.

Apocalyptic horror: 28 Days Later (2002)

Commercially and critically successful, *28 Days Later* marks another generic shift for Boyle. Often heralded as a genre-busting work, it is worth considering whether the film does really challenge the generic expectations of apocalyptic horror films or just develops existing conventions by combining them in new ways. The main narrative follows Jim (Cillian Murphy) as he awakes in a London hospital to a world ravaged by a virus that turns those it infects into murderous savages. Initially alone, he subsequently befriends a series of other uninfected individuals, including Selena (Naomi Harris), and father and daughter Frank (Brendan Gleeson) and Hannah (Megan Burns), and tries to make his way north to apparent safety at an army compound near Manchester.

Using the opening of the film to reveal the virus to be government-

8   Derrida in Mitchell (ed.) 1981 p 61.

produced and tested on primates is certainly not a new approach. *The Lawnmower Man* (dir. Brett Leonard 1992), *Monkey Shines* (dir. George Romero 1988) and the ITV series *Chimera* (dir. Lawrence Gordon Clark 1991) all follow a similar idea. What perhaps is new here is the very opening shot, with the camera pulling out slowly from a montage of global civil unrest, only for this to be revealed as part of a bank of monitors which are exposing a test subject, a chimp, to repeated images of brutality. The effect of cinematic violence on a test subject who cannot look away evokes the treatment given to Alex in Kubrick's *A Clockwork Orange* (1971), a film that Boyle has cited as one of his earliest influences.

Animal rights' protesters break in and seek to free the chimps, who are being used by the government for medical research. One of the animals, infected with an experimental drug that induces aggression, known as 'Rage,' instantly sets upon the group, leading to the national outbreak of disease that the film dramatises. We cut to black and silence in the opening attack of the chimp. After its initial ferocious attack, the use of gore here is relatively restrained, something that is also true of the rest of the rest of the film. Threats are more often suggested by flickering shadows than by the physical appearance of infected individuals, and on-screen killing is usually shown by victims disappearing under a mass of flailing arms. There are no lengthy special-effects sequences showing methods of killing – a staple element in the zombie subgenre. In the café, which Jim later explores whilst the other survivors search for petrol, he is surrounded by bodies, all slumped like waxworks, but they are only shown relatively briefly and in half-light, except for an iconic girl, face-down with a doll. The effect is not the visceral shock of a conventional zombie film but the horror of the situation on a human scale. Here, Jim has to kill for the first time, defending himself against an attack by an infected little girl. Boyle does not show us the fight but Jim emerges from the café bloodied and, by implication, with a new sense of the brutality that is needed to survive.

Boyle's presentation of the Infected draws on a number of guiding principles. In the production notes, Boyle comments that 'the general idea was to try and shoot as though we were survivors too,' and the grainy quality of some of the digital video imagery suits the bleak apocalyptic nature of the narrative.[9] The strobe effect used for the Infected is created by filming at up to 1600fps (normal speed is 24/25fps) with Canon XL1 DV cameras, which produces a jumpy, staccato look.

---

9 Boyle at http://www.cilliansite.com/production-notes/28-days-later-prod-notes.pdf, p.6.

This technique is also used for Jim in his climactic fight at the army base, emphasising how he must discover an animal survival instinct within himself and also making it more ambiguous as to whether he has become infected, especially as he is now bare-chested and sprayed with blood. His movement is also differently choreographed from earlier scenes, his sudden movements reminiscent of the descent of Roy Batty (Rutger Hauer) into comedic lycanthropia in Ridley Scott's *Blade Runner* (1982). Jim is forced to learn the brutality of survival now, smashing the head of a soldier before putting his fingers through the man's eyeballs (another similarity with Batty's despatching of Tyrell in Scott's film).

In the opening sequence at the animal research centre, where protestors attempt to free the animals, Boyle uses extreme close-ups on eyes, signalled as abnormal by being bloodshot, tinged with yellow and used in combination with a red colour-wash. The first example of this is the escaped chimp in shots that strongly evoke the extreme close-up of devilish eyes in *Rosemary's Baby* (dir. Roman Polanski 1968). Boyle removes the red – associated with the Infected – from the colour palette elsewhere in the film, so that it can be instantly linked with an attack at close quarters, such when an Infected individual jumps onto the back window of the cab as Jim, Selena, Frank and Hannah try to escape London in Frank's black cab via a road tunnel. The red colour-wash even extends to the crow's (literal) bird's-eye view of Frank, just before a drop of infected blood drops straight into his eye.

Edwin Page's assumption that the horror genre always portrays violence with tongue-in-cheek references marks him as a post-*Scream* film viewer: he name-checks *The Shining* (dir. Stanley Kubrick 1980) as an example of sober horror but fails to explain why this is relevant in a discussion of the zombie subgenre.[10] Although it is frequently described as a zombie film, leading in part to some harsh criticism from horror fans expecting the sorts of serial, gory pleasures delivered by a George A. Romero film, *28 Days Later* is not part of that sub-genre. As Boyle states himself, 'we stole lots of bits from zombie movies but *28 Days Later* is a thing in itself'.[11] Feeling perhaps that a slow, lumbering threat to eat people's brains was too much part of a cinematic past and difficult to place in a realistic context, writer Alex Garland and Boyle opted for a more likely source of mass panic: viral infection. Its characteristics – transmission by bodily fluid, haemorrhaging, and speedy death – link it

10 Page 2009 p.133.
11 Boyle at http://www.cilliansite.com/production-notes/28-days-later-prod-notes.pdf, p.6.

with known phenomena such as the Ebola virus, SARRs, and bio-terrorist attacks. In *Survivors* (BBC 1975-77; remade 2008-2010) the virus, which wipes out up to 99 percent of the population, is man-made and its spread is due to a laboratory accident. Boyle's notion, in collaboration with Garland, was to dramatise an experimental drug which exaggerates existing psychological traits rather than to create a purely external explanation for the virus. During shooting, the notion of the virus changed from a global epidemic to one that only affects Britain, cut off from the world and effectively quarantined. The leader of the military group, Major West (Christopher Eccleston) and his second-in-command, Sergeant Farrell (Stuart McQuarrie) suggest differing readings of the situation, but the film does not dwell on this as such considerations would need to take place in lulls in the narrative pace, of which there are few. In any case the hero, Jim, has no means of communicating beyond Britain, itself an unconventional setting for this horror subgenre (see Chapter Four for further discussion of national identity).

John Carpenter's *Ghosts of Mars* (2001) also features an airborne virus (whose own sentient point-of-view is suggested by a red colour-wash) that induces in sufferers a self-harming, murderous rage. Carpenter's film, like Boyle's, creates tension through the use of blurred figures that pass close in front of the camera, accompanied by a whooshing sound effect. This combination of a visual and aural trope is used by Boyle to suggest danger, such as when Mark (Noah Huntley) and Selena rescue Jim from his first experience of the Infected, during their exploration of the blockade and later when Jim lures the soldiers, who have proved to be a threat to survivors rather than their saviours, into a trap. This whooshing effect is a combination that Boyle also uses in *Sunshine* for the communication towers, prior to their destruction. Indeed, Boyle states on the *Sunshine* DVD that 'the only way that CG images look like they've got weight as opposed to looking real, they sort of feel real in an invisible way, is sound'.

Page mentions, but does not explore, the influence on *28 Days Later* of Richard Matheson's 1954 novel *I Am Legend* and all its subsequent cinematic versions. Although released after Boyle's film, Francis Lawrence's 2007 version starring Will Smith provides an interesting contrast. In Lawrence's film and in *The Last Man on Earth* (dir. Ubaldo Ragona 1964) the hero is a virologist and thus is part of a potential solution. The symptoms are akin to vampirism and the virus is rapidly spread with little distinction between those infected and those who are not. For Boyle, on the other hand, any hope of a cure lies outside the scope of his hero. All Jim can do is try to survive. Boyle maintains the vampiric overtones by having the Infected transmit their infection by direct blood contact but Selena's advice that the uninfected should not travel at night is not really explained. Lawrence uses CG effects for his monsters rather than Boyle's preference for actors, make-up, and adjustment of film speed. A lower level of technology actually packs a more visceral punch. With a bigger budget, Lawrence can include scenes of mass evacuation and panic, but it is the very absence of people that make Boyle's opening so powerful. *The Last Man on Earth* ends with the hero being shot and stabbed; Lawrence also makes him a martyr in *I Am Legend*, killing himself with a grenade to help others escape. Boyle rejects such closure, opting for hope.

There is a slight nod to Romero's *Night of the Living Dead* (1968) in the amoral action of the Infected, who are prepared to turn on members of their own family in their sheer determination to attack. Other Romero films are also referenced. From *Dawn of the Dead* (1978) Boyle uses a battle in a grocery store and a confrontation with an infected child in a café. From *Day of the Dead* (1985), Boyle takes two ideas: of an infected man who has been cruelly chained like an animal in order to be studied and of a military enclave which appears to offer sanctuary to women but actually preys upon them sexually.

A more direct precursor of Boyle's film is George Romero's 1973 *The Crazies*, which portrays the effects of a leaked government-produced bio-weapon. Like Romero's characters, Boyle's Infected also become homicidal or die. *The Crazies* also includes a highly contagious virus that induces homicidal rage, and the film follows a group of survivors as they seek to avoid capture by army units. However, what marks Boyle's Infected as different is speed. The zombie sub-genre is characterised by slow-moving, lumbering creatures who may retain a small element of their humanity. Boyle's creatures, on the other hand, are turned instantaneously by the virus into snarling killers, using every ounce of energy to rush at those not infected and claw them to death. The speed of infection (15-20 seconds) and speed of attack reflect one of Boyle's underlying aesthetic guiding principles – cinema is about forward motion. Like the survivors, you move or die. There is literally no time for sentimental goodbyes. Mark, Frank, even Major West are all despatched without ceremony. 'Frank' and 'Dad' become quickly designated as 'the body' that the soldiers have to move in a matter of seconds. This is also a difference between Boyle's shots of an empty city and previous apocalyptic visions – nearly all the shots of the city show Jim walking through them, partly for scale, but also to show that he keeps moving.

The unpredictability and speed of the sudden appearance of the Infected could be said to increase suspense but it is also a little too easy, as they can pop up at any given time, for no specific narrative reason other than to introduce some spectacle, such as the figure that crashes through the glass of Jim's parents' house. However, it does also keep self-conscious philosophising or romantic interludes to a minimum, as such activities would seem ludicrous given the imminent threat that prevails throughout much of the film.

The belief of Sergeant Farrell, that since humanity has only existed for a relatively short time in evolutionary terms, 'if the infection wipes us all out, that is a return to normality' is undercut by the assertion by Major West that all he sees is the same situation as before the outbreak of the virus – 'people killing people'. In West, there is something of Jack from William Golding's *Lord of the Flies* (1954) – the loyalty of followers to a 'chief', who believes in mankind's innate bloodlust, is secured by allowing them to give vent to their sadistic impulses. Farrell, as a Piggy-type character, tries to be logical, talk sense, and keep his soldiers' lust for Selena in check but is ultimately killed by them in their pursuit of it.

The survival of the remaining humans is made more difficult, not less, by the actions of the army. In apocalyptic narratives, the source of supposed comfort often turns out to be a source of threat: this idea can be traced back from Robert C. O'Brien's novel *Z For Zachariah* (1973) at least to Peter Watkins' *The War Game* (1965). After being picked up by the army at a blockade, Jim and the others are offered hospitality by Major West at the mansion house that is his base. Boyle goes beyond the abuse of power shown in Romero's zombie films by making the rank-and-file soldiers seem childish: Jones, as typical of the lower ranks, is shown larking about with the taxi once it has been commandeered, driving it in circles with a soldier on the roof. It is more than just underlining the age difference between the men and their commander: they seem unfit to be given weapons and their active enjoyment of picking off the Infected in the nightly turkey-shoot on the front lawn horrifies Jim. The gradual revelation of West's so-called plan underlines the psychosis of the military ethos here. After avuncular invitations to shower, eat well and make themselves comfortable, West reveals to Jim that the radio broadcasts he sends out, apparently offering shelter, are a fraud, designed to draw survivors, especially women, for the prospect of gang-rape.

Many elements of *28 Days Later* are familiar to post-disaster narratives

– London is empty, the army is hostile, the church is powerless and West proves initially charming but ultimately psychotic. Boyle adds to this an updated view of infection, moments of narrative stillness (discussed in Chapter Six) that have a poetic power of their own, and an innovative visual style. His hero survives partly by luck and partly by finding within himself a necessary streak of brutality and resourcefulness. It is a horror film: not one dependent on gory special effects, but on the intrinsic drama of survival.

Science fiction meets philosophy: Sunshine (2007)

Sunshine takes a familiar premise, the threatened extinction of mankind, and gives it a new twist by focusing not on global warming but on a future earth needing more warmth from a dying sun. The crew of a spacecraft, the Icarus II, led by chief physicist Capa (Cillian Murphy) are sent towards the sun to try and reignite it with a giant bomb, replicating a failed mission that took place 16 years earlier during which the spacecraft mysteriously disappeared.

It is a staple of science fiction and horror genres that characters are placed in a position of maximum isolation and helplessness, but when it is announced that the spacecraft will lose contact with earth sooner than expected, the effect is psychological rather than cinematic: the mental strength of each character is tested by being separated from those they know. One of the premises of Alex Garland's script is that despite knowing that they face inevitable cosmic annihilation, the crew continue to function. As the captain of the first mission, Pinbacker (Mark Strong), says, 'there will be nothing to show that we were ever here' and he seems to have found some consolation in giving up his mission to re-animate the sun and placing his faith instead in God's apparent plan to annihilate humanity. The sun has an increasingly hypnotic effect on Pinbacker (and his parallel character, Searle, on the Icarus II), leading to both men exposing themselves to larger and larger doses of harmful rays. Viewers of the film would know that the death of the sun, although a scientific possibility, is not foreseen as happening for another five billion years, so the full force of the crew's situation remains extremely distanced in time, undermining Boyle and Garland's attempts to create a sense of narrative jeopardy.

Boyle seems determined to do things slightly differently. From the very opening of the film, the Fox Searchlight logo sequence runs backwards so that the film opens with a shot of what we assume will be the sun but is revealed to be the golden heat-shields of the spacecraft. We are challenged to look and think about our diminutive role in the cosmos, a question linking the film generically with a more innovative, philosophical strand of science fiction. However there is also a strongly derivative element running through the whole film. On the one hand, this derives from the very nature of science fiction set in space (one of the most distinct cinematic genres, inevitably reminding audiences of other films) but on the other, there is also a highly allusive quality to much of the narrative which, like Garland's work discussed elsewhere in this book, could point either to a lack of originality, or to creative use of intertextual cross-referencing.

Like Kubrick's *2001* (1968), *Sunshine* features an emergency space-walk and an argument over the voice-related authority of an on-board computer at a moment of crisis (the need for someone to sacrifice themselves to reset the heat-shields), evoking comparisons with HAL in the earlier film. Boyle opted to keep Chipo Chung, the voice of the computer, on-set so that, in the same way that the special effects personnel were also present for some of the filming, a greater sense of coherence could be created. This gave the actors a greater sense of their own performance at the point of delivering it, rather than it becoming merely a post-production technical exercise.

There are some obvious parallels with Ridley Scott's *Alien* (1979) – the emergency sequence with its flashing lights, sirens and people running down corridors; the knowing joke from Mace (Chris Evans) that they 'might get picked off one-by-one by aliens,' and, as the ship approaches the sun and heats up, there are several more corridor shots accompanied by the grinding sound of shape-changing metal. It is as if the sun is animating the ship and it is groaning in pain. As in *Alien*, there are cutaways to little executive toys to show movement in the ship, but also to provide ironic juxtaposition with the main action. We see a close-up of a round-faced, nodding, smiling orange figure, specifically echoing the colour palette surrounding Pinbacker (only ever shown in a blurry, fiery shot), contrasting with the shots of the interior of the Icarus II, which is dominated by more sober blue, grey and green.

Page contrives to make *Sunshine* seem a direct descendant of *Alien*, but on nearly every point, it is a matter of contrast rather than similarity. He suggests that the femininity of Corazon (Michelle Yeoh) or Cassie (Rose Byrne) is somehow made androgynous by their uniforms in an attempt to parallel Ripley, but this is just not so, something that is reflected in Cassie's observation in a flat, bored voice, watching a scuffle between Mace and Capa, that they are suffering 'an excess of manliness breaking out in the Comms Centre'. Male aggression seems something that female crew tolerate as if observing a lower evolutionary life-form. Page criticises the film as a missed opportunity for failing to make a female character as dominant as Ripley, but this is clearly not what the film is trying to do: Page does admit, however, that the characters were originally written without a specific gender, which is actually a braver directing choice.[12] Unlike the mix of ethnicity in *Aliens* (dir. James Cameron 1986), the dominant influence here is Asian–American, as this reflects the most likely source of capital to fund space exploration in the near future. What *Sunshine* primarily shares with *2001* and *Alien* is a sense of gradual pacing, especially in the first half, and a sense of melancholy realism that shifts into the fantastical with the appearance of Pinbacker as the apparent normality breaks down.

The 'botanical garden,' on which the crew of the spacecraft depend for oxygen, masterfully created by production designer Mark Tildesley, owes much in concept to *Silent Running* (dir. Douglas Trumbull 1972), which also features an obsessed botanist whose life is centred on the nurturing of precious plants and whose character becomes much more brutal once threatened with their loss. When Capa sends a message home, this is shot against a green, dripping background and is inter-cut with the garden, suggesting that he at least appreciates what its keeper, Corazon, is trying to create. Like Tarkovsky's *Solaris* (1972), Boyle suggests that lengthy space travel makes human psychology turn inward, here most obviously because it is dwarfed by the size and power of the sun. In the face of something that threatens to render meaningless all that they know, it is perhaps not surprising that some of the crew buckle under the stress. As with *Solaris'* visual phenomena which could be interpreted as visions or projections, such as the appearance of Hari (Natalya Bondarchuk) the dead wife of the captain, *Sunshine* problematises what it is that the crew sees in looking at the sun, and the effect it has on them. This is shown particularly in relation to their captain, Kaneda (Hiroyuki Sanada) who repeatedly watches the video log of his predecessor on Icarus I, the log showing a madman with a distorted physical form and manic eyes, ranting at the camera before the transmission freezes. The crew share their visions: when Capa wakes from a nightmare of falling into the surface of the sun, Cassie's questioning suggests that she often has the same dream. This sharing, and the difficulty of distinguishing between such experiences and objective reality, are also a centrepiece of *Solaris*. In

12 Page 2009 p.193.

John Carpenter's *Ghosts of Mars*, the psychological problems associated with lengthy travel in space (even on the Mars train) are acknowledged: like Mace, police officer Melanie Ballard (Natasha Henstridge) takes a drug which induces a pleasant dream of earth (also featuring waves), which seem to make both characters feel peaceful.

In Brian De Palma's 2002 *Mission to Mars*, (itself extremely derivative of *2001*), as in *Sunshine*, a spacecraft disappears in unknown circumstances and we follow the rescue mission, effectively blending science fiction with detection. As the crew receives a cryptic message from the first ship, there is a realisation that they can only find out what happened by exposing themselves to the same dangers and possibly sharing the same fate. As with Boyle's film, there is a greenhouse zealously guarded by one crew member, Luke Graham (Don Cheadle), and a captain, Woodrow 'Woody' Blake (Tim Robbins), who heroically sacrifices himself for the good of the mission while on a spacewalk. His demise, in first freezing and then burning up, is effectively split by Garland and Boyle between the fate of Kaneda, who sacrifices himself to the rays of the sun in repairing a heat shield and Harvey (Troy Garity), who is knocked away into an instant frozen death during the desperate 'jump' between Icarus I and II, after Pinbacker has undocked the two spacecraft.

An even clearer precursor is Paul W.S. Anderson's *Event Horizon* (1997). Like *Sunshine*, it has the same basic plot of a missing spacecraft, found apparently abandoned with someone, or something, on board that should not be there. We have another self-sacrificing captain (played by Lawrence Fishburne), frozen bodies shattering, drama at airlocks, a distorted tape from the previous captain warning them to save themselves, and — the most obvious parallel of all — a Pinbacker-type figure called Dr Weir (Sam Neill). He guards the 'gravity-drive' that lies at the heart of the ship and which distorts time and space at the climax, transforming him into a scarred, shape-shifting creature, described as 'the Weirbeast' in the credits. Like *Sunshine*, Anderson's film also uses brightly lit space helmets (allowing us to see facial expressions), a score that includes Boyle-favourites Orbital, and a largely British crew at Pinewood.

In *Sunshine*, the bomb is often referred to euphemistically as 'the payload,' but in John Carpenter's *Dark Star* (1974), which also features a bored, listless crew, it is named explicitly in witty dialogue as 'Bomb'. In Carpenter's film, there are hilarious philosophical discussions between Lt Doolittle and the Bomb, in which Doolittle tries to teach the bomb the basics of phenomenology to distract it from detonating. Ironically the Bomb eventually rationalises that it is God, declares 'let there be light' and blows itself up. Perhaps the most obvious link, picked up by Mark Kermode, is the connection between Sergeant Pinback (Dan O'Bannon) in *Dark Star* and Pinbacker in *Sunshine*. In Carpenter's film, Pinback's identity is based on a mistake: he tries to save a character (whose name is Pinbacker) from committing suicide and by accident dons his spacesuit and assumes his identity.[13] Boyle's Pinbacker appears to want to be taken seriously, but by linking his name with Carpenter's absurd figure, whose whole character is based on a fraud, this is undermined.

The narrative twist of picking up a distress signal from the previous mission on Icarus I is the first major turning point in *Sunshine*'s narrative and is important for a number of reasons. As a genre staple, it is a way to reference other works (notably *2001*), to inject suspense, and to underline that it is Capa's judgement which carries the most weight in any matter, such as whether they should change course to respond to the distress signal. This is important because although the group appears relatively egalitarian, sitting and discussing problems together, this is not a democracy. The vote that is taken later about whether to kill Trey (Benedict Wong) in order to save oxygen for the rest of the crew, is only tokenistic – although Cassie refuses to support the idea, Mace clearly intends to carry out the act whether everyone agrees or not. As in *Solaris*, there is a sense of déjà vu in the attempt to solve something inexplicable that seems to happen more than once (the mysterious failure of an earlier mission and the apparently impossible appearance of a new crew member on board the spacecraft). Reminiscent of George Sluizer's 1988 *The Vanishing*, there is also the sense that the character investigating the mystery, in this case Capa, can only solve it by submitting himself to the same fate as the previous victim.

A key problem with the narrative is that it works against empathetic engagement with character. As soon as the mission starts to unravel, the notion of characters having a valid role becomes progressively undermined. Trey is a master mathematician but, after failing to re-set the heat shields at the correct angle, he becomes a blank of self-loathing and suicidal tendencies. Four of the crew – Capa, Mace, Harvey and Searle – are trapped on Icarus I when Pinpacker undocks the two spacecraft and leaves the men with only one spacesuit between them. The captain, Kaneda, dies trying to fix the heat shields, and although communications

---

13   Kermode in *The Observer*, 25 March 2007.

officer Harvey frantically tries to assert his authority (he is theoretically next in command), he is reminded by Mace that he is a communications officer on a ship without any communications towers: in other words, with no visible function. Corazon could also be said to be lacking a clear function once the garden is destroyed. The absence of the garden certainly changes her character and her nurturing quality seems much reduced, being prepared to let Mace kill Trey so that the rest of the crew can survive.

The character of Capa has greater depth than it might at first appear. Delivering his final message home, he says 'I know everything you want to say,' which may sound arrogant but also at the same time avoids the kind of empty sentiment that is antithetical to his nature as a scientist. Similarly, his final promise – 'I'll see you in couple of years' – might suggest either that he expects to return or that he does not expect to survive and is referring to some kind of afterlife. Unlike other crew members, Capa does not become fearful about the decreased level of oxygen or the reduced prospect of a return journey, as if deep down he knows their return is impossible. As in the horror genre, with Jim and Selena in *28 Days Later*, science fiction also generically resists the development of romantic scenarios – the focus on action struggles to accommodate dialogue that seem sentimental and self-indulgent when dealing with matters of life and death. There are hints of some romantic potential between Cassie and Capa as she helps him into his spacesuit, comforting him (and possibly herself too) that he has 'done this' (a repair drill) 'a 1,000 times in training'. The closing of the helmet momentarily frames her eyes looking at his. Boyle originally had plans for a love scene between the two, but the pressures to maintain forward narrative momentum meant this had to be dropped. Checking later on the payload, they have a more intimate discussion (accompanied by a softer, more sentimental score than elsewhere) about the prospect of death, during which she asks him if he is scared. Capa answers as a physicist, imagining the incredible nature of witnessing a new star being born from an old one, not just being partly responsible for this but being allowed to see it too. This suggests that from a scientific point of view he is actually closer to the evangelical spirituality of the psychologist, Searle (Chris Curtis), than it might seem. The scene was originally shot with Searle as Capa's interlocuter, but using Cassie instead allows the dialogue to be more intimate and draw on the possibility of a romantic relationship.

The decision about whether to divert the spacecraft to answer the distress beacon, apparently emanating from Icarus I, is theoretically democratic with the crew gathered around the table and points of view expressed, but the crew are framed as blurred figures in the background – the real decision-maker, framed in sharp focus, close to the camera, looking up, is Capa (almost in pop video pose like Bruce Gowers' 1975 'Bohemian Rhapsody' for Queen). The loneliness of his role, designated by his intellect, not by politics, is emphasised by this framing and the Dietrich-like top lighting, picking out his prominent cheek-bones and suggesting he needs spiritual help from above, as down here he is very much alone.

Kaneda is closer to a conventional hero, wrestling with greater responsibilities which he shoulders alone. Whether he becomes obsessed with the fate of Icarus I is hard to judge but we see him alone, watching Pinbacker's increasingly irrational video transmissions, in which he talks of the beauty of watching the sun. It might seem that Pinbacker communicates something here and that it is as a result of seeing this that the captain sacrifices himself. It is apparently the action of a hero, but perhaps he has already been seduced by Pinbacker's theory of acquiescence to the sun. An opening chess scene with Capa (filmed but not included in the final cut) might have suggested the beginnings of a battle of minds, or even that the captain has become too inward-looking and contemplative: in cutting himself off from contact with the crew possibly he has become more susceptible to Pinbacker's doctrine. The captain's continued presence was to be denoted by the carrying of a chess-piece through the narrative, but such symbolism would have given the captain a greater, epic weight than his character really has in the narrative.

In terms of visual style, the interior of the ship with its long, bright corridors and billowing, shiny plastic, evokes Michael Jackson's video for 'Scream' (dir. Mark Romanek 1995) which, at $7 million, is still the most expensive pop video ever made. For budgetary reasons, the set for Icarus II was covered in thick dust, re-lit and re-used as Icarus I. Garland's concept of a whole set turned on its side (evocative of the Zeebrugge ferry disaster) proved too expensive and might have had distracting overtones of *The Poseidon Adventure* (dir. Ronald Neame 1972). The gold colour of the spacesuit suggests it might derive from the same technology as the golden heat shields, but it still seems highly stylised and the ultimate revelation of its splendour is made more dramatic by a preceding sequence of tight shots, depriving us a sense of the whole suit. There is a strange blend of anachronisms in the cumbersome suit, reminiscent of a Victorian deep-sea diving outfit but with a Medieval-style slit in the helmet, and something much more alien and futuristic in the mixture of curved and flat surfaces in its design. There is even a nod to Kenny's ever-present hood in Trey Parker and Matt Stone's animation *South Park* (1997-present), also signalling the likely fate of the crew (as Kenny dies in virtually every episode). The film may be set in the future, but the lack of visibility provided by the helmets and the poor mobility of the suit as a whole, show that these are both fairly contrived dramatic constructs which place obstacles in the way of the characters, and are there in order to create opportunities for suspense. Boyle overcomes the logistical problem of not seeing astronauts' faces by having a camera positioned within the helmet with a wide-angle lens at 45 degrees to the wearer's face. This creates a sense of claustrophobic tension, and of visibly rising heat as we see the sweat beading: it also means we can take in both what is visible, and the wearer's reaction to it, in a single shot. *Alien's* use of grainy images from cameras mounted on the helmets themselves is used later in Harvey's discovery of the thriving garden on Icarus I. This technique references the earlier film's exploration section with obscured visuals so we do not know if the new environment is hostile or not. At the beginning of the space-walk, the in-helmet view is then used as part of several juxtaposed images – the control room in the middle, the captain on the right, and Capa on the left. Movement is difficult, both inside and outside the spacecraft in these suits, reflected in the disembodied sense of seeing Capa observing his own hands through the slit, as if alien to himself, and of course preparing us for his trip and fall en route to the bomb at the climax.

There are many striking and memorable images, such as the space-walk sequences in which tiny humans are dwarfed by the scale of their surroundings, and the mini-montage alongside the closing credits which reminds us of all that we have seen. After Trey's miscalculation with the heat shields causes direct rays to strike the Icarus II, Corazon is effectively in a glass cage surrounded by images of fire as she tries to gain access to her precious garden, housed in a sealed-off area whose oxygen is now feeding the flames. Capa's panic, in fleeing from Pinbacker, is suggested by close-ups of his face, inter-cut with shots from a camera mounted on his head, conveying a sense of claustrophobia in being chased down corridors. This ties in with two earlier shots: the tight close-up shots of both he and Corazon using scooters to get around the ship and the head-on shot of the captain looking straight at the camera, the sun's rays approaching in the reflection on his visor.

The attempt to get back to Icarus I by being blasted from one airlock to the other while clinging to one another, seems strangely primitive amid all the complex technology, but does yield one of the film's most memorable images. We see Harvey, knocked into the freezing depths of space, in profile as he expels his final breath, which seems to be transformed into golden dust (reminding us of Searle's final words to Capa: 'we're only stardust'). Harvey passes a reflective shield, giving him a Poe-like image of impossibility – he sees the moment of his own death. It is poignant and we are encouraged to see the transformation as strangely beautiful as Harvey passes close before the camera, his eyeballs visibly freezing. In passing an arm of the communications towers, ironically his responsibility, his arm strikes one and instantly shatters.[14] He is a pitiable Everyman figure, apparently surrounded by more proficient and assertive astronauts, but is largely out of his depth, longing to get home and is one of the first to be vaporised when exposed to the sun.

The flash-cuts used of the former crew as Capa, Mace, Searle and Trey enter Icarus I would normally be too quick for the human eye to register, but the contrasts in light and colour and their repeated nature means that most viewers will pick them up (unlike, perhaps, David Fincher's use of images of Brad Pitt as Tyler Durden in the hospital and at the self-help groups in *Fight Club* (1999) which are really only visible on DVD freeze-frame). Here we have a strong juxtaposition of images of light with darkness, life with death, and clarity with mystery. Fincher's favoured device of flashlights piercing the gloom is also used here, and each flash-cut is motivated by a torch shone straight at the camera. On a first viewing of *Sunshine*, the flowers around the crew's heads in the glimpse of a group snapshot (which represents a Hawaiian-style homecoming) may even seem like blood when seen at normal speed. The dust that covers everything may not be composed of human skin, as Mace jokes to unsettle Harvey, but there is a sense that the men have entered a tomb and that these flash-cuts in some measure represent the souls of those who lost their lives here. Like the final shot in Kubrick's *The Shining* (1980), we see a smiling posed shot of the first crew juxtaposed with what became of the figures in the photo, in the shots of incinerated bodies in the observation room. The technique also anticipates the later use of flash-cuts in Capa's apprehension of a blurred orange figure who turns out to be Pinbacker and who seems to spirit himself unseen between the ships, apparently leaving no trace in the dust, perhaps suggesting that he is not fully mortal either.

14 See Garland 2007 pp.142 and 144 for storyboards by Martin Asbury and James Cornish.

Boyle's only previous attempts at science fiction had ended with the aborted *Alien Love Triangle* (2002) project, a three-part film, only the first part of which was ever made and now exists in commercial limbo, unavailable on DVD and never given a general release. With features such as teleportation and aliens posing as humans, even the plot outline has the intriguing feel of a Cronenberg remake of *Mork and Mindy* (ABC 1978-82). Boyle himself notes that film is primarily a medium of action, rather than contemplation, and it may be that viewers assumed any movie categorised as science fiction would involve spectacular special effects and explosions. In terms of the former, *Sunshine* certainly has powerful special effects sequences, but they are philosophical and cerebral rather than visceral. A key element of science fiction, which may lie behind Boyle's observation that directors tend to 'visit' this genre only once, is the sheer pressure of creating a fully realised world in a studio. Shots that may look undramatic, such as the simulation of zero gravity, are immensely time-consuming and difficult to set up and film.

Sunshine is certainly not a flawless film. There are some strange plot-holes and at times the derivative nature of the script threatens to overwhelm the narrative, making it a patchwork of allusions. The dialogue sporadically echoes one of Scotty's exclamations from *Star Trek* (Mace's 'it sounds like she's tearing apart') or Han Solo's warning to Luke in *Star Wars* (Corazon's reply: 'I know what it is, fly-boy'). However, more broadly, the film also shares (especially with Kubrick's *2001*) the notion that spaceships, even bombs, can be things of beauty and we are invited to view them contemplatively as they move, turning slowly through space. All the other films mentioned here include a key element of long-haul space flight – how space-travel demands a sense of perspective on your own planet and its meaning in the wider cosmos. Conventional science fiction avoids such larger questions, usually opting for special-effects-driven excitement and drama, creating a hellish environment rather than seeking to explore the transcendent and the divine. If *Sunshine* fails in part to meet the genre expectations of mass audiences, it does so due to the scope of its ambition.

CHAPTER THREE

· PERFORMANCE VERSUS TECHNOLOGY ·

'We wanted the film to have vibrancy – a humour,
an outrageousness, we wanted it to be larger than
life really'

Boyle on *Trainspotting*[1]

A key part of Danny Boyle's approach to filmmaking is to marry intense performances with cinematic technology. All directors do this to an extent, but it is Boyle's blend of the emotional realism of his cast with what might be termed the 'hyper-realism' of its presentation, which makes his visual style distinct.

The notion of what constitutes 'realism' is a huge question in film (appearing on early stages of almost any Film Studies degree course) and it would be very easy to dig this chapter into a lengthy, and ultimately unhelpful, digression. I will therefore focus consideration on where notions of realism are relevant for Boyle's work. As someone who did not go to film school, Boyle seems comfortable using different modes of realism in his work, from the raw emotion of his actors' performances to the stylised heightened reality of sequences where he uses technology to convey a different kind of emotional intensity.

The term 'social realism' is applied across a range of art-forms including painting, and it generally relates to the presentation of the harshness of life, especially for those at the bottom of the social spectrum. In film, it grew out of post-war Italian neo-realism, associated with directors like Vittorio De Sica and Roberto Rossellini. The relevance for this study is its application to films made in the UK in the late 1950s and 60s and often dubbed 'kitchen sink drama'. Films like *Saturday Night and Sunday Morning* (dir. Karel Reisz 1960), *A Taste of Honey* (dir. Tony Richardson 1961) and *A Kind of Loving* (dir. John Schlesinger 1962) brought working-class stories to a mainstream audience for the first time: they were often based in the north of England and dealt with issues of regional identity and sexuality previously only discussed in the margins of films.

In some ways Boyle's work continues this tradition. Northern England certainly features in his films (see Chapter Four for a detailed discussion

---

1   O'Hagan in *Sight and Sound* 6:2, February 1996 p.11.

on regional and national identity) and his protagonists are often working class, as in *Trainspotting*, *Shallow Grave*, and *A Life Less Ordinary* – and in *Slumdog Millionaire* they are under-class. That said, Richard in *The Beach* seems to be affluent enough to afford a long-haul flight and an addiction to video games, and the single parent family in *Millions*, moving to a new estate, seem closer to aspiring middle class. As for sexual politics, this only really appears at the periphery of Boyle's cinematic vision, in Diane's rather contrived sassiness in *Trainspotting*, or where, in the same film, sexual gossip is covered by claims to be talking about football and shopping. *A Life Less Ordinary*'s uneasy appropriation of screwball comedy motifs does not take notions of sexual politics beyond fairly predictable banter. With the exception of Renton escaping at the close of *Trainspotting*, Boyle's narratives do not feature a 'local boy made good' motif and none of his male heroes display the anger typically associated with kitchen sink drama. On the contrary (apart from *The Beach*), they display an enduring and charming wit, denying Boyle's films the power of polemic but allowing his work to reach a wider public than overtly political statements might achieve. With the exception of *Sunshine*, which is set in the future, it is the 'nowness' of Boyle's film output is striking. His interest is resolutely contemporary; he tells stories about the world in which we are living today.

Preparing the actors

Boyle's theatrical background resurfaces in the way he prepares his actors, encouraging them to develop a better understanding of the roles they are to play by reading books and viewing relevant films.[2] This is his priority rather than suggesting that they undergo a psychological 'becoming' as advocated by the school of method acting, a practice that evolved in the US via the Group Theatre in New York through the 1930s and 40s, influenced by the Russian theorist and teacher Konstantin Stanislavski. The term is often (mis)used as shorthand for immersing oneself in a role, most obvious in roles requiring physical changes, such as Robert de Niro in *Raging Bull* (dir. Martin Scorsese 1980) or Daniel Day Lewis in *My Left Foot* (dir. Jim Sheridan 1989) and can involve remaining in role during the entirety of a shoot, often leading to tensions and difficulties on set.

Actors, his male leads especially, often wish to work with Boyle more

---

2 Part of Boyle's prescribed reading for *Sunshine* was Andrew Smith's *Moon Dust* (2005), comprising interviews with astronauts and their feelings of being in space/away from the earth, especially the effect of being completely out of sight of their home planet.

than once (think of Ewan McGregor, Robert Carlyle, Cillian Murphy or Christopher Eccleston) because of his attention to the craft of acting. There is an inevitable tension between performance and the technical means by which it is presented to the audience, but what makes Boyle's approach distinctive is the depth of theatrical performance he coaxes from his actors and the degree of fantasy that he then allows to operate on this filmed footage.

He used an element of the method approach in bringing his cast for *Shallow Grave* and *Sunshine* to live together in confined conditions prior to production (in the latter case, in a university hall of residence). This gave both films the sense that the cast were a tight-knit group, who knew each other well enough to be able to deliver almost overlapping dialogue lines – even to the point of being irritated by one another. To anticipate the experience of weightlessness in *Sunshine* and the sensation of inhabiting another world entirely, Boyle arranged a scuba-diving course for the cast, had them use a flight simulator, and sent Michelle Yeoh to the Eden Project in Cornwall to get the flavour of becoming a credible botanist. Brian Cox, the scientific consultant for the film, gave lectures to the cast on elementary quantum physics, the sun, and the back-story of the plot in which the sun has been rendered weaker by a so-called 'Q-ball,' thereby threatening life on earth.

For *127 Hours*, the very title of which implies a specific timeframe, Boyle had to condense certain parts of the story, including the final scene in which Ralston cuts off his own arm. In his book, Ralston describes this as taking 45 minutes but Boyle has to suggest this by the intensity of his hero's emotional journey. He did not allow his props department to step in and help James Franco, in the role of Ralston, with easy solutions to problems like tying knots with one hand (his left), which he wanted his actor to struggle with alone (as Ralston had done). Franco is on screen for large parts of the film and it is his performance that holds the film together.

The DVD for *Slumdog Millionaire*, as with the disc for *Millions*, includes a snippet of Boyle directing a child actor. Orders are barked intensely at Ayush Mahesh Khedekar to create the scene and every few seconds he is set a new challenge so he has little time to think. It seems a brusque style but it leads to a powerful sense of engaging realism in the performance. The children display such an instinctive knowledge of film, because cinema pervades Indian culture so powerfully, that performing on camera seems very natural to them. Much of the power of the first half of *Slumdog* comes from the acting performances of the three leads, (especially the youngest trio, all played by non-professionals). The children's characters are defined early in the film: Jamal endures the ultimate in visceral horror, jumping into the latrine pit, in order to achieve a romantic ideal – an autograph of his film idol – and his brother Salim brutally steals and sells it. Jamal, Salim and Latika refer to themselves as 'The Three Musketeers', even though Alexandre Dumas's 1844 novel is largely unknown in India and perhaps this might therefore seem a heavy-handed cultural imposition. It is, however, a fitting literary allusion, linking the reading matter in their crowded classroom, the code whispered from Salim to Jamal before fleeing from Maman, the notion of 'all for one and one for all' (a notion persistently undermined by Salim), and the final quiz-question that Latika cannot answer but which Jamal guesses correctly. The question, the identity of the third musketeer, is implicitly linked with Latika herself as the third in a tight-knit group (Salim and Jamal, having earlier been ironically called 'Aramis' and 'Porto' by their teacher as they read *The Three Musketeers* in class). Like Damian and Anthony in *Millions*, the brothers are both affected by the loss of their mother, the younger more obviously than the elder. In a sense, the older brother displaces his loss into selfish activity, but we see from Salim's wide-eyed inability to sleep (he turns away from Jamal but still faces the camera) in the container on the night after the death of their mother, that he too is affected.

Boyle's attention to detail does not only apply to main roles but to a host of memorable off-centre minor characters which people Boyle's films, including Tod Johnson in *A Life Less Ordinary*, the policeman in *Millions*, and Prem in *Slumdog Millionaire*. In *A Life Less Ordinary*, a comic highlight is provided by the arrival of Johnson (the late Maury Chaykin) at the door of the protagonists who are hiding out in a cabin in the woods. Chaykin is perfect at playing camp eccentrics who can be, by turns, childish or extremely menacing (think of Major Farnbrough in Kevin Costner's 1990 *Dances with Wolves*). Here the exchange with Robert is enlivened by Celine pretending that she is a newly wed and that Robert is a pop-star seeking some privacy. She is presenting Robert, Tod, and possibly many male members of the audience with an ideal fantasy life of fame, riches…. and Cameron Diaz in a flimsy sheet, draped provocatively around her, slowly mounting the stairs, causing Johnson to tilt his head as the door closes. Besides planting a gag for later, when Robert is introduced by Tod to the crowd in a bar as Richie Vanderloo, a famous country and western star, the scene also shows Celine's desire for role-playing, a trait that also emerges when, playing at being a tortured victim, she screams on the phone for help. The scene however belongs to Chaykin, who recounts asking his friend Felix, who 'hasn't been the same since the war' if the newcomers in the cabin are good or evil: 'one bark for good, two for evil'. Naturally enough Robert assumes, stifling a giggle, that Felix is a dog, provoking Johnson to declare 'do you think that I would talk to a dog? What do you think I am? Some kind of a crazy, backwoods lunatic? With a handful of human skulls and a scythe that I sharpen every day in readiness for Armaggedon?' The level of precise detail – that goes way beyond what the plot requires – of this individual who only watches 'the Biblical channels' is what makes this funny. By the end of the exchange, we have been given so much detail that we feel we have a sharp insight into his eccentric life, so that his assumption of a friendship with Robert, considering they have only just met, does not seem quite so illogical. Tod feels close enough to say 'take care, Richie' as if he has made a friend for life.

In *Millions*, the local policeman (Pearce Quigley) is played almost exactly like Ricky Gervaise's David Brent character in BBC's *The Office* (2001-2003). This was developing a cult following just prior to the production of Boyle's film, with a performance style dominated by unfunny jokes, sporadic giggles, throwaway remarks and general insensitivity. The officer warns the assembled new neighbours, in between unsubtle hints for toast and tea, that they will be issued with a crime number when, not if, they are burgled and there is no mention about the prevention or detection of crime – just the procedure with insurance claims. After a break-in at Ronnie's house (presumably by the unnamed robber looking for the cache of money the boys have found), he asks if they had any special security-coded items, then admits it would not make any difference anyway.

In *Slumdog Millionaire*, in his first film role in English, Anil Kapoor gives an assured performance as the smarmy but threatened TV-show host, Prem. He shifts from mocking distain at the beginning (calling the protagonist Jamal a 'chai-wallah') to apparent concern for him in the scene in the toilets, where he writes the answer to a question on a misted-up mirror, although we subsequently learn his supposed help is a deliberate attempt to mislead. The revelation that he, too, is a child of the slums is surprising, but provides a motivation for his determination that the only person whose fame will rise on this show is his own. Threatening to lose his cool when Jamal wins the money at the end, he nevertheless retains his composure and even reclaims some of the initiative with an improvised little celebratory dance.

As a relief from the pressures of the everyday, Boyle's characters seek an escape into fantasy worlds. These might be based on tricks, lies, or flights of imagination but they are a testament to the power of creativity to escape one's situation. The term 'hyper-realism' is a useful one when it comes to Boyle's cinematic aesthetic. As defined by theorist Nobuyoshi Terashima, hyperreality 'is nothing more than the technological capability to intermix virtual reality (VR) with physical reality (PR) and artificial intelligence (AI) with human intelligence (HI) in a way that appears seamless and allows interaction.'[3] It describes film sequences in which what we see cannot literally take place, but are plausible because the actions relate to what we already know of the emotional lives of the characters. Renton's headlong dive into the toilet in *Trainspotting* to retrieve the heroin, or Richard's jungle walk in *The Beach* where he appears as a character from a computer game, would fit this mode most closely but it bleeds across Boyle's style as a whole into transition sequences too. In *Slumdog Millionaire* for example, as Jamal and Salim tumble from the train, we shift from the first to the second set of actors (from Ayush Mahesh Khedekar and Azharuddin Mohammed Ismail to Tanay Chheda and Ashutosh Lobo Gajiwala), which Boyle achieved by spinning the young boys in a drum. Later, there is a second transition, involving a jump in space and time but not a change in cast, as Jamal is shrouded in the steam of a worker spraying pesticide and emerges into the red light district of Pila Street.

For some theorists, hyper-realism might best suit the notion of completely artificial, virtual environments, but Boyle's take on this is less technologically all-embracing. It usefully describes the creation of alternative worlds in which at any given moment, it is not always possible to say what is 'real' and what is not, but through which the protagonist moves without questioning the reality of his new surroundings. Dream sequences draw on this a little, such as in *Trainspotting* during Renton's nightmarish visions of a baby crawling on his ceiling or in *The Beach* when Richard's dreams of Daffy firing a machine-gun. In both these examples, however, there is the narrative presence of drug-use to motivate a visionary sequence. Boyle certainly uses CGI where it is unavoidable, such as the explosive effects in *Sunshine*, but he retains in the scenes discussed in this chapter a strong sense of enhancing human performance rather than replacing it with its simulacra. Many of his 'special effects', such as how the Infected are portrayed in *28 Days Later*

3　Terashima 2001 p.4.

or the initial chase of the children by security guards in *Slumdog Milllionaire*, are achieved by choice of camera and film stock and by the power of close-up images of protagonists, accompanied by memorable pumping contemporary music.

A key part of evoking the hyper-real is sound. In *Trainspotting*, Renton talks of Begbie 'getting off' on 'his own sensory addiction' and the latter's destructive personality is connected with aural transgression in smashing bottles, breaking pool cues and just the sheer volume at which he speaks. *Trainspotting* also offers the viewer similar pleasures in its kinetic camerawork and unconventional aural structures throughout the film. A significant but easily missed example of this hyper-realism is how the mundane sounds of everyday life are largely faded out to be replaced by a soundtrack and an occasional 'whooshing' noise as the protagonist, Renton, undergoes experiences that are beyond his mundane existence. These are either via drugs (as he realises he needs to find a toilet quickly), emotional shock (as he reads Diane's letter about Tommy's worsening condition), or fear (hearing Begbie ringing his doorbell after he thought he had escaped his old life). Locations at doorways in particular seem to signal not just the need to summon up courage but the imminence of stepping over a threshold, into a new life.

Through much of the film, the soundtrack appears conventional, with what we hear generated from what we see on screen (diegetic sound) but in a heightened, stylised sense. In the sequence featuring Renton's self-imposed detox programme, the visuals not only cut ruthlessly from one element to the next, but aurally we are almost hit in the face with buckets thumping as they hit the ground, bolts being slammed shut and nails being hammered into planks. Sounds seem matched to their source, but are suggestive of an addict's world that is so numb in its sensory awareness, that sound has to be ratcheted up to register at all. Spud's awareness of having soiled his sheets is signalled by the rumble of a passing plane. The distorted sucking sound that accompanies the depression of a syringe when Renton injects himself amplifies the physical action and marries it with the transcendent out-of-body experience that the drugs induce.

Sometimes intertextual references rather than sound act as a bridge to the hyper-real. There is no record of shark attacks in the specific area of the Thai islands shown in *The Beach*, and these are imported solely to heighten the drama. The swim to the island alludes very obviously to *Jaws* (dir. Steven Spielberg 1975) in the underwater, low-angle shots of figures swimming framed against the sun above the surface, the scenes of panic, and a girl disappearing. At this point, Richard's panicked reaction is played for laughs as Françoise and Étienne expose his pose of bravery by pretending to be pulled under by sharks. However, the later appearance of a real shark avoids *Jaws*-style shots, probably due to budgetary reasons, and limits itself to a flash of a fin close to the camera. Even with the opportunity of including some real jeopardy, the episode is mediated into a campfire story, told in retrospect. Bearing in mind Richard's status as a serial liar, it is debatable how much of this fisherman's tale is true. The inter-cut shots of the battle with the shark end with a shot of the animal's mouth opening and closing as if talking, delivering the 'enjoy your dinner' punch-line, and casting the episode in the realm of the fantastic, like the toilet scene in *Trainspotting*. Richard's story is laced with exactly the kind of 'pretentious bullshit' Françoise rejected earlier (Richard claims events transpire 'just as nature had ordained'), but here we are supposed to believe that it wins over the group, securing his position as 'alpha male'.

The Beach contains examples of camera positioning and movement which shift from the stylised to something more suggestive of Richard's distorted state of mind, such as the vertiginous angle from above Richard, Françoise and Étienne as they look down over the edge of the waterfall, and the high-angle wide shot of the three struggling ashore, taken apparently from a headland and momentarily suggesting a watchful presence. At the burial scene, Boyle uses a strange point-of-view shot into the grave of the shark victim (one of the minor Swedish characters), rotating it 45 degrees, effectively converting a portrait-format shot into a landscape-format, reflecting the distorted nature of the values of the mourners, that allows them to indulge in grief one minute and then ignore suffering the next. Their walking away from the grave in separate directions suggests their essentially egotistical nature. Later, as Richard retreats to the shadow of a hut, there is the use of a wide-angle lens and an iris on the image of Keaty, conveying effectively that Richard is not listening and is literally distancing himself from an unwanted truth. The same effect is used in *To Die For* (dir. Gus Van Sant 1995) when the psychotic Suzanne Stone (Nicole Kidman) does not want to hear her husband dismiss her dreams of media stardom.

As Françoise and Richard lie on the beach at night, looking up at the star-filled sky, the potential for dialogue of a romantic or philosophical nature is undermined by Françoise's portentous and faintly ridiculous dialogue ('essentially you are photographing yourself in a parallel universe'), which applies more closely to the process of filmmaking than to her action with the camera on the beach. We see a character on screen, mimicking Boyle's role in looking down a lens and framing a shot, first of the sky, then human figures, then distorting those figures for a particular effect. Like the shot just prior to the waterfall jump as the camera pulls back from Françoise, Étienne and Richard to reveal the drop immediately below them (produced with a remote-controlled helicopter), there is the sense that the time-lapse plotting of the character across the screen is contrived to inject some filmic spectacle into a static plot. Like the 'bullet-time' sequences in *The Matrix* (dir. Wachowski Brothers 1999), this idea to create on-screen dynamism where the dialogue cannot provide it, but in *The Beach* it only underlines a generic mismatch rather than complementing it.

Horror tropes appear sporadically, such as the *Evil Dead*-style, ankle-height racing camera shot up to Richard, wide-eyed, holding his hand over Françoise's mouth as they and Étienne crouch in the marijuana field. Later, in Kho Pha Ngan, a hand drops on Richard's shoulder, only to be revealed as one of the backpackers he met before he came to the island. The moment when Richard confronts the petrified female tourist, one of the group who have followed his lead (and his map), he is shown in close-up giving what might be described as a vampiric hiss, causing the girl to freeze in shock, at which point she is gunned down. Generic markers from action and horror reflect the distorted subject universe that Richard inhabits but, without the humour of Renton in *Trainspotting* or Ralston in *127 Hours*, such grandiose aspirations make the protagonist just seem pathetic.

The influence of Anthony Dod Mantle's cinematography on Boyle's films from 2001 onwards should not be underestimated. Mantle's innovative use of small, lightweight cameras, such as he used when working with the Dogme95 film movement, allows him to explore more fully scenes of fantastical movement – from the way the Infected move in *28 Days Later*, to the fluid transition sequences in *Millions*, and the chase in *Slumdog Millionaire*. It is a good example of technological decisions having an impact on creative choices (or Boyle selecting to work with certain technology to give him a greater range of creative opportunities, depending on how you look at it). Mantle's work on the first three accredited Dogme films, particularly *Festen* or *Celebration*, (dir. Thomas Vinterberg 1998), followed the 'rules' of this revolutionary group of filmmakers, which was inspired largely by Lars von Trier, and which dictated that all shots should be taken with handheld cameras.[4] Not all

4   Kelly 2000 pp.226-228.

of the ten commandments of the Dogme 'manifesto' apply to Boyle's work, most notably their outlawing of non-diegetic music, genre films, or crediting a director. Music is very important to the kinetic nature of Boyle's films; he has produced films that explicitly play with genre conventions such as *A Life Less Ordinary*; and while he may be generally democratic in his method of working, the films definitely bear his name – it is his will that drives projects forward.

The hyper-real just below the surface

Even in films that have an apparently simple visual style, there is complexity too. In *Millions*, Boyle dramatises the world through the eyes of a devoutly religious 11-year-old boy, Damian (Alex Etel) whose life is turned upside down by the discovery of a mysterious sack of money in his garden. The title frame, which is slowly revealed to be made up of a mass of the word 'Millions,' that gradually fades to reveal just one single word, feels almost like a concrete poem. It is simultaneously a visual pun of being one in a million, the pieces literally being millions in number but all being representations of the word itself, and the impossibility of expressing unimaginable wealth. Text in the same font is also used later in the film for introducing the school nativity play, breaking the dramatic illusion temporarily, reflecting the increasingly professional technology used in school plays and encouraging us to connect this scene with the opening – it prompts the viewer to consider what has changed between these two points in the narrative, more particularly whether Damian and his family are any happier for finding the money.

The setting for the film, Portland Meadows, is a newly built estate of houses in an unnamed, generic town in the north of England (Cottrell Boyce's novel mentions Widnes in passing). In the opening 20 minutes of the film, there are a number of wide shots of the flat landscape, composed of 80 percent sky (such as the sequence where, via dissolves, Damian pushes boxes containing doves up a hill). Whereas for writers like Thomas Hardy, such picture composition implies a hostile sky pressing down on a lone individual, as in *Tess of the D'Urbervilles* (1891), here it is the expansive, bright possibilities that are emphasised (in part due to the skilled work of Mantle as cinematographer). These shots are similar to the artwork of Alfred Bestall in his Rupert books and Daily Express column, which feature a similarly fantastical landscape. Vapour-trails streak the sky like meteors and even the less aesthetically pleasing imagery of billowing chimneys suggests an environment that is being left behind in Damian's move to a pristine new housing estate.

Later, the central protagonists, Damian and his brother Anthony (Lewis McGibbon) buy mobile phones and – despite sitting only a few yards apart – call each other, the signal shown by a red line on screen, disappearing off-frame and then coming down again. The absurdity of communicating by phone when they are close enough to speak face-to-face reflects the problem that the money represents, as well as the problems they have in talking to each other. This is also alluded to in the shots of Damian opening Anthony's bedroom door during the night: through the use of back-lighting, he casts a long shadow within the room, a shot that carries some expressionist weight, as the ever-present reality beneath their daily lives is the loss of their mother and the difficulty they have in articulating this.

Transitional devices signal the hyper-real just beneath the surface. We cut from Damian's classroom to a playground scene via the appropriate effect of a board being wiped and later there are several uses of blurred diagonal wipes – a device often associated with another fairy-tale narrative, *Star Wars* (dir. George Lucas 1977). At one point, a computer screen opens out as a cube in a scene transition, something that seems visually anachronistic, evoking a cross between a Rubik cube and a playground folding game, and filmically like an early visual effect from the BBC's *Top of the Pops*.

There are some elaborate effects used in the film which, viewed out of context, almost seem gimmicky. In the sequence where Anthony and Damian are discussing how to give money to the poor, they appear as moving parts of a copy of estate agents' details, and then the camera pulls back to show them examining those same details in a shop window. It is certainly clever, but it is unclear whether it really justifies the time it must have taken to achieve. A similar effect in *Fight Club* places Jack (Ed Norton) in an IKEA catalogue, but this is a film where the protagonist is intimately connected with issues of empty consumerism. Here, there is a link with Anthony subsequently going to a property and precociously telling the agent that he is looking to buy as part of an investment portfolio, which is a light-hearted comic moment of youthful precocity, but carries little more resonance. Elaborate effects are also used in a house-building fantasy sequence. The boys see their new home materialise before their very eyes as stop-motion sequences are used to make the blueprints stand up to form a 3D structure, and turf to unroll itself, as if Boyle does not want to lose the physicality of the filmic experience even within a fantasy sequence.

The story of the mail train robbery, the source of the money, is dramatically relayed by one of Anthony's friends whose father is a policeman, rather than conveyed via computer screens as in Cottrell Boyce's novel. The effectiveness of this sequence in the film owes much to Chris Gill's rapid editing and the use of film stock which emphasises the reds and blacks, positioning the robbery as a little film-within-a-film, an action film within a family drama. It also represents the violent adult reality underlying the childish fantasy of the main plot and, after the gleeful revelation of the truth, Damian's world-view is questioned. 'I thought it was a miracle from God', he says, but it does not provoke in him a crisis of faith. For him, this is an immense realisation – what he had thought was a message from God turns out to have a very human explanation and he immediately cuts off Anthony's attempt to spin the story as still God-directed ('God does not rob banks' he tells his brother).

For *127 Hours*, for the first time, Boyle used two cinematographers – in addition to Mantle, he brought in Enrique Chediak with whom he had worked in his capacity as a producer on *28 Weeks Later* (dir. Juan Carlos Fresnadillo 2007), to use small cameras (the SI-2K, 35mm film camera with occasional use of the digital Canon DSLR). Part of this decision seemed to be based on the practical difficulties of securing either man for the full length of the shoot, but it did allow Boyle to be creative, alternating the two cinematographers almost at will. Originally this was an attempt to set up a 'good cop – bad cop' dynamic which would elicit genuine confusion from actor James Franco, but he seemed to have worked well with both, so ultimately there is no distinctive 'look' to footage shot by either one of them. Boyle's preference for continuous shooting, which gives performances a particular intensity and credibility, especially when dealing with a developing focus on one individual, extends to his desire for the production crew to work seven-day-weeks, which labour legislation forbids. He managed to work round that a little with his use of two cinematographers and by filming Franco in unusually long takes.

As with Mantle's innovative camera placement in *Strumpet*, we have a point-of-view shot from inside Ralston's water bottle and different, grainy film stock used for the footage he takes with his own camera. Where *Slumdog Millionaire* uses jump-cuts to pull back from the slum, giving a progressive sense of scale, Boyle pulls straight up (separate camera shots blended digitally to mask cuts) to show the insignificance of one human life in the broader landscape. Boyle's preference for long takes and the corridor-like set in Salt Lake City on which much of the film was made, made reverse shots difficult: Boyle's editor, Jon Harris, helps to add a sense of visual dynamism by jump-cutting around a single frame rather than moving to a new one.

It is worth considering the opening of *Shallow Grave* in some detail as it was Boyle's first feature film, often the one he quotes as his best, and can be read as a statement of intent. The visual ambition, in particular the drive beyond gritty realism, is present even from the opening frame, a complete screen of red, the colour the film returns to at moments of extreme horror. Credits start to run, ticker-tape style, across the top third of the screen. Like the opening of *Trainspotting*, this feels closer to the style of a pop video and the beat picks up as we follow a tight shot, tilted down at cobbled streets, creating a sense of headlong motion. The film speeds up as we race through the streets, only to switch to slow motion in reaching the townhouse where the main events are to take place.

Again, as with the beginning of *Trainspotting*, the film opens with a passionate, first-person narration, direct to camera by David (Christopher Eccleston), which introduces the central theme: 'I'm not ashamed. I've known love. I've known rejection. I'm not afraid to declare my feelings. Take trust, for instance, or friendship. These are the important things in life. These are the things that matter. That help you on your way. If you can't trust your friends, well what then? What then?' The narrator tells us 'this could have been any city,' but from the accents and the architecture, we become aware that this is an Edinburgh story. Similarly, he tells us that 'we're all the same' but actually it will be the extraordinary nature of the characters rather than their typical, representative function, which will be most striking.

The opening rotating close-up of David, to which we return at the end, lulls us into the false assumption that we will see things from his point of view and that, as he is telling the story, he will survive. In retrospect, knowing what we know by the end of the film, this an impossible shot. This framing motif also appears in a further rotating shot as a figure, subsequently revealed as prospective flatmate Cameron (Colin McCredie) makes his way up the vertiginous stairwell of a desirable flat where he would like to live. The protagonists, a group of friends, literally live in an ivory tower, their wealth and professional status (accountant, doctor and journalist) allowing them to lead detached lives from which they pour scorn and derision on the world below, members of whom they invite up from time to time to humiliate. Cameron's point-of-view eventually alights on the 'welcome' mat, proudly emblazoned with 'Not Today Thank You', giving us an introduction into the world of the film, most of which is played out in the top floor of the large townhouse.

The flatmate interviews are an exercise in bullying. This could be carried out (and filmed) in a way that would emphasise realistic dramatic conventions, but instead the protagonists are shown in a purposely non-naturalistic fashion. Low-angled shots of David, Alex (Ewan McGregor) and Juliet (Kerry Fox), all sitting in chairs, give them a predatory, looming air. These are alternately cut with shots of the interviewee, placed in the middle of a couch, looking small and lost. Alex brazenly forgets, then misuses, Cameron's name, setting the tone. He recounts the qualities of the flat, describing it as 'spacious, bright, well-appointed', to which Cameron nervously agrees, only for Alex to unsettle him with a more throwaway 'all that sort of crap.' With rhetorical flourishes, Alex builds to a climax and then delivers the punch-line – 'so what on earth makes you think that we'd want to share a flat like this with someone like you?' The drum-led music kicks in at this point as Cameron realises he is the victim of a cruel joke. Alex continues a list of articulate insults – 'my first impressions – and they're rarely wrong – is that you have none of the qualities that we normally seek from a prospective flatmate. I'm talking here about things like presence, charisma, style and charm and I don't think we're asking too much. I don't think we're being unreasonable.' Cameron is led, not for a further tour, but to the door by David who keeps his head down to stifle his giggling. The cold delivery of lines, bewildered reaction shots and apparently unconnected action in the background (Alex cycling around inside the flat during the interview) creates the sense of a highly unusual group of characters who seem to lack completely any sense of sympathy or empathy – a key trait of psychopaths.

We now know we are in the presence of a group of characters who, despite their apparently respectable professions, are deeply unpleasant individuals, bound together by their lack of fellow feeling. Indeed, one of the provisional titles of the film was *Cruel*. A rapid montage of interviews with further victims intercuts quick-fire questions, some clearly irrelevant (Alex asks about the best way to sacrifice a goat), some just plain insensitive (Juliet asks if the man's affair is with a man or a woman), some more subtle and satirical (Alex asking a Goth how she knows what shade of black to wear), and some just to humiliate (David asking to name a singer and subsequent singles by some music he plays, as if this is a quiz show). The sudden rush to sit next to interviewees and have their picture taken is also calculated cruelty: these are not best friends on holiday. Rapid inter-cutting between interviews conveys the speed and random nature of the questions and the fact that they are not really listening to the answers, suggests extreme boredom. The theatrical humiliation underlines just how empty are their lives, that they need to be entertained in this way, treating the interviewees as performing animals in their own private zoo. The following scene, featuring highly combative squash games, suggests their so-called friendship is based largely on competitive rivalry.

As with *The Beach*, intertextual references are also part of the 'portal' to episodes of hyper-reality. We can see Boyle's admiration for the work of the Coen Brothers here, especially *Blood Simple* (1984). Like the earlier film, the plot devices of the discovery of money, the problems involved in disposing of a body and several double-crosses, all begin with a character introducing the narrative in a first-person voice-over and who is ultimately revealed to be dead. There are stylistic echoes too – David's drilling through the floor so that the attic to which he retreats is punctured by rays of light is prefigured by Visser (M. Emmet Walsh) shooting through a wall at Abby (Frances McDormand) in a darkened room, achieving a similar lighting effect. Page compares *Shallow Grave* to *Reservoir Dogs* on the grounds that it features a limited setting, a plot revolving around money, and a low budget. There are other parallels that could be drawn too: apart from the use of overlapping dialogue is the initial shot of the case, opened by Hugo but away from the camera so that we do not see its contents, foreshadowing Quentin Tarantino's use of mythic contents in *Pulp Fiction* (1994).

The edgy hipness of Tarantino can also be seen in aspects of *Trainspotting*, particularly in the protagonists' self-aware, ironic dispositions, easily referring to icons of pop culture. The dynamic shooting and editing style of the film also borrows stylistic devices from *la nouvelle vague* (freeze frames, split-screen and subtitles) and from the vibrant pop culture films of Richard Lester (such as when The Beatles race to escape fans in *A Hard Day's Night* (1964)). However, Boyle takes such influences a stage further in episodes where we begin in the everyday world but, without warning, suddenly shift into a related fantasy zone, what might be termed the hyper-real.

Where fantasy meets the everyday

What Philip Kemp, writing in *Sight and Sound*, finds 'remarkable, given its subject-matter, is that the lasting after-effect of watching *Trainspotting* is a sense of exhilaration'.[5] For example, both Welsh's novel and the film feature the recovery of the opium suppositories in a disgusting toilet, but in the film Boyle shifts into another realm of fantasy altogether. The first shot from within the toilet reveals a hellish *Blade Runner*-style set and we are likely to share Renton's reaction as we sporadically cut back to his point-of-view, recoiling from the stench in the cubicle. Camera-positioning jumps around, from a bird's eye view to an ecstatic close-up of Renton as he empties his bowels, to the shot up through the bowl as he realises what he has done. At first there is no music in the scene, underlying its grim reality, but as Renton pokes about in the disgusting water, the music from the earlier detox scene comes up on the soundtrack and, as the level of fantasy increases, so does the light, dreamy nature of the music.

Renton not only puts his hand into the bowl, but slowly dives in head first in an act of impossibility. There are no fictive markers, so what we see is a surreal expression of the lengths to which addicts will go to support their habit. Strong overhead light, clear water and a sea-bed that casts the drugs as naturally occurring pearls, all create an otherworldly beauty to the underwater scenes, as if just below the surface there is the presence of beauty and freedom, if only we could access it. Sarah Street believes that the scene 'communicates Renton's desperate idea of the value of his search.' However, there is genuine originality here, unlike the hyperbole used by Stephen King about his 2001 novel *Dreamcatcher* and the subsequent 2003 Lawrence Kasdan film, claiming that he was breaking taboos in showing toilets in a new way to open up debates about cancer. The sound of sonar blips and a passing mine are engaging elements of childish fantasy and indicate that there is still part of Renton's psyche, which is marked as imaginative and thereby redeemable.

There is even a fantastical element in transition scenes and some bleeding of the fantasy elements back into the reality. The scene immediately following the dive into the toilet shows Renton entering his flat with soaking wet trousers. Later, there is a spatial impossibility in the cut from Renton's jump from the pub wall, to his landing, frog-like, in the extreme foreground of Mother Superior's flat (John Hodge's screenplay describes him 'executing a somersault in mid-air'). The effect is strangely theatrical and reminiscent of Steven Berkoff's 1969 stage adaptation of *Metamorphosis*, especially the highly stylised manner in which McGregor then uncoils himself from his landed position. Boyle also uses text on screen, not just to introduce the character's names, but

6 Street 1997 p.125.

also to provide subtitles for dialogue between Renton and Spud in the nightclub, for a chronological exposition of 'the first day of the Edinburgh Festival,' and for framing the simple toilet sign in the back of the betting shop with 'the worst…in Scotland' after Renton has already gone in.

Like the toilet scene, Renton's supposedly final hit begins with a heightened sense of gritty reality and then fluidly shifts into the fantastical. Renton falls backwards in ecstasy as we have seen him do before, but here he appears to be swallowed up, along with the carpet, into a chasm that opens up in the floor. The reverse angle gives us his point of view looking up, as if out of a grave, and then Mother Superior's looking down at the shivering wreck he has become. Lou Reed's 'Perfect Day' (1972) on the soundtrack manages to blend the euphoria of the experience and the dissonance in the horrific visuals – the day is far from perfect. Reed's song bleeds over the following scenes so that its climactic line ('You're gonna reap what you sow') is juxtaposed with attempts to revive Renton in hospital. The melodic calmness of the song also complements the reaction of Mother Superior, whose measured response suggests that dealing with overdoses or bad reactions to drugs is all part of a dealer's job, and the matter-of-fact attitude of the hospital doctors. Renton's drug-induced point of view continues as he is carried down the steps, his vision still cropped as if he is looking up at the world from the bottom of a grave, reflecting his medical condition. In A&E, Renton's vision is sometimes edged by borders, apparently made of carpet, making the sequence unclear as to exactly how much is only a drug-induced fantasy. As elsewhere, wide-angle lenses reflect a hallucinogenic state as we see Renton on a hospital trolley: his head is distorted and sharp but his feet remain blurred, conveying a sense of bodily disconnection.

As Renton's parents impose a strict 'detox' regime on their son, we experience the room as his drug-craving body perceives it. As well as the painful reality of convulsions that wrack him, the walls seem to lengthen and the bed pulls back. A thumping dance track starts and Boyle uses the overtly low-tech, theatrical device of Renton in agony under the sheets, meeting his friends, one by one, evocative of Banquo's ghost or even Scrooge's visions of his past and potential future life. The baby crawling on the ceiling is the peak of the nightmarish images that plague Renton in withdrawal. Shown first in long shot, the baby crawls nearer, increasing Renton's dread which reaches a climax as the baby falls down towards his face. The fact that this is clearly a hallucination and its head is rotating

180 degrees are both small nods to William Friedkin's *The Exorcist* (1973), but the stress here is physical rather than spiritual distress. His visions – of Sick Boy (Jonny Lee Miller), parroting the government slogan 'Just Say No,' Spud sitting on top of the door dressed in a pantomime prison uniform, and Tommy, introduced by a shadow prefiguring what he will soon become – underline the hollowness of Renton's clichés about drugs as 'better than sex'.

Boyle does not shy away from the occasional self-consciously constructed shot, like the image of Anthony in *Millions* reflected in the mirrored door of a cupboard, and here we have Renton and Spud entering the newsagents John Menzies as seen in the reflective panels above the door. Later he uses a shot through a left-luggage locker in which Renton leaves some money for Spud and which is lined with mirrors that frame Renton in an effective three-shot as his face is reflected, suggesting both a capacity for duplicity and a multifaceted personality. The technique is used again, right at the end of the film, to record Spud's surprise at being left any money at all. In the final sequence we also see a shot tilted at 45 degrees, which then pivots 180 degrees as Renton walks past, reflecting the point-of-view of an addict lying on the ground from whom Renton, now free of drugs, can walk away. However, the shot also feels more like some bravura styling from a pop video, notably Cabaret Voltaire's 'Sensoria' (dir. Peter Care 1984), Leftfield's 'Original' (dir. Mike Lipscombe 1995) and The Sundays' 'Summertime' (dir. Pedro Romhanyi 1997), all of which use the same camera movement.[7]

Boyle often uses slightly low angles to convey the skewed world of a group of addicts whose life is based around their next hit, such as Renton's pep talk to Spud, shot over a pub table-top; the wide angle-lens and tight shots used to distort Renton's face as he goes into the betting shop; and Renton and Spud's appearance in court. In each case, these low angles do not make the subject seem empowered and important but create an ironic belittling effect. The use of freeze frames motivates the addition of some back-story. Begbie, in mid-boast about a fight he supposedly had, is instantly undercut by cutting to Tommy telling us the real story, and the moment that Begbie and Sick Boy leap from a cupboard in a desirable property whilst prospective clients are being shown round, effectively puts an end to Renton's estate agent career.

7 Leftfield also contributed the title track for *Shallow Grave*, 'A Final Hit' for *Trainspotting* and 'Snakeblood' for *The Beach*.

In the bar-scene in *A Life Less Ordinary*, Celine wins the drinking game against Robert and the sequence morphs into a fantasy, but exactly where is unclear. A spotlight falls on Robert who stands, makes his way to the stage, saluting the crowd en route and delivers a fairly polished performance of 'Beyond the Sea'. The choice of song seems a strange one – although it was first released in France in 1946, it is most commonly remembered as a Bobby Darin hit from 1959. Robert is denoted as a smooth Sinatra-like lounge singer from a previous, but unspecified, bygone era. Celine joins him and the pair perform a song and dance routine on the table and the bar, by which time she miraculously appears in a different dress and he is now in a suit. The musical is one of the few genres that Boyle has yet to attempt but with such sequences, he is able to indulge a guilty pleasure. By placing this scene in the context of a bar, he can blend reality into fantasy without characters bursting into song for no apparent reason, although rehearsed choreography in a tango sequence, dress changes and a full orchestral score, all signal this as a subjective fantasy of Robert's. The fantasy elements start to become more pronounced as the bar scene is inter-cut with close-ups of Robert strapped to a Catherine Wheel-style apparatus of neon lights on a game show called 'Perfect Love'.

In *28 Days Later*, narrative exposition is conveyed in a range of ways, some more subtle than others, ranging from the conventional to the more stylised, to sequences approaching the 'hyper-real'. Our first sight of Jim (Cillian Murphy) is a close-up of one of his eyes anxiously looking around, trying to orientate himself in a hospital where he has awoken. Shot from above, he is shown to be completely naked, his body looking physically small and almost boyish. Indeed, Kermode talks of his 'oddly ethereal charm'.[8] Jim is forced to grow and change during the course of the film, finding within him the will to fight and even kill when necessary, but Boyle does not let us forget Murphy's physically diminutive stature. He is shown naked twice more: shaving and cutting his hair in Frank's flat, and showering in Major West's improvised army base, his appearance reminding us that he must use cunning, rather than force, to outwit the Infected and the soldiers.

Some shots are fairly conventional: Boyle uses, for example, a standard montage to indicate the passage of time in his footage of the taxi, tilting up from a close shot of the tarmac (reminiscent of the opening of *Shallow Grave*) to the cab driving past the camera, a passenger point-of-view

8 Kermode in *Sight and Sound*, 12:12, December 2002 p.60.

from within, panning right to left through the windscreen, the side of the vehicle showing the wheel hub (usually used to suggest speed), and the empty road ahead.

Other shots of the taxi use more oblique stylisation: as Frank drives Jim, Selena and Hannah out of London, we see the image of Jim's face looking out of the cab, overlaid with the reflection on the window of the scene he is looking at – piles of bodies on the pavement. It is an example of what cultural critic and philosopher Slavoj Žižek calls 'the metasuturing of the interface,' in which a shot contains its own counter-shot, a technique increasingly used in this kind of context where a character looks out from a passing car (see James Spader in Cronenberg's 1996 *Crash*, Ralph Fiennes in Cronenberg's 2002 *Spider* and Morgan Freeman in David Fincher's 1995 *Seven*).[9] This condensed shot shows a moment of contemplation, where we literally see a character looking outwards as a reflected image plays across his face, using moving images to represent the act of thinking.

The act of thinking is also conveyed in the scene at the house of Jim's parents, where he finds the dead bodies of his father and mother (who is still clutching a photograph of Jim). He caresses his mother's recipe book and the pictures on the fridge, motivating a flashback of sorts. He looks off-frame to the right and we cut to a grainy image (shot on Super-8mm) of a return from an ordinary shopping trip. There are no fictive markers here that could indicate we are seeing a memory; Jim even seems to interact with the pictures, speaking to them. His repressed grief is captured in the tiny gesture of rubbing the door slightly with his hand on the way out of the room.

The hyper-real and point-of-view

The narrative point of view in *Millions*, not just in Damian's voiceover but in everything we see on screen, proceeds from the unfettered fantasy of a young boy. Boyle is very good at evoking iconic moments in childhood: the start of the opening bike race, framed by railway arches, and the subsequent slow motion procession through brilliant yellow rape fields, all convey a powerful sense of uninhibited movement. We have images of the impossible (saints appearing, soon-to-be-built houses springing up before our eyes and a bag of money, apparently defying the laws of physics like Barnes Wallis' bouncing bomb, before striking

9 Žižek 2001 p.53. In *Slumdog*, the presence of the Orpheus myth in Jamal's pursuit of Latika is also seen in the image of Maman being shot through a mirror, in a nod to Jean Cocteau's *Orphée* (1950), as Salim passes through a magic mirror into a world of fantasy.

Damian's 'hermitage'). Camera shots from within the family home when it is first constructed (looking out through the pillar box-style flap or a high-angle rising up the central chimney section) emphasise that we are seeing events through Damian's innocent, but celebratory, point-of-view. Speeded-up motion (such as Damian watching the trains, or pupils putting up a welcome sign to him with magnets) pushes the narrative along but also underlines the subjective nature of time, especially to children.

There is a constant tension between an adult and childish view of the world, with the harsher adult view only intruding sporadically – in the robbery flashback, the decision by Ronnie (James Nesbitt) to keep the money, and in the threatening presence of the unnamed robber himself. The sequence where the two brothers take the bag of money to a bank and try to open an account evokes the library scene in Ken Loach's film of *Kes* (1969) where again, without the presence of a parent, children are denied access to the adult world. Mostly it is the child's view which predominates: the experience of moving house, seen as a great adventure rather than a logistical nightmare; constructing a hermitage close to a railway line (this proximity and the final burning of the money on the tracks were the source of the 12A certificate); the sudden and unexplained appearance of representatives from various charitable causes during the night; and the final fantasy sequence of what could be done with the money. The clear continuity contradiction between the Christmas setting of the narrative and the boys' playing coatless outside amid bright blue skies, underlines the upbeat optimism of Damian's view of the world, where the sun always seems to be shining.

On the DVD commentary, Boyce mentions Frank Capra, suggesting that exaggerated action which is not fully explained indicates that what we are seeing is a subjective fantasy (one of the early taglines for *Millions* was 'keep it unreal'). The slightly odd Latter Day Saints (portrayed largely at the level of stereotype) all blond, dressed in suits, speaking robotically and cycling in unison around the roads also evoke the sporadic appearance of nuns in Andrew Davies' TV comedy *A Very Peculiar Practice* (BBC 1986-92). Even the shot of the playground from above, with its giant red play-balls, seems to distort perspective, and the name of the family's new house, shown briefly, is Serendipity, suggestive of the making of pleasant discoveries by accident.

The sequence where Damian first approaches his neighbour opens with a crane-shot that drops down close behind Damian's head. It may be intended to suggest that we should try to anticipate what he is thinking, but it is also a stylistic nod to indie filmmakers like Paul Thomas Anderson, who are given to creating shots that draw attention to themselves by breaking conventions over picture composition (such as the sequence between the boy rapper and the cop in *Magnolia*, 1999). Humorous examples of similar quirky shots include the nativity donkey riding with Damian on the top deck of a double-decker bus. On the DVD, Boyce notes the similarity between this scene and Nick Park's *Wallace and Gromit* and certainly the donkey's lack of expression as it is wheeled in and out of shot feels a little like the typical movement of Shaun the Sheep in *A Close Shave* (1995). Boyle also notes a slight evocation of Nic Roeg's *Don't Look Now* (1973) with the camera placed in the dark recesses of the bus and all the light out in front, casting Damian and the donkey virtually as silhouettes.

As in *Millions*, Boyle also uses a quiz-show reference and text-on-screen in *Slumdog Millionaire* but in the later film there is a *Who Wants to Be a Millionaire*?-style question about the narrative itself, that is not in the script but that was added by Boyle himself. Thus, from the outset we are invited to consider the methods by which we are being told the story, as well as the story itself. The familiar mise-en-scène of the TV quiz-show, dominated by soft blue light and percussive synthesiser, is contrasted with the yellowy background of the torture sequences. Boyle uses dramatic means to cut between the two, using a graphic match between the slap of Jamal as a prisoner and his sudden shock at the reality of the pressure of the quiz-show.

Like the flash-cuts of the crew in *Sunshine*, we are then given an iconic image, the significance of which we return to later. Jamal looks directly at the camera and we cut to a high-angle view of a beautiful girl, dressed in yellow, at a train station (a shot that appears again later during the scene in which Jamal and Salim sneak into an open-air opera), reflecting the difficulty of finding romantic love as well as emphasising that it is never far from Jamal's mind. Much of the film is concerned with memory, and this image represents the driving force in Jamal's life. It is, we learn later, finding the girl that is his prime motive in being on the show, not the money. As with the shots of the Infected in *28 Days Later*, Boyle uses a Canon Mark 3/EOP 3 camera here (and at moments of key memory 'snapshots' like signs to the Taj Mahal or the interior of the call-centre) which is more commonly used for stills to give an extra density of colour and a different, more grainy texture.

Strict realism is by-passed, as it is in Bollywood film. There is a slight ellipsis about precisely how Jamal got on the quiz-show: showing him at the call-centre implies he had the opportunity to phone in, but we do not see this explicitly. The number of questions is even lost in the narrative momentum – Simon Beaufoy's deletion of a question about architect Sir Frederick Stevens, designer of Chhatrapati Shivaji Railway Terminus (and the corresponding shot of Jamal sitting by a statue of him at the station) is barely noticeable and would perhaps have felt like another reference to India's imperial past, rather than to the generation of the protagonists who firmly belong to the present.

The chase of the children through the slums in *Slumdog* is key to the film's appeal and a further example of heightened realism. It establishes early in the film the nature of the setting from which the characters come and shows a way of life rarely glimpsed in western cinema. We are catapulted into a different world, full of colour, movement and life. What makes Boyle's sequence easier for audiences to engage with is that ultimately in *Slumdog* we see small children enjoying the pleasure of running and being chased – like the interrupted cricket match on the airport runway, it is a different kind of exciting game. More generally, *Slumdog* is a film that celebrates the child over the adult, the fantasy over the prosaic, love over money and possibility over likelihood. The boys' crime, trespassing on the runway, and their likely punishment, a beating at most, means that there is a joyous feeling of liberation in the chase, represented by their turning to taunt the guard just before their luck runs out and they are caught.

The chase sequence starts with an unnamed boy, sporting the name of the film on his vest – a non-naturalistic element and a tongue-in-cheek visual gag that problematises easy distinctions between fiction and reality. Such knowing references to the mechanisms of filmmaking appear throughout the film, such as when the security guards outside the call-centre look directly at the camera and declare 'no filming,' or when Jamal looks straight down the camera lens at a powerful memory of Latika, reflecting his motivation in making direct contact with her through the means of television (and echoing Strumpet calling out to Strayman while on live TV). We see the pressure mounting on him in the TV studio as we become a producer for a second or two, watching from behind a boom camera as it hones in on him for a close-up.

The chase scene, which in film terms lasts just over three minutes, took Boyle as many months to shoot and edit (making its production speed closer to that of stop-motion animation). The finished result is like a master-class in direction, not necessarily because it is flawless but because it shows the full range of available shots – we have variations of angle, a static and moving camera, differences in film speed, and varied distances from the subject of the shot. The rapid rhythm of cutting and the alternating extreme high and low angles, along with A.R. Rahman's pulsating soundtrack give this sequence the features of a trailer. Kinetic camerawork, with forward and reverse tracking shots in front of and behind the children, gives us the sense of being part of the group. The close-up of the significant characters here, revealed later as Salim (Azharuddin Mohammed Ismail) and Jamal (Ayush Mahesh Khedekar) is complemented by broad smiles and a high-five, encouraging the viewer to celebrate with them.

The chase does not give us a precise sense of geography but more a generic feel of slum-life as the children run over a rubbish tip. They seem used to evading authority, jumping a low wall and pelting the guards from the rooftops with anything to hand. The cramped alleyways necessitated lighter, smaller cameras and this also meant the use of handheld cameras with tight shots, tilts and whip-pan movements to keep the children in shot. The alternating extreme high and low angles make us feel like part of the group on the roof outsmarting the guards, but we also can share the pursuers' frustration in being blinded by low rays of the sun as they look up at the crowds of children throwing things at them. Cutaways show other everyday activities such as scavenging recyclable material from the river and a long shot, through which everyone runs, emphasises the comic difference in scale between the pursuers and the pursued.

Boyle uses a range of camera speeds, including slow motion, catching the kids as they jump from the roof to the exaggerated speeded-up effect, also used in *28 Days Later*, to convey the confusion and disorientation of the pursuing guard. Close, tight shots with rapid movement contrast with longer, static shots as the pursued and the pursuers run through the shot. The brightness of shots framed into the sun, glimpsed above the rooftops, is juxtaposed with shots from within dark shops watching the routine spectacle of kids outsmarting adults.

In a sense, the whole film is constructed around a series of chases, all representing a flight from poverty, but in different circumstances. The night-time flight of the two boys from Maman's camp is cinematically the least effective (paradoxically possibly because it is the most dangerous, placing youngsters close to a life-threatening train). What is powerful, however, is Salim's betrayal of Latika as the brothers board the train (unseen by Jamal, he lets go of her hand so that she is left on the tracks) and the following shot of the brothers inside the carriage, looking at a sea of faces of other non-paying passengers, each possibly with their own stories to tell but about which the narrative remains silent. It is both a nod to a similar scene in the Coen Brothers' *O Brother, Where Art Thou?* (2000) and an example of what Stanley Cavell, philosopher and cultural theorist, calls 'the ordinary as the uneventful'.[10] For a moment we glimpse other shadowy men in a snapshot of countless other parallel lives, played out in the midst of similar forces.

Not all pursuits are light-hearted. The second slum chase, when anti-Muslim fanatics conduct a sectarian attack, has a deadly outcome: the mother of Jamal and Salim is killed. The promotional tag-line that described *Slumdog* as 'the feel-good movie of the decade' is only partly true. There is some humour, such as the joke Latika plays on Jamal, putting chillies down his underpants while he is sleeping, and the 'dancing' scene between the youngest incarnation of Jamal and Latika, pulling faces while earnestly discussing their future. There is also the joyous scene, evocative of the toilet-diving in *Trainspotting*, when Jamal jumps down into the unspeakable in order to achieve something transcendent – here, a signed photo from screen idol Amitabh Bachchan. We see Jamal, who is standing in the latrine, take out the treasured folded photo, look at it for a second, look down the hole, hold his nose and jump, but keep his hand held high. As with much of the chase sequence, as Jamal approaches the crowd, Boyle keeps the eye-line shots at waist height to convey a child's point-of-view. This 'feel-good' film, however, opens with scenes of Jamal being tortured and memorably includes the deliberate blinding of slum children who have been tempted away to live with the apparently benevolent Maman (Ankur Vikal) who uses bottles of Coca-Cola to lure them into to a life of petty organised crime. The elements of the love story between Jamal and Latika, which fall into the category of romanticism and Bollywood myth, are given greater resonance by being contrasted with starker images, such as the man on fire stumbling behind the boys as they beg the troops for help. The institutions of government, especially the police, seem at best indifferent and at worst corrupt, prepared to torture Jamal to please Prem, the quiz show host. Jamal, after all, has committed no crime, merely presumed to challenge their assumptions about the ignorance of slum dwellers by answering questions correctly on a TV quiz. The fact that the guard apologises to Javed Khan (Mahesh Manjrekar) for bumping into his the large white car during the chase, suggests a cosy relationship between

10   Mulhall, (ed.) 1996 pp.260-294.

gangsters and the police. Bizarrely, the Indian government did not object to the presence of torture in the script so long as it was not condoned above the rank of inspector, underlining the tacit acceptance of such practices. It is perhaps surprising, too, that Celador, who even part-funded the film, allowed Boyle to use all the iconography of their quiz show, even though the film showed the quiz as clearly open to corruption.

Boyle's film does not operate in a generic vacuum. There is a debt to Italian neo-realism, particularly to *Bicycle Thieves* (dir. Vittorio De Sica 1948), which also features a child-centred narrative (using some non-professional actors in key roles), involving a search around the poorer parts of a city. The big eyes and open features of Ayush Mahesh Khedekar, the youngest incarnation of Jamal, constitute an Indian version of Enzo Staiola who plays the boy in the Italian film. The use of non-professional actors and low-budget shooting on location can be traced back to *Pather Panchali* (dir. Satyajit Ray 1955), which features children at its core, including the brother-sister relationship of Apu (Subir Bannerjee) and Durga (Uma Das Gupta), which mirrors the innocence of Jamal and Latika. Ray's film also includes a fascination with moving images (a glimpse of a traveling bioscope), which is a feature shared by *Slumdog* as we see the boys worship Bollywood stars, literally in Jamal's 'toilet dive' in order to see his idol but also subsequently in the tiny cinema where Salim trades Jamal's prize autograph for cash. There is even an allusion to one of Ray's iconic long-shots of a train through the vast Indian landscape before the shift to the Taj Mahal section of the narrative.

The core group of a girl, two boys and a gun on the run, has elements of *Jules et Jim* (dir. Francois Truffaut 1962) but in a childish universe with an uplifting rather than downbeat ending. Both films feature a charismatic girl and the shifting romantic dynamic between two men who share a sense of shared destiny, unable to strike out on a life separate from the others, but also unable to live together harmoniously. The slum chase (and Boyle's kinetic style more broadly) demonstrates many of the signature stylistic devices of the French new wave (such as a constantly moving point-of-view using innovative lightweight cameras, freeze-frames, panning and wipes). Latika and Catherine (Jeanne Moreau) from *Jules et Jim* share a sense of iconic, stylish beauty and an influence across the whole narrative, even in scenes where they are not actually present.

David Fincher in *Benjamin Button* opts for computer-generated effects (over 350 visual-effect shots used in the whole film) and one main protagonist (Brad Pitt) to convey the change across a far greater age span, but it is a central feature of Boyle's bravery as a director that he chose to use three sets of different actors to play three ages of his protagonists (at 7, 13 and 18). Originally, Jamal was conceived to be older but once the 17-year-old Dev Patel was cast, it shifted the other age-stages downwards, compounding the casting challenges. On the DVD commentary, Boyle notes that 'most films are about control' but that 'India's different. If you seek that kind of control, it will drive you insane'. In a city that seems to be evolving almost daily, that kind of flexibility is a crucial quality in a director and a further difference with Fincher, who often insists on dozens of takes to gain the shot he wants. It is worth noting that Jamal wins the game and 'gets the girl' partly because it is his destiny but also because he is curious: we see Jamal 'hoover up' cultural knowledge of the UK at the call-centre. Despite the full title of his film, *The Curious Case of Benjamin Button*, Fincher's protagonist never shows any curiosity whatsoever. He can speak from birth, we never see him reading alone and he is given life-lessons from a sequence of characters (Daisy, played by Cate Blanchett, tells him, 'we're supposed to lose the ones we love') but there is no evidence that he actually learns from any of them.[11]

Like *Trainspotting*, *Slumdog* uses occasional fantastical elements without fictive markers, momentarily disorientating viewers, such as Jamal's fantasy of pushing Salim off the roof of a building, juxtaposed with the 'real' event in which he just punches him. This kind of unsignalled fast-forwards is extremely rare in mainstream film, unless in the genre of the supernatural, in Walter Mitty–style cases, where characters are serial fantasists, or in more edgy scripts by figures like Charlie Kaufman, who question the fabric of film narrative itself (see Michel Gondry's *The Eternal Sunshine of the Spotless Mind*, 2004). It indicates Boyle's preparedness to slip into the subjective universes of his characters, making them more interesting and encouraging a sense of empathy from the viewer, who may feel that momentarily they are being given rare and privileged access to an individual's thought processes.

There is some great shot composition, such as the night-time shot through the container where the boys are sheltering, whilst Latika (Rubina Ali) huddles on the ground in the rain, a tiny figure in the distance. There are closer shots that also draw attention to themselves as consciously artistic, such as the close-up shot through a keyhole, when the brothers discover Latika in one of the disreputable houses on Pila

---

11 Browning 2010 p.126.

Street. Jamal walks into extreme close-up, only to be hauled out of focus by Salim who wants to see Latika and whose image we see reflected on his eyeball. There is also the use of freeze-frame for Jamal's vision of the god Rama (it seems unlikely that this is a real child, more a reflection of the religious affiliation behind the attack on the group of Muslims, in which his mother is killed). The fixed camera, point-of-view shot on the tea-tray as Jamal negotiates the desks at the call-centre, and the reflection of Jamal in Salim's sunglasses (a further example of Žižek's idea of a shot containing its own counter-shot, mentioned earlier in relation to *28 Days Later*) are examples of carefully crafted shots which create depth of meaning, but do not require greater effort from the audience: the narrative is not slowed down to accommodate such artistry, neither do we have to scan the whole frame for meaning. They are examples of the richness of Boyle's composition, rewarding repeated viewing, especially on DVD, when images can be replayed or frozen. Boyle seems to be simultaneously addressing audience needs of at a mainstream, art-house and cineaste level.

Time out

A couple of examples of Boyle's work outside film are worth briefly mentioning here as they also contain a blend of powerful theatrical performances and fantastical sequences. The BBC TV dramas *Strumpet* and *Vacuuming Completely Nude in Paradise* (both 2001) followed the critical disappointment of *The Beach* and mark a period of Boyle taking stock, before returning with *Millions* in 2004. Page recounts the basic narratives of these two dramas at some length and implies they represent a turning point in Boyle's filmmaking career. It is true that he met Anthony Dod Mantle, the cinematographer with whom he would work with on his subsequent films; that both dramas gave him the opportunity to experiment with mobile digital cameras, and that in *Strumpet* he teamed up once more with Christopher Eccleston. However, while both films are very watchable, they represent a hiatus or even a nostalgic throwback rather than a development for Boyle. Extremely limited casts, highly personal narratives with great emotional intensity focusing on one main relationship in a northern English setting (complete with a working men's club in *Strumpet*, and Blackpool as the venue for the annual prize-giving in *Vacuuming*), all evoke the kitchen sink dramas of the 1950s and 60s.

Strumpet is a fairly slight tale of a homeless poet named Strayman (Christopher Eccleston) who wanders round an unnamed urban wasteland, squatting in any available council flat with his pack of dogs. He stumbles across a singer, the 'Strumpet' of the title (Genna G) and they enjoy a brief rise to fame when a wannabe manager, Knockoff (Stephen Walters) hears them singing together. Knockoff steals a camera and, on the basis of a filmed impromptu performance, persuades some record executives to take notice. *Vacuuming Completely Nude in Paradise* dramatises the soul-destroying life of Tommy Rag (Timothy Spall), an unprincipled door-to-door salesman explaining his craft to a trainee, as he is locked in competition to be top of the regional sales list. Both *Strumpet* and *Vacuuming* seem on paper quite small-scale and perhaps an odd choice for Boyle after *The Beach*, but that is precisely the point. They represent a going back to his roots, particularly in northern subject matter and the larger-than-life, theatrical performances of the two leads, but they also express a profoundly cinematic sensibility.

The performances of Eccleston and Spall are the dramas' most memorable features. Spall especially, as the foul-mouthed salesman Rag, spends virtually his entire on-screen time snarling and swearing aggressively at other drivers and at his hapless new trainee Pete (Michael Begley). Rag represents naked capitalism, turning his aggressive charm on the most vulnerable (badgering the elderly in sheltered housing, brazenly walking past signs reading 'strictly no traders'). Spall's grotesque snuffling of Puffa Puffa rice for 'breakfast' seems a fairly obvious caricature of Willy Loman in Arthur Miller's *Death of a Salesman* (1949). Boyle uses surveillance footage and experimental camera positioning (possibly inspired by Mantle's previous work in the dance scenes for Thomas Vinterberg's 1998 *Festen*), where the camera is strapped to the protagonists' heads at points of particular disorientation or to objects (a pen in *Strumpet*, a vacuum cleaner in *Vacuuming*), but the result is anachronism rather than gritty realism. The presence of a stereotypical working men's club, the Ford Sierra that Rag drives, and the dated and unfunny dance routine at the close, to Sheena Easton's 'Nine to Five', all make it seem a decade overdue.

Strumpet's riotous scene when itinerant musician Strumpet and the enigmatic poet Strayman improvise a song while dancing around his decrepit flat is the nearest Boyle has come to capturing the euphoria of music on film. Generically, this scene is closer to a musical as Strumpet joins in without apparently knowing the words. At the climax, there is an intrinsically impossible attempt to reprise the spontaneity of this first performance in the *Top of the Pops* studio, which may have the illusion of rebellious behaviour, with characters jumping on stage and singing live, but where 'liveness' is packaged as just another entertainment feature. More telling perhaps is the film's opening with Eccleston's delivery, not of one of Strayman's own poems, but of John Cooper Clarke's profanity-strewn 'Chickentown'. Eccleston's Strayman feels almost like a showreel for his subsequent portrayal of Dr Who – literary, eccentric, dynamic and essentially theatrical; quite literally 'performance poetry'.

Both dramas feature typical Boyle stylistic devices: in *Strumpet*, a point-of-view shot through a confectionery stand in a newsagent; and in *Vacuuming*, a similar shot from a car glove compartment. Even within two quite predictable plots, there is some stylistic innovation, particularly in matters of scale – in *Strumpet*, there is a surreal shot in which an apparently giant Strayman looks down on Lilliputian-sized passers-by, and in *Vacuuming* Rag's death is shown with his face in extreme close-up, lying lifeless on a beach with his hapless girlfriend calling for him in the extreme background. Boyle is interested in bravura transition devices, such as the titles of *Vacuuming* being sucked up by a Hoover that Rag is demonstrating, or the action of Knockoff, the manic pop manager in *Strumpet*, turning to the camera and literally turning the screen 'off' with a TV remote.

What makes these two TV dramas significant, however, is that they represent the point at which Boyle seems to have taken a step back from his career trajectory and concluded the way he produces his best work is through smaller crews and budgets, actors who he knows and respects, and a balance between intense individual performances and the eruption of the surreal/impossible into the everyday life.

Conclusion

Boyle shows similar key qualities to those of Stephen Daldry, another British theatre-director-turned-filmmaker, whose films include *Billy Elliot* (2000), *The Hours* (2002) and *The Reader* (2008). Daldry also worked for a while at The Royal Court and is co-director, with Boyle, of the opening ceremony for the Olympic Games in 2012. The two men share the same attention to detail, the ability to coax powerful performances from lead actors, and a strong sense of celebrating the humanity of a film's characters.

Bearing in mind the films discussed in this chapter, it should perhaps not be surprising that Boyle's direction of *Frankenstein* at London's National Theatre in 2011 took an innovative approach to the blend of technology and acting style with the two lead actors, Jonny Lee Miller – with whom Boyle had worked in *Trainspotting* – and Benedict

Cumberbatch, swapping roles on alternate nights, so that they played both the Monster and his creator. As Boyle himself states, 'it puts the accent on performance and not on make-up.'[12]

The sensitive performances that Boyle manages to get from seven-year-old Alex Etel and nine-year-old Lewis McGibbon in *Millions* (as Damian and Anthony) are typical of his work with children: the results are especially impressive given that they were both first-time actors upon whom the entire project rested. On the DVD commentary, Boyle admits that the full realisation of that risk only came later. The two brothers appear in most of the scenes and yet, due to their age, there were legal limits on how many hours they could work per day, which was frustrating for Boyle but meant that he had to make the most of what valuable contact time he had. The 'spirit of the film' mentioned on the DVD extras extends beyond the credible family unit that Boyle attempted to construct. It was the innocence and optimism of the young actors themselves, and the trust that Boyle and writer Frank Cottrell Boyce put in them, that is astonishing in retrospect. Damian's mother's advice to 'have faith in people' is exactly what holds the production together. In the 'Raw Attic' sequence, part of the DVD deleted scenes package, in which a frightened Damian hides in the attic of his old house, we can hear Boyle's direction to Etel. What is striking is the vitality and energy of Boyle's instructions, so that almost every movement is accounted for, including breathing to simulate fear, such that Boyle can almost appear bullying in his directorial technique – but it works.

Boyle has particularly strong faith in the people around him and believes that, if correctly chosen, they will work together to create something greater than the sum of their parts. Intelligent (and perhaps lucky) casting plays a part here and he has been helped on all his productions by the astute choices of casting director, Gail Stevens, Boyle's former partner, with whom he has retained an effective working relationship. More than this, however, it seems that Boyle retains a faith in the process. In *Shakespeare in Love* (dir. John Madden 1998), Philip Henslowe explains to Hugh Fennyman that the natural condition of the theatre business is 'one of insurmountable obstacles on the road to imminent disaster'. Like him, Boyle probably believes that there is nothing that can be done about it but that, given good will and commitment, all indeed will 'turn out well'. As Henslowe replies when Fennyman asks how this can possibly be: 'I don't know,' he says. 'It's a mystery'.

---

12 See 'Sherlock star Cumberbatch to play Frankenstein on stage,' 29 October 2010, www.bbc.co.uk/news/entertainment-arts-11651495

CHAPTER FOUR

· REGIONAL AND NATIONAL IDENTITY ·

'He has taken us places we've never seen'

voiceover on the trailer for *127 Hours*

The trailer for *127 Hours* features brief shots from a number of Boyle's films up to this point, including Richard jumping from the rock in *The Beach*, Salim and Jamal in front of the Taj Mahal in *Slumdog Millionaire* and Jim alone walking through London in *28 Days Later*. It is such places, the trailer suggests, that make Boyle's films distinct. The term 'places' here connotes not just geographical locations but emotional experiences. Place is an important part in the emotional journey that we take with the characters. Although Boyle draws upon a range of locations in his work, this chapter considers how he portrays notions of nationality, and Britishness in particular.

The notion of what constitutes a national cinema is quite subjective. The films of Merchant-Ivory, often taken to represent Britishness through a series of literary adaptations of novels by Henry James and E.M. Forster, such as *The Bostonians* (1984) and *Room With a View* (1985), are directed by James Ivory, produced by Ismail Merchant and typically use scripts by Ruth Prawer Jhabvala. However, as Merchant himself once commented, 'it is a strange marriage we have at Merchant Ivory... I am an Indian Muslim, Ruth is a German Jew, and Jim is a Protestant American.'[1]

Locations, stars and financial backing may originate from one specific country but in an increasingly global marketplace, this is unlikely. Although the mood of Scottish militancy and national pride that seemed resurgent through the mid-1990s frequently appropriated the language and iconography of *Braveheart* (1995), the film itself was directed by and starred Mel Gibson, who was born in America but grew up in Australia. It took sizeable liberties with historical fact about the rebel William Wallace and shot many sequences in Ireland rather than Scotland, such as the Battle of Stirling Bridge which was filmed in County Kildare. Boyle's first two feature films, *Shallow Grave* and *Trainspotting*, both set in

---

1   Merchant in *The Times*, 26 May 2005,
http://www.timesonline.co.uk/tol/comment/obituaries/article1079969.ece

Scotland, challenged established representations of Scottishness, particularly in their uncompromising use of vernacular language.

Scotland

Prior to *Shallow Grave*, the popular perception of Scottish cinema was dominated by certain key figures such as Bill Forsyth, known for his low-budget whimsical dramas like *Gregory's Girl* (1981), *Local Hero* (1983) and *Comfort and Joy* (1984); the gritty realism of Ken Loach (although not Scottish himself, he used stars like Robert Carlyle and shot in Glasgow locations) in work like *Carla's Song* (1996); and family-based, almost sociological records in the work of Bill Douglas in his bleak black-and-white trilogy *My Childhood* (1972), *My Ain Folk* (1973) and *My Way Home* (1978). Even the cultural spectre of *Brigadoon* (dir. Vincente Minnelli 1954) still hovered over the limited representations of Scottish national identity on film, with its kilts, bonnie lassies and sense of Celtic mystery and romance. The establishment of the Scottish Film Production Fund in 1982 laid the groundwork for the provision of institutional support for an indigenous film industry, but Boyle's work also acted as a catalyst for a doubling of Scottish-based production through the 1990s (from five to 10 features a year), including Loach's *My Name is Joe* (1998) and Lynne Ramsey's *Ratcatcher* (1999). Where Boyle's work differs, however, is in the speed and energy of his style and in the engaging humour that pervades his films.

Shallow Grave was very well received at Cannes in 1994 and became the most successful British film of 1995, with *Trainspotting* taking the same accolade a year later.

However, these films did not suddenly appear from nowhere. Stefan Schwartz's *Soft Top, Hard Shoulder* (1992) anticipates some of the quirky humour and concern with Scottish identity as hero Gavin, played by Peter Capaldi (a visual reminder of Forsyth's *Local Hero*, in which he co-starred), acts like a Renton-in-reverse. Whereas Renton leaves Edinburgh to begin a new life in London, Gavin is forced to travel back from London to Scotland for a family gathering and, en route, re-evaluates how he feels about his homeland.

A key part of *Trainspotting*'s appeal is its specific positioning in opposition to heritage representations of Britishness, and Scottishness in particular. Released around the time of a mini-renaissance in Scottish film, *Trainspotting* sets out to subvert clichéd elements in the portrayal of identity. A central way in which it does this is by drawing on music: not the music traditionally associated with Scotland, but ambient dance music and bands from the Britpop movement of the mid-nineties. The vibrancy of Welsh's prose in the novel already seems to possess a musicality of its own but, in seeking to bring this to a mainstream audience, Boyle and screenwriter John Hodge downplayed Welsh's more obvious linguistic excesses in terms of dialect and phonetic delivery which might disorientate audiences, and transposed this sense into rapid cutting and a thumping soundtrack.

Rather than a backward-looking view of culture, its focus is resolutely contemporary. Ang Lee's adaptation of *Sense and Sensibility* (1996) was released on the same day as *Trainspotting* in the UK, but Boyle's film takes its inspiration less from the written word than its aural context – the way that DJs juxtapose different tracks and beats to create moods for mass audiences on club dance-floors. Martin Stollery notes that Renton is a 'poacher' who assimilates himself into whatever situations he finds himself.[2] This is most obvious when Renton adopts the language of a Thatcherite estate agent, but his traits are like those of a successful music sampler, taking linguistic elements and redeploying them in a new context.

Will Self called *Trainspotting* an 'extended pop video' which was probably intended as a dismissive comment but from which Boyle might take some pleasure.[3] Although he has never made a pop video, music is clearly important to Boyle, both personally and as a filmmaker: his use of contemporary music in his work, particularly in scenes with rapid cutting and oblique camera angles, often denotes intense experiences of a transcendent kind.

Boyle stated that he 'wanted the film to pulse, to pulse like you do in your twenties.'[4] In *Trainspotting*, when Renton dives into the toilet, we hear Brian Eno's 'Deep Blue Day' (1983), giving the sequence the restful feel of a chill-out room in a club, the exact opposite of where this scene ostensibly takes place. We have an escape, an interlude from the everyday to which Renton must return, spluttering back into the disgusting cubicle some seconds later, but providing us with a momentary glimpse of another, more beautiful world. Murray Smith notes how Sleeper's version of 'Atomic' (1996) is heard over the three sex scenes in the film, giving them a sense of coherence and of simultaneous chronology; the melody of Pulp's 'Mile-End' (1996) reflects the emotional poverty of Begbie's existence; and the grinding rhythm of Underworld's 'Dark &

---

2   Stollery 2001 p.24.
3   Will Self cited in Morace 2001 p.83.
4   Danny Boyle cited in Callaghan, 'The Scottish Invasion,' *New York Magazine*, 15 July 1996, p.39.

Long' (1994) captures Renton's nauseous heaving while undergoing withdrawal.[5]

As producer Andrew Macdonald describes it: 'the music allows us to travel in time, which is why the arc of music was from washed-up punk, to the King of Punk – Iggy Pop – right the way through dance music and a quick trip to London's dance culture, right the way through Brit Pop, with Pulp and Blur.'[6] Sleeper's 'Statuesque' (1996) also plays over a bar scene and Blur's 'Sing' (1991) accompanies the second time we see the chase sequence with which the film opens. Murray Smith analyses at some length the music choices that Boyle makes, underlining how the film manages to interweave contemporary British dance culture (bands such as Underworld and Leftfield), the then-emergent Britpop sound (Blur and Pulp), and references to American counter-cultural icons of the 1970s (Iggy Pop and Lou Reed especially).[7] The use of indie Britpop and ambient dance broadens the cultural reference and appeal beyond Scotland to Britain more widely. Polygram, seeing an opportunity, spent at least a million pounds on marketing the soundtrack (unusually high, in comparison to the film's overall budget, which was only half a million more). More than just a slick piece of marketing, the CD for *Trainspotting*, packaged like the accompanying advertising for the film in distinctive orange with the protagonists lined up and posing for the camera, was a successful expression of contemporary British music culture, which at the time was dominating sales across Europe and even making inroads into America.

Boyle's interest in music extends not just to selecting existing, known tracks for particular scenes (as with Lou Reed and Iggy Pop here), the music often being used ironically, but helping to bring little-known bands to a wider public. In *127 Hours*, we have Free Blood's 'Never Hear Surf Music Again,' whose driving baseline helps to emphasise the kinetic nature of the opening sequence of Ralston on his bike. It is a measure of Boyle's high status following *Slumdog Millionaire* that, whereas he had to sacrifice his choice of music for *28 Days Later* (he had wanted The Clash's 'Hitsville UK'), he can now use a virtually unknown band to 'open' a film.

Conventionally, film directors avoid using voiceovers as it is seen as 'too easy'; it appears to break the rule of 'show rather than tell'. As Brian Cox, playing script guru Robert McKee, states in *Adaptation* (dir. Spike Jonze 2002), 'any idiot can write a voice-over narration to explain the

---

5   Smith 2002 p38. and p.62.
6   Andrew Macdonald cited in Finney 1996 p.180.
7   Smith 2002 pp.65-74.

thoughts of a character.' However, with *Trainspotting*, Boyle challenges this head-on. Renton's opening monologue is not just any first-person narrative but a speech that is lengthy, delivered in an accent many viewers might not often hear, and which is intercut with explanatory flashbacks to introduce the main characters. After reconsidering the effectiveness of Martin Scorsese's *Goodfellas* (1990), which uses, right from the opening, unremitting voice-over from the point of view of Henry (Ray Liotta), Boyle states, 'I started off thinking it's a substitute for the visual, but actually you need to visualise a lot more because you need to create a lot of material to allow the voice-over to have its time.'[8] Welsh's novel, comprising several juxtaposed narrators, is thus given coherence in the film by giving Renton ownership of the narrative.

Both *Shallow Grave* and *Trainspotting* established the screen persona of Ewan McGregor as a young, dynamic actor of considerable talent, particularly effective in roles requiring witty, loveable rogues. *A Life Less Ordinary* continued McGregor's partnership with Boyle but his character, Robert, is much less assured. In all three of these roles, McGregor used his own relatively soft Scottish accent – part of his acting persona that he was subsequently forced to modify in later bigger-budget roles for other directors, such as Christian in *Moulin Rouge* (dir. Baz Luhrman 2001) and the young Obi-Wan Kenobi in the *Star Wars* trilogy *The Phantom Menace* (1999), *Attack of the Clones* (2002) and *Revenge of the Sith* (2005), where he adopted the clipped Home Counties accent that would make him believable as a young Alec Guinness, who plays Kenobi in the earlier films.

Shallow Grave contains glimpses of Scotland but the film, supposedly set in Edinburgh, was actually shot mostly in a huge warehouse in Glasgow, underlining the blurriness of 'Scottishness' in the minds of many cinema-goers. It is perhaps worth noting that of the main three characters, Ewan McGregor is the only genuine Scot. Most of the city-specific references are in small cutaways or tight shots. We tilt down from 'The Scotsman' building (a broadsheet paper based in Edinburgh) to the three protagonists, crushed into a Mini, returning from their squash game. Later, as Alex is flicking through TV channels, we hear mention of regional news ('Scotland Today') and a football commentary. There are stereotypical images of Scottish culture in the country dancing at the charity dinner ('Strip the Willow'), with men in kilts, even Alex in a tartan jacket in the same scene, and there are glimpses of beautiful

---

8   Boyle cited in Smith 2002 p.179.

Highland scenery, when Alex, Julia and David are driving out to dispose of the bodies of the thugs that David has killed.

Much of what was written about *Trainspotting* at the time of its release focused on its Scottishness as this was a buoyant time for Scottish cinema and culture in general, with the establishment of a Scottish Parliament following the Labour victory in 1997. It was, and continues to be, viewed as a 'Scottish' film due to its location, cast and, above all, its language. Indeed, Boyle himself was so strongly identified with his subject matter at the time, especially by American audiences, that occasionally he was mistakenly described as being Scottish himself. Filmic representations of relationships to the English, like *Braveheart* and *Rob Roy* (dir. Michael Caton-Jones 1995) were big-budget and historical in nature, straying towards heritage more than seriously revisionist. *Trainspotting* does touch upon heritage Edinburgh, such as the Festival, but this is only the starting point for some choreographed violence and chastising of stereotypes, as Renton and the others march in step behind Begbie to give an American tourist a lesson in raising his voice in a public bar (described by Renton as one of 'the good times'). The film could be viewed as an ironic commodification of images of Scotland, rather than the novel's attempt to challenge the literary dominance of the west of the country. For example, when the protagonists go up to the Pentlands, the contrast with the natural landscape shows up the absurdity of their appearance: they stand on the railway platform in skin-tight trousers, with no coats or outdoor-wear, some swigging beer. They have no interest in trying to explore this quintessential Scottish countryside and Renton reacts cynically to the clichéd suggestion that they go for a walk. On the platform, just as in the march into the toilets behind the hapless American or the parade across a London street, there is a choreographed element to the movement of the group across the screen, often moving in synch together. Their shared background, especially their drug habit, reduces their individuality, making them act as a unit.

On the one hand, the desire to produce a film that would be popular in the American market led to a heightening of what is distinctive, a ratcheting-up of features signalling regional and national identity. However, this railway scene, shot at Corrour Station, near Loch Ossian, is the sole example of the Scottish countryside in the whole film. In Welsh's novel, Renton's rant about being Scottish appears during a scene in a pub in central Edinburgh and not as a speech declaimed to others, but as part of Renton's interior monologue. In the film, Renton is rejecting the colonising force, the English, as weak and effete but those colonised, the Scots, as even more so for allowing it to happen. It also acts as a moderation of a more blunt expression in the novel – 'Ah've never felt British, because ah'm not. It's ugly and artificial. Ah've never really felt Scottish either, though. Scotland the brave, ma arse; Scotland the shitein cunt.'[9] In the film, Renton is using a gendered expression of a parasitical relationship and the speech certainly has power, especially as forcefully delivered by McGregor. However, by choosing to place it against the backdrop of sweeping hillsides, it could be said to be using a Scottish cliché (the landscape) for the recognition of international audiences as much as for the purpose of questioning it. As a polar opposite to the patriotic calls of faux-Scot Mel Gibson, up in the Highlands, Renton is expressing a much more bitter, some might say realistic, view of how it feels to be Scottish.

Viewed as pure background, there is a glimpse of quintessential Highland landscape, a view of Princes Street, and the interior of a spacious Georgian flat in Edinburgh's city-centre, but in the foreground we have a very different kind of heritage. We are presented with a daily ritual chase between security guards and shoplifters, Renton's realising that he has slept with a schoolgirl and Spud declaring the very idea of walking in the countryside as 'not natural'. The fact that the film opens with a flight from store detectives suggests lives going nowhere, and Renton recognises, before being rugby-tackled out of shot, that 'sooner or later this kind of thing was bound to happen'.

The fact that Renton expresses his feelings of post-coital euphoria by comparing it to a Scotland game in the 1978 World Cup, not only shows how drugs have blunted his sex drive but also the importance of that particular match in popular memory. The image of Archie Gemmill's goal, in which he skips around several tackles and scores for Scotland from an acute angle against Holland, articulates the hopes of a small but patriotic nation, apparently on the brink of a moment of national pride and self-definition of Scotland's status as gutsy underdog.

For Steven Blandford, *Shallow Grave* and *Trainspotting*, with their rejection of clichéd representations of Scotland or a moralistic representation of drug culture, 'form an acute vision of 1990s Scotland that has little to do with social realism and everything to do with situating Scottish filmmaking in the vanguard of international independent cinema.'[10] In effect, accents and the opening scene apart,

---

9 Welsh 2004 p.228.
10 Blandford 2007 p.71.

Boyle has crafted a tale with more universal applicability, which displeases some viewers, especially devotees of Welsh's writing who see in this a mirror of Renton's betrayal of his roots. Boyle presents us with a Scotland that is grubby and urban, rather than scenic and rural, and a country that is not associated with kilts, shortbread and the Festival, but with heroin.

England – North and South

Boyle's choice of his apocalyptic setting for *28 Days Later* (2002) gives us a view of England which is partly derivative but which has already proved influential, inspiring Edgar Wright's 2004 parody, *Shaun of the Dead*. The hero in Boyle's film, Jim (Cillian Murphy), wakes up to an apparently empty world, something that also happens in John Wyndham's novel *The Day of the Triffids* (1951). A recent BBC version of Wyndham's narrative (dir. Nick Copus 2009) attempts to emulate Boyle's realisation of a deserted hospital and equally deserted streets, including Westminster Bridge, but cannot match his arresting visual images. As Jim, wearing his ill-fitting green hospital gown, scavenges for food along corridors, Boyle juxtaposes a line of telephone receivers, hanging lifeless and sharply focused in the foreground against the blurred background of a Costa Coffee outlet, symbolic of the global branding that no longer has any meaning. Outside in the hospital grounds, alternating extreme high- and low-angles of angular tower-blocks create powerful images of alienation as the lone figure of Jim is framed as tiny and insignificant, dwarfed by his environment. An almost surreal, three-layered image shoots him in extreme high angle as he looks down at a rank of ambulances below, and yet trees in the extreme foreground, apparently above, look almost like a window-box. He seems detached from his environment without, at this stage, knowing exactly why. The hospital scenes, shot in a real hospital, look like stills from a J.G. Ballard photography exhibition, juxtaposing cold images of technology with a familiar cityscape made alien to the hero.

Moving out into the streets, Boyle uses extremely wide shots to encompass recognisable London landmarks such as Westminster Bridge. He shoots through a double-decker bus lying on its side, to film Jim's approach, then switches to an extreme high-angle shot of the bus, making it look almost like a toy. Jim shuffles through souvenir models of Big Ben before the camera swings round 180 degrees to frame him in front of the real thing itself, just as lifeless. Other films have attempted to depict the emptiness of a post-apocalyptic London, including the 1984 video for The Human League's 'Life On Your Own' (dir. Simon Milne), which in turn was supposedly inspired by *The Omega Man* (dir. Boris Sagal 1971), and in which we see lead singer Phil Oakey, apparently the sole survivor of some kind of Armageddon, stumbling about empty London streets, amidst deserted tube stations and overturned double-decker buses. *Daleks' Invasion Earth: 2150 A.D.* (dir. Gordon Flemyng 1966) opts for a Blitz-like vision of a destroyed city, rather than just emptying out the one people know. Boyle's version is powerful, not just because of the lack of the one key ingredient of major, bustling cities at eight o'clock in the morning – people – but also the strange beauty of cities without people, the stillness and relative quiet. A.O. Scott describes the camerawork of cinematographer Anthony Dod Mantle here as having 'an ethereal, almost painterly beauty. The London skyline takes on the faded, melancholy quality of a Turner watercolour.'[11] Unlike a purely digital effect, or crude crowd-control, like the packed pavements visible behind Bond's Las Vegas car chases in *Diamonds Are Forever* (dir. Guy Hamilton 1971), Boyle used groups of attractive young women, including one of his own daughters, to persuade pedestrians to stay out of shot.

As Jim wanders through the streets, Boyle places the Cenotaph in the background, a memorial to those killed in wars, ironically underlining the loss that Jim's brain cannot comprehend. We see him instinctively scrabbling around to bag up cash strewn in the road but which now has lost all meaning and value. Boyle drains these street scenes of strong colour, with exceptions for significant objects such as the bus, so that Jim's green gown stands out against the dominant grey of the cityscape as his tiny figure walks through the bottom of extended wide-shots. The first major use of colour is on an advertising hoarding at Piccadilly Circus, featuring girls whose smiles contrast sharply with the scene of emptiness in front of them. Sound is important too – but for a few birds the city is silent, so that when Jim touches a car, setting off an alarm, it makes him (and possibly us) jump. Boyle's camera positioning also creates an element of suspense in that he uses a tilt-shot down to Jim as he walks through the streets, as if he is being observed from a rooftop, and even in the scene in which he approaches a car that is stopped in the middle of Piccadilly Circus, we momentarily cut to a point-of-view shot from the car window, which could be that of someone in the car watching him. Later, there is a slow tracking shot through an interior door of Jim's parents' house, again as if he is being watched. Mantle's use of digital

---

11 A.O. Scott cited in Murray, Heumann 2009 p.187.

video for the urban scenes gives them the grittiness of surveillance footage (an effect he played with in *Strumpet*). As Boyle states in production notes for the film, 'this is the way we record our lives.'[12]

The board in Piccadilly Circus, on which survivors have pinned pictures and notes in their search for loved ones, was inspired by real news reports and it is only when Jim is faced with the sheer number of missing people that the human dimension of the situation comes crashing in on him. As he walks away, the camera tracks in on the photo of one particular unknown boy, before fading to black. It is also an example of a typical Boyle camera technique, moving across or in the opposite vector to his subject, thereby exaggerating their movement (the same device appears as Frank, Hannah, Selena and Jim leave a supermarket and in the shots of an army convoy turning off the motorway). The use of the pin-board provoked some negative chatroom reaction at the time of release because it was similar to ones erected after the 9/11 terrorist attacks and Boyle has said that with hindsight, he might not have used it.

The sequence in the road tunnel, leading out of London, seems close to a more powerful sequence in Stephen King's *The Stand*, both in his 1978 book and Mick Garris' 1994 TV mini-series, where a group of survivors from a government-produced plague are fleeing New York and must pass through the Lincoln Tunnel – a much longer and more frightening prospect than in this film. Here, the attempt to place obstacles in the path of the cab that the protagonists are travelling in – abandoned vehicles, a puncture, rats and finally a horde of Infected – all seem a little obvious and the means of escape, apparently simply driving *over and through* any obstruction, smacks more of *Chitty Chitty Bang Bang* (dir. Ken Hughes 1968) than apocalyptic horror. The gleeful squeals of the passengers, the sheer wish-fulfilment that such action will be physically possible, and the apparent lack of damage to the car, shift the narrative temporarily into the style of a children's adventure story. This continues in the interlude in a deserted supermarket, where Frank (Brendan Gleeson) secretes four bottles of expensive whisky and makes a show of leaving his credit card at the till. There is a childish, playful element at work in the possibilities of limitless chocolate, and even a mundane shopping trip becomes a comic interlude with a point-of-view shot of Selena from her trolley, with a wide-angle lens producing a distorted

---

12 Boyle, *28 Days Later*, Production Notes, at http://www.cilliansite.com/production-notes/28-days-later-prod-notes.pdf, p.6.

image as if we were a baby being pushed along, redolent of Pulp's video for 'Common People' (1995).

The mood continues to lighten as the cab moves out of London, and Boyle shows us images of beauty, such as a field full of flowers (although this is potentially ambiguous: the scene is unpolluted but the blooms will also remain unpicked). This is not an unbroken interlude, however, which might feel too sentimental, and the necessary stop for petrol creates tension in the combination of low-angle shots and the vulnerability of the group's situation. We might expect Hannah (Megan Burns), who seems the most physically vulnerable, to be the target of any attack but it is Jim who is set upon by a young boy. The attack marks a turning point in Jim's character: for the first time, he must kill to survive, and must kill an infected child in a direct and brutal fashion. This rite-of-passage changes him and he is now closer to Selena in knowing what survival entails. The sequence is closed by Hannah driving the cab straight at a petrol tanker, her rage suggesting that she has become infected but she twists the wheel around at the last minute, signalling her as a normal thrill-seeking teenager, in an effective manipulation of our expectations.

On the motorway, the scene appears strange as we may never have seen the roads so empty, except on black and white film from the 1950s of the opening of the M1. The sequence where the cab they are driving slows down and Frank says 'must be Manchester' is followed by a tilt-shot up the length of a straight road, absolutely empty as far as the eye can see (the speed of setting up shots with digital video was a key factor in making it possible to close major roads). There is a fantasy element here, reminiscent of car advertisements, when a completely empty road suggests limitless possibilities. In *Strumpet*, the journey on virtually empty motorways is towards the south as the source of fame, fortune and material wealth – but also metaphorically and literally contagion and death. Here the metaphor is given concrete reality as the characters resolutely head north as a means of escaping the virus. The uncanny beauty of the scene is reflected in the colour-contrast of sharp green verges with tarmac and the picture composition uses a huge wind turbine, initially as an otherworldly background to the cab as it crests a curve in the road, but then in a reverse-shot from behind the turbine, so we hear a sudden whoosh of its blades.

Mark Kermode terms the film 'quintessentially British' but more precisely it is resolutely English in its setting and its production, from the Cambridge-based research centre of the opening, to the desolate London streets, to the outskirts of Manchester and the denouement in the Lake

District.[13] The supermarkets, Frank's Christmas lights and the setting around Frank's flat all evoke a typically English late-twentieth century urban landscape, complete with light industrial units, a gas tower, high-rise blocks and blocks of terraced houses. Boyle tilts down from the road sign 'The South' to a scene of gridlock, suggesting almost a modern version of Hadrian's Wall. This military roadblock/check-point, around which the cab gingerly edges, also suggests a cultural division, as if one is entering a very different part of Britain.

Other films by Boyle may not have attracted the attention given to *Trainspotting* or even *28 Days Later* in their depiction of modern Britain but nonetheless have something to say about it. The setting for *Millions*, for example, strikes a tone that is affirmative and optimistic. On the DVD commentary, Boyle describes modern estates in the north of England of the kind he shows as 'places of optimism and hope' and he intended the boys' school to represent New Labour's investment in primary education: the classrooms are all newly decorated and seem exciting, positive places to be. More widely, he speaks on the DVD about wanting to celebrate a move away from a cynical selfish era (seen in *Shallow Grave*) towards a more generous sense of community. The small elements of regional identity are celebratory, even when drawing on stereotypes – the lucky recipient of the free meal that Damian and Anthony give in Pizza Hut screams 'you must be minted' in vibrant Scouse. Anthony wishes he could buy a house in Reading (not just because the price would go up but also because it would not get broken into) and the newly built housing estates are not portrayed as uniform and stultifying, but part of an aspirational dream. The north of England is evoked by blue skies, space and optimism, symbolised by the scene of St Francis of Assisi releasing doves, rather than by grimness, rain and constriction. The robbery sequence involves an elaborate plan of distraction so that a robber can hide himself on a train carrying money and then throw bags of cash out to waiting accomplices at pre-arranged locations along the route. On the DVD commentary, Boyce talks about the robbery in particular as evocative of classic British films relating to trains, especially *Night Mail* (dir. Harry Watt and Basil Wright 1936), and of the cultural impact of the Great Train Robbery in 1963.

It should be said that the narrative strand that places the story within the final days of the British pound tries to introduce a rather strained element of jeopardy and pace into the film. Currencies rarely become

13 Kermode in *Sight and Sound* 12:12, December 2002 p.60.

worthless the day after a changeover, but the idea does allow Boyle to invent a TV public information film featuring Leslie Phillips, who plays to type as a lecherous cad, warning us about the impending changes (apparently Boyle was advised by advertising companies of the need in such circumstances for a known figure with whom older generations could identify). The currency change also motivates consideration of notions of value, particularly in the juxtaposed views of Anthony, who is looking to invest and accumulate and Damian, who wants to do good with the money.

India

Edwin Page claims that the story of *Slumdog Millionaire* 'could have been told using any cultural background,' but this is clearly not so.[14] There are numerous culturally specific aspects, from the Taj Mahal sequence, the ubiquitous use of Hindi, the very specific slums, the portrayal of Mumbai, which make this a truly Indian film. Beaufoy's script, like his work on *The Full Monty* (dir. Peter Cattaneo 1997), foregrounds the background, so to speak – the setting is a vital part of the film's conception. People in India were surprised that Boyle chose to film in a real slum rather than recreate one in a studio and he shows us a city with a pulsating sense of life. Boyle read all he could (particularly Suketa Mehta's 2004 *Maximum City*, a blend of historical study and numerous stories about life in Mumbai) to immerse himself in the culture, and sought to avoid stereotypical shots, such as livestock in the streets (although a cow is glimpsed in the first wide shot of Maman's gang going to work). Jamal and Salim try to find Latika in a city that threatens to swallow her up (first in Cherry Street and later at Khan's house, which *was* actually owned by the developer of the blocks behind it, reflecting how the slums have given rise to a new generation of entrepreneurs, some legitimate, some less so). The shots of the brothers sitting on the edge of a vertiginous drop, looking down over a Mumbai that appears to be growing before their very eyes, may in part have been inspired by Jia Zhangke's *Still Life* (2006), which also features a search for spouses and love and in which images of natural beauty are juxtaposed with rapidly changing urban environments (the Three Gorges region in China).

Boyle shows a city undergoing massive change at an extraordinary pace. We see the boys walking along a huge pipeline and later helicopter-shots across the cityscape convey the scale of change. At several points we

14 Page 2009 p.199.

see an immense rock outcrop, Gilbert Hill, next to huge tower-blocks, juxtaposing the modern with the primitive. The protagonists playing in the huge empty Tulip Star hotel dramatises the playground of western visitors and an emerging Indian middle class, in a contrast of scales (wide angles emphasising the children's progress through the lobby, and high and low angles following their progress up the stairs). This sequence, using a real hotel stuck in the limbo of a legal dispute, avoided the difficulty of the trio being filmed in a hotel open to the public (filming anywhere in Mumbai generates instant crowds).

There is a disturbing parallel between Maman's exploitation of the children and the film's use of real children from the slums for its own dramatic purposes. The use of non-professional, child actors is a powerful crystallisation of the notion of seeking a pure 'innocent' performance, and the inevitable destruction of that innocence by the filming process itself. Like the boy in *Bicycle Thieves*, who could not be cast again in a similar role, the child stars of *Slumdog* have been changed by the process. Similarly, in *Millions*, Etel and McGibbon matured through the production process, conducting their own media interviews and emerging more knowledgeable about how films work. This is not to vilify Boyle specifically. The film, as with any film using non-actors, is offering an escape from poverty, but only on its own terms. Boyle did everything he could to minimise this (paying for schooling and setting up trust funds to be activated on its completion) but it was foreseeable that, to some, bringing the child stars to the Oscar ceremony was about exploitation of the cast as much as recognition of their achievement.

Maman's gang bears some similarity to Fagin's group in Dickens' 1838 *Oliver Twist* (a novel also concerned with the slum-life of children against a background of rapid industrialisation). Fagin used threats of physical violence alternated with apparent benevolence (giving free food and shelter) to make him richer through organised street crime, and this is what Maman does here. This is taken a step further in deliberate mutilation for begging (Swarup suggests this is a detail that is more mythic than realistic in the film).[15]

There is a similar balance between raising the viewer's awareness of such activities and sentimentalising them as a source of pity. Is it really better to starve than eke out an existence as a blind beggar? (Latika calls Maman 'a saint' for giving them food). What is missing in the film, but

---

15 See Sonia Shah, 'Hollywood Puts on the Dog: We're All Slumdog Millionaires at Heart,' http://www.finebooksmagazine.com/issue/200907/slumdog_millionaire-1.phtml

present to some extent in Swarup's book, is Dickens' philanthropic middle-class, in the shape first of the Brownlow family and then the Maylies, who eventually help Oliver escape a life of crime and poverty. A Dickensian universe, without the twin fantasies of film or TV quiz as escape route, relies entirely upon such philanthropy as the only hope for its protagonists.

What is often missed by western audiences of *Slumdog* is that the key Indian cast members playing the parts of the inspector, the sergeant, the gangster Khan and the host Prem are all well-known Bollywood stars, directors and writers. Therefore, there is some calculation at work in casting too, that in the scenes not featuring children, the experience of familiar actors can balance the sense of risk elsewhere in the narrative. Bollywood actor Amitabh Bachchan questioned, via a blog, whether the film would have been so warmly received had it been made by an Indian director (a comment that could be interpreted as being motivated by envy as he was the original TV host of *Who Wants to be a Millionaire* in India – a detail mentioned explicitly in the novel).[16] Bachchan is perhaps correct that all major cities in the developed and developing world have similar underclasses but that this has not been given such prominence by a global media who are quick to confirm a stereotype linking India and poverty. Boyle certainly went to great lengths to try and avoid the sense of a westerner's eye-view of an exotic, unknown culture. He used a largely Indian crew (including a Hindi-speaking co-director, Loveleen Tandan, who should share much of the credit for the performances of the child actors); he worked on the script for many months; he shot on location in Mumbai rather than in a studio (unusual for a film in India where the presence of stars brings traffic to an instant standstill); he cast indigenous non-professionals as well as unknown actors; and he agreed to a significant part of the film's dialogue being in Hindi (this latter decision was forced upon him as finding English-speaking children of this age proved impossible).

Like all of us, Boyle is a product of his own culture and the film, made with western money, reflects to some degree the commercial tastes of a western audience. Buildings like the Taj Mahal are icons of a tourist's view of India and yet that is precisely why they are useful to a filmmaker keen to tell a detailed story and needing some easily identifiable cultural markers. To be fair, Boyle also uses the Taj Mahal in a satirical way as a smooth-talking Jamal easily infiltrates the tour guide industry in order to

16 Swarup 2006 pp.16-17.

dupe gullible westerners, all just wanting their Princess Diana-style snapshot in front of the building. We see culture being manufactured on the spot, when Jamal ironically dismisses the official guide-book as 'written by a bunch of lazy Indian good-for-nothing beggars,' suggesting his improvised version of his own culture is no less valid that the 'official' version. Importantly, such cultural references underline the relative nature of knowledge. Jamal does not know facts about his history as dictated by its colonial masters (such as the face on a 1000 rupee note, or the text beneath the national emblem), but he does know his culture (who recently stole a bicycle, or how much food costs at a particular place).

The grandiose opera staged in front of the Taj Mahal is for rich, western audiences, allowing an underclass of the indigenous culture (a group including the brothers) to gain some revenge in stealing bags from under the stage. The parallel between the opera's tragic storyline (Orpheus travelling to the underworld to find his beloved) and the Latika/Jamal romance is a little heavy-handed (one reason why Boyle cut the scene between Jamal and an Australian woman who explains the plot to him). This cut was the source of some disagreement with Beaufoy but on balance, it was probably the right decision.

The American couple, who 'aestheticise' the panorama scene by the river, while their car is stripped of everything of value, are shown as deserving their fate. Examples of such cultural revenge pepper the narrative, making claims of exploitation more complex, such as when Salim fills up the mineral water bottles with tap water and glues the tops back on, to serve to rich hotel customers. What appears to outstrip any cultural material from either east or west is television. The TV set placed in front of the Taj Mahal at the climax dominates the interest of the crowd rather than the beauty of the building behind it. Success on a TV show represents the sharing of a collective, possibly even global, aspiration.

Wes Anderson's *The Darjeeling Limited* (2007), also made by Fox Searchlight and also set in India, did not attract the same kind of criticism. Anderson's protagonists are all played by Americans (Owen Wilson, Adrien Brody and Jason Schwartzman), who do not speak the language of the country they pass through and who really understand very little of what goes on around them. Trains also appear here (the prime setting for much of the film) but the point-of-view is unremittingly western, casting long shots of the train passing through the landscape (also used by Boyle) as exotic but unknowable. Boyle shows his characters hustling for a living on the train, buying and selling anything;

Anderson shows us the consumers of such services. His three protagonists, also brothers, are not trying to escape poverty – if anything they are fleeing an empty life of western materialism on an undefined 'spiritual quest'. Boyle features the young brothers trying to steal food through a window, with one lowering the other upside-down by a rope, which seems to suggest a move in the direction of the comedy genre, but the underlying motive for Jamal and Salim's dangerous act is poverty. Even the soundtrack, especially 'O...Saya' (Rahman with MIA) feels like an effective fusion of cultural influences. Almost every Indian-specific feature of Boyle's film is absent from Anderson's – no Hindi-speaking child actors, no focus on the reality of daily life of ordinary people and little sense of place: it is about visitors to a country, not the inhabitants. All the suffering (very visibly represented by plasters across Wilson's face) happens to the white protagonists and is largely self-inflicted. There was, however, no campaign to criticise Anderson for his apparent exploitation of Indian culture.[17]

Boyle's scenes in the call-centre, where Jamal gets a job, show a different process of cultural appropriation, in which Jamal appears to know some aspects of Britain better than his own country (learning about soap operas and celebrity gossip), but cannot help a caller from Scotland (ironically voiced by a German actress) with her gas/electricity bill. Ultimately, the film provides a series of powerful glimpses and memorable images of a culture rarely seen in western cinema and with some element of Indian 'ownership', reflected in the largely Indian crew used and in narrative features such as the unnamed woman who accosts the taxi en route to the TV studio and who Jamal expects to beg for money – but who actually wishes him good luck.

A landscape of the mind

Hollywood's portrayal of landscape has created its own network of mythic values. The Canyonlands National Park where climber Aron Ralston was trapped is not far from Monument Valley, whose iconic scenery was used to such great effect in John Ford westerns like *The Searchers* (1956), reflecting the pain of the lone hero Ethan Edwards (John Wayne). It is a landscape like none other on earth and due to its appropriation in film, has evolved into a repository of cultural, cinematic, philosophical and even religious values, to represent a mythic land of possibilities, self-expression and freedom.

17 See Browning 2011 pp.123-126.

127 Hours appears to offer the pleasure of contemplating a spectacular landscape as backdrop to a gutsy survival tale, but Boyle fairly quickly undercuts this expectation. The film moves from kinetic action to literal stasis as Ralston is trapped, but this does not lead to a desperate search for movement or spectacle in the landscape with tracking shots across the Utah skyline. Physical isolation is the cue for an exploration of mental isolation: Ralston has cut himself off from those around him and the film traces an emotional, and even spiritual, journey as he reconnects with them. We do not learn about the setting during Ralston's 127 hours, much of which takes place without dialogue – the real location is inside his head. It is ultimately not a film about landscape but an urban narrative with its more urgent driving rhythm. The challenge of realising this contradiction may have drawn Boyle to the project, an apparently bizarre choice with little commercial potential but one which he had begun researching before the success of *Slumdog*.

It is Boyle's first attempt at a true-life story with all the limitations this brings, such as the simple fact that much of the audience will know of the hero's final desperate action before they see the film. It therefore also becomes a challenge to Boyle as a filmmaker – how can you make such an apparently grisly experience interesting, when many people already know what they assume is the central key fact about the arm? What leads us to the interior however, is a kinetic establishment of Ralston's existence – a life led in raw and untamed settings. Visual ambition is central to Boyle and he often forces the viewer to question what we think we know, as in *Sunshine* when Fox's logo transforms itself into what appears to be the sun, only for this assumption to be then overturned with a sweeping shot that reveals it to be the heat-shield on the front of the spacecraft, Icarus II. In a dynamic shot in *127 Hours*, Ralston jumps from the back of his truck, the shot taking us through a flap, like a theatrical curtain, with Ralston jumping over the camera itself, taking us into the setting. The landscape is not a backdrop to be looked at and admired; it is a playground, almost an adversary to pit one's wits against. This, together with the clear reference in Fox's marketing copy that the hero ultimately decides to 'choose life,' evokes the kinetic opening of Boyle's breakthrough feature, *Trainspotting*.

127 Hours might seem, on paper, to be a film about exteriors, an opportunity to celebrate landscape. Certainly musicians have used a similar backdrop for videos, such as The Killers' 'Human' (dir. Danny Drysdale 2008), Dead By Sunrise's 'Crawl Back In' (dir. P.R. Brown 2009) and even Morrissey's 'November Spawned a Monster' (dir. Tim

Broad 1990). In all three examples, a lead singer is framed against spectacular desert rock-forms, while miming to a song (and accompanied by musicians in the first two instances). The Killers add out-of-place animals like a tiger, and Dead By Sunrise include pieces of sculpture, but in each case, the landscape is only used to suggest high production values and fairly empty spectacle – there is no narrative taking place within the setting.

What links these examples visually are matters of scale (the human figures are small in contrast to the expanse in which they stand), colour (the backdrop is usually drawn from a palette of golden brown through to red) and aridity (desert and a lack of water predominate). The human figures look out of place and thereby our attention is drawn to them. This setting lends the songs a supposedly epic quality, elevating mundane lyrics to the heights of grand poetry and transposing connotations of ruggedness from the landscape to the singers, all of whom are male. It is an unforgiving landscape, which historically has tested and defined those who have sought to colonise it.

There is a closer similarity between Boyle's film and Robbie Williams' video for 'Bodies' (dir. Vaughan Arnell 2009) in terms of style and content. Both feature sweeping helicopter-shots, edited together with small jump-cuts, focused on a lone male figure, who is off-roading on a bike, including pulling wheelies for no other reason than the sheer pleasure it brings. The landscape is dusty, iconic of the American west (Arnell shot in the Mojave desert; Boyle in Utah). Williams' video differs from the other examples mentioned in that it shifts to the more conventional 'miming mode' only in the final section of the film (and it does feel closer to a film than a video) as he stands upon the wing of an abandoned aircraft. Both heroes suffer technical problems and both are 'rescued' by the convenient attention of attractive women (Williams' motorbike breaks down and he is picked up by a girl, Ayda Field, in a buggy; Ralston crashes, picks himself up and later comes across two attractive female hikers). However, whereas Williams' video suggests the arrival of a woman provides a saviour for the hero, for Boyle women play a more tangential role. The backpackers that Ralston meets, Kristi (Kate Mara) and Megan (Amber Tamblyn), find him attractive but too self-absorbed to be worth pursuing and the narrative focuses firmly on a tale of male hubris transformed into chastened self-preservation. Ralston's sister Sonja (Lizzy Caplan) and girlfriend Rana (Clémence Poésy) exist to provide material for his mental processes: shown like alternative films, they are the means by which he works through his thoughts.

The rugged, unforgiving landscape evokes the nature of America as a frontier nation, created in a spirit of westward expansionism that celebrated individual freedom and connoted a sense of religious destiny, as well as requiring qualities of endurance and toughness stereotypically associated with masculinity. All of these qualities, especially the notion of individual freedom, are conveyed in the juxtaposition of singer and setting. It is an impossible situation – we know the singer is not performing, since there are no trailing wires from the instruments, no microphones and in Williams' case, not even a semblance of performing the song we hear until the end of the video. It has become a convention of music videos which audiences rarely question but it does mean our attention is drawn away from the non-existent performance to the setting in which it takes place.

Stylistically, the Williams and Boyle pieces are close. Boyle tends to use aerial movement over and across his lone hero, rather than rotating around him but even so, there is a similar blend of sudden increases in film speed and then a few frames of slow-motion and time lapse photography as the sun passes across the landscape (also reminiscent of *The Beach*). Both feature close-ups of spinning tyres – in *127 Hours* as an overhead, point-of-view shot of Ralston looking down at his front wheel, and in 'Bodies' as a wide-angle-lens shot of Williams getting onto his bike and spinning dust into the camera. Both men are casting themselves as heroes in their own fantasy adventure, akin to the lone male biker figure popularised by stars like Steve McQueen. The landscape also has spiritual overtones, drawing on America's historical westward colonisation, justified by notions of Manifest Destiny. Such spiritual connotations in music videos are rarely explicit, except by openly Christian bands such as The Lighthouse Family, or in country and western, where the setting can be as much of a cliché as the lyrical content. Musically, even the opening bars of Williams' song with its echoing choral style, before we reach the explicitly religious content of the chorus, suggest that the lone figure is undergoing some kind of spiritual epiphany, an impression enforced by the shot of Williams raising his hands aloft from the handlebars at the music's climactic moment.[18]

In *127 Hours*, Ralston's struggle can either be seen as being about the smallness of humanity in the face of a natural world created by a benevolent God, or the rebellious hubris of humanity struggling against

---

18 The British duo The Lighthouse Family also used similar awe-inspiring landscape as a backdrop for the video for their debut hit, 'Lifted' (dir. Leigh Richards 1996), which complemented their overtly Christian lyrics.

an inhospitable environment. The ultimate lesson Ralston learns is not to humble himself before an all-powerful creator but to accept his role in the fabric of society, particularly amongst his friends and family (the subject of his flashbacks): the resolution is therefore a humanist one.

Although Williams is British and much of his fanbase is in Europe, he still has ambitions to break into the American market and he lives for much of the year in Los Angeles. Williams had already tapped into Americana with the video for 'Feel' (2002), also directed by Vaughan Arnell, in which we see Williams on horseback surrounded by rugged snowy scenery and iconography more explicitly associated with westerns (he lies in a water-filled trough, watches a rodeo and pursues a girl (Daryl Hannah), also on horseback. Such an extreme landscape in a wealthy country like America also signals confidence in the performer from the record company and a willingness to embrace large production values to promote them.

As with the opening of *127 Hours*, in Williams' video we see an individual testing himself against the elements (and by implication, the spiritual entity that created them). Yet unlike Richard in *The Beach*, the figure here is completely alone, not consciously seeking to impress anyone (at least until the girls appear in each narrative). However, Ralston does carry a camera everywhere and the speed with which he naturally records his thoughts and feelings even prior to being trapped, suggests a character for whom technology represents an alter ego with which he naturally and almost instantaneously communes. When he crashes his bike, there is something almost insane about the low throaty laugh that is his response to the self-induced pain. There is the sense that Ralston's thrill-seeking has numbed him from 'normal' emotional responses: his apparent addiction to risk acts like a drug of which he needs progressively stronger doses. On meeting the girls, he takes his picture with them all together, and it is unclear whether this is a souvenir for them, of which they should be proud, or one in a long line of trophies for him.

Both Boyle's film and Arnell's video for Robbie Williams use a split-screen effect of a particular kind. Rather than the typical use of split screen in film narrative, which in Brian De Palma's *Snake Eyes* (1998) or Richard Fleischer's *The Boston Strangler* (1968) signifies simultaneous action in different locations, in Boyle's film we are presented with a single frame divided into three across the middle of the screen, but all three frames are from the same location and time. This is both redolent of a stylistic motif from the 1960s, where new technology was used to add an air of sophistication to a static scene (such as the chess game in Norman

Jewison's 1968 *The Thomas Crown Affair*) and from the early 1970s in music shows like *Top of the Pops* (BBC 1964-2006), when the developing use of video technology allowed producers to play with performance footage, constantly re-framing or moving frames around the screen.

The effect of choosing such stylistic devices, also prevalent in TV car commercials, is to give the sequence, especially when accompanied by a pumping soundtrack, a feeling closer to pop video – small-screen fare yearning for a larger canvas. This small-screen flavour also links with the basic plot premise of *127 Hours* ('man trapped in canyon amputates his own arm'), a type of plot that in the US is very much associated with prime-time shows which focus on a sensationalised, 'amazing-but-true' aesthetic, and have even spawned their own channels like The True Movies. Using members of the public rather than actors, telling 'true-life stories', favouring video footage over staged material – these are features associated with low-cost, prime-time TV, rather than cinema.

As in *The Beach*, we are shown amazingly beautiful scenery but it seems to represent little more than a playground for the bored thrill-seeker. In *127 Hours*, Boyle adds a lagoon known only to his hero, into which he initiates his newly found 'subjects' by demonstrating how to drop into it from a crevice. Ralston seems to need acolytes/followers to bolster his sense of self, but realises through the course of his narrative that he has much to learn himself. In both films, Boyle seems less interested in what characters do than what they are thinking. In Richard's case in *The Beach*, the problem is that he does not seem capable of particularly mature thought, beyond childish fantasies of being an *Apocalypse Now*-style action hero. For Ralston in *127 Hours*, his near-death experience proves to be a more chastening experience, acting as a catalyst for some genuine introspection. Richard shares some of Ralston's basic features (a young, self-centred, thrill-seeking male out to seduce any girls he can), but we do not really care about his fate, whereas Boyle manages to make us care about Ralston. Both men enter a largely uninhabited paradise, reflective of an emotional (and possibly spiritual) deficit in their lives but whereas Richard translates his near-brush with death into a campfire story with the climactic embellishment 'no, I will not die today', Ralston makes that pledge a reality.

The result of this reduction of scale is that we see a hero taming a wilderness, battling an elemental foe and winning, thereby asserting his masculine mastery over the elements and emulating male heroes of classic Hollywood westerns, which are predicated on polemic gender roles. Huge natural landscape formations are reduced in scale by being framed and then re-framed in a series of shots that cast the landscape as manageable and secondary to human concerns. We are not invited simply to look at landscape in awe or in a moment of contemplation.

A key element here is pace, achieved in part through rapid editing and partly through A.R. Rahman's energetic score. We judge Richard's character more harshly perhaps because we have time to do little else – here we are not afforded the luxury of contemplation until Ralston is trapped. The title card only appears 20 minutes into *127 Hours* at the point at which the hero is trapped and we may then re-evaluate a figure whose dominant characteristics are restlessness and boundless energy (features shared with Boyle too perhaps). As with Renton in *Trainspotting*, Boyle seems to find it hard to be too judgemental towards characters who display excessive amounts of youthful energy. Despite Ralston's situation, Boyle was at pains throughout the shoot to imbue the filming process, as well as the performances, with energy and drive. So much so, in fact, that during the climactic severing scene, James Franco cut through a prosthetic arm containing a steel pin, which special effects experts thought was impossible.

In *Cast Away* (dir. Robert Zemekis 2000), Tom Hanks has a fictional sounding-board (a volleyball with a face painted on it) in order for the protagonist to have a notional person to address. Boyle does not do this, but has a similar problem of how to make a narrative with a lone survivor interesting. His solution, taking inspiration from Ralston's book, is to move beyond the setting, using flashbacks (especially to his girlfriend), delusions due to dehydration, and Ralston's recorded farewells to family members as constructs to add back-story and to make Ralston's character more likeable. Ralston has two challenges: to survive but also to record that survival, both in memory and – crucially – on film. Of all Boyle's heroes, Ralston is the first to obsessively frame, record and convert experience into media images at the point they occur, casting him in the guise of a proxy director. He uses his own camera to record his experience, and eventually writes an account of it in the book that became Boyle's source material for the film. The visions that Ralston has of a future son, a cute blond boy (Peter Joshua Hull), evoke the similar thoughts of a lone, demented individual in *Jacob's Ladder* (dir. Adrian Lyne 1991). For both men, these represent their fleeting thoughts at the very point of death, but whereas the hero in *Jacob's Ladder* does die, Ralston severs his arm and breaks free.

For the first time, Boyle and his leading man have not just a script, a fictional account of an experience, but the living testimony of the survivor himself. After initial qualms about the ability of a feature to convey the power of his experience, the real Aron Ralston relented and was a great help to actor James Franco, talking him through his emotions in the canyon, even down to the exact movements he made at various points of his captivity. The idea of making video messages to family (which Ralston describes doing in his book and which he agreed to show privately to Franco and Boyle) also appears in *Sunshine*, and Ralston's delusion about appearing on a morning radio programme has precursors in the game-shows in *Trainspotting*, *A Life Less Ordinary* and of course, *Slumdog Millionaire*. It almost seems that becoming mini-directors is the default setting for Boyle protagonists faced with a situation of emotional pressure. When Ralston falls from his bike before the ordeal in the crevice begins, he takes a picture of himself mugging for the camera. His life is very much mediated through cameras. There is no complete immersion in a fantastical episode but we do see Ralston clearly constructing a fiction, playing both host and guest, and recording his bittersweet feelings on his own camera. While some might question the addition of the lagoon scene, it is true that the real Ralston did edit some of his final messages to his family: in other words, there are several levels of fictional representation here – it is not a simple matter of truth juxtaposed with fiction. Boyle adds to this a technological sensibility with the theatrical technique, often used by fellow director Ken Loach in achieving scenes of gritty realism, of shooting the film mostly in chronological sequence. This is highly unusual in contemporary filmmaking as it is more inconvenient (and expensive) – shooting out of sequence and then editing footage together has been the norm since D.W. Griffith's *Birth of a Nation* back in 1915 – but it does allow an actor the luxury of a sense of emotional progression and arguably yields more powerful performances.[19] It also allows the director to be less focused on technological manipulation of footage and to concentrate on what is happening in front of the camera at a given moment.

Boyle is dealing with a true story, a living survivor and a written account of events, all of which constrained his flexibility in terms of the setting. For Ralston in the film, the landscape represents freedom, but it is a narcissistic freedom in which he indulges himself in hedonistic pleasure, alone. He runs into the girls; he does not plan to meet them or extend the time he spends with them. He is a man alone with his technology (his camera especially). The landscape provides him with an

19 Gunning 1993 p237.

opportunity to test himself bodily in increasingly extreme scenarios without the difficulty of dealing with people. The film is ultimately about a character who tries to deny his social nature, that his natural environment is really in towns and cities, and who is brought to this realisation in an extreme text of his will to survive.

There are some similarities with Boyle's first film, *Shallow Grave*, in the intensity of the limited location. Granted, *127 Hours* opens with spectacular scenes of immense landscape but once Ralston is trapped, the film's focus narrows down to a lone individual and his battle for sanity and survival. Boyle opens out the narrative with flashbacks and delusional sequences but like *Shallow Grave*, which is fundamentally three adults in a single Edinburgh flat, it seems the film's greatest drama (and greatest challenge for Boyle as a filmmaker) is to make the literally static location seem emotionally dynamic.

Boyle appears to relishes the challenge of how to engage his audience with a story they think they know and how to make his viewers not want to run screaming from cinemas yet remain true to the visceral horror of what Ralston has to do. There is in particular a kind of perverse delight in appearing to offer the viewer one kind of film, while really smuggling in something else. Superficially, the narrative is a tale of the country and of human isolation. In actuality, the opposite is true. Boyle filmed a series of dialogues with Ralston's mother, sister and girlfriend, which served to complete the narrative by giving the viewer the consolation of redemption, in other words giving the hero the possibility of atoning for his emotional neglect of those closest to him. However, on reflection, the tone of such sentiment seemed false to the body of the film and Boyle chose instead to end the film with a triptych-style shot of crowds because ultimately it is about people and engagement with people – not about the desert landscape at all. Like Ralston himself, this is a connection we really only make at the end of *127 Hours*, a lesson for which we too have to wait and which is part of the sense of viewing satisfaction that the film ultimately delivers.

Conclusion

It seems that when Boyle bases his films on areas with which he has a personal or aesthetic connection, such as Scotland or the north of England, he conveys the narratives with confidence. It is also worth noting that his main leading men (McGregor, Eccleston, and Murphy) all hail from areas other than southern England (Scotland, Northern England and Ireland, respectively). The further from home he gets, the less assured he seems. The Thailand of *The Beach* and the California of *A Life Less Ordinary* seem sketchy and peripheral to the action and it is tempting to see both films, the latter especially, as unsuccessful experiments, a flirting with a trans-Atlantic aesthetic with which Boyle seems not wholly comfortable. It is a pity, for example, that the opening section of *The Beach* was cut from the final version. This would have shown water fights between tuk-tuks as part of the New Year celebrations in Bangkok. Its omission means that the finished film does not really show Richard-as-appreciative-traveller: in these scenes we would have seen his attraction to mock-combat and his engaging sense of playfulness, as well as overtones of baptism. The real culture, which is not packaged for western tourists, is glimpsed only in the reclining Buddha figure and fleeting shots of the Khao San Road. Garland's novel has a more detailed account of the train journey on the way to the island, but this does not find its way into the film. Symbolic of the undeveloped vision of *The Beach*, despite its more profound aspirations, is the map of the island. Drawn by Garland himself, who is given the rather grand title of 'cartographer' on the end credits, it does not look mysterious, but more like the childish scrawl that might be found in an episode of Scooby-Doo.

In his TV films, *Strumpet* and *Vacuuming Completely Nude in Paradise*, Boyle's evocation of place is also less assured, relying largely on stereotypes, especially juxtaposing northern poverty with southern wealth. The two protagonists in *Strumpet* are seen driving south in a battered van to London, the mythical source of their potential fame and fortune. While it may be true that the *Top of the Pops* studio is in London, there is the sense of two diametrically opposed worlds with little in between. We cut from the filth of a squat filled with a pack of feral dogs in the north, to the high tech of a meeting room with record executives in London. *Slumdog Millionaire*, clearly the furthest from Boyle's own background, should (according to this argument) be the weakest in terms of setting but this is not so. Here, we see the world through the eyes of children and where this applies, the connection with environment seems to remain intact (think of *Millions*, too). Even in *Trainspotting* and *Shallow Grave*, although dealing with gritty and sometimes grisly subject matter, the protagonists – Ewan McGregor's characters especially – retain a certain child-like innocence or flippancy. Where the protagonists are adults and the setting is some way from Boyle's home ground, as in *The Beach* and *A Life Less Ordinary*, they struggle to convince and involve viewers and partly as a result we do not care as much about what happens to them.

CHAPTER FIVE

· MORAL CHOICES ·

'It's much easier to make cynical films...I wanted to make something more emotional'

Boyle on the DVD commentary for *Millions*

Debate over the moral content of film has been present since the very earliest days of the medium, moving from silent-era controversies to the introduction of the Motion Picture Production Code in 1930 which made efforts to control moral content. The Code became unsustainable after World War II, under pressure from ground-breaking films like *The Lost Weekend* (dir. Billy Wilder 1945). A voluntary code followed, linked to a process of certification that regulated audiences by age, a process which still exists today but which can be evaded by increasingly sophisticated technology, delivering films straight to computer screens or mobile phones.

Recent published criticism tends to focus on a number of key points: historical elements of censorship such as Gregory D. Black's 1996 *Hollywood Censored*, controversial genres and directors such as Michael Bliss' 1993 *Justified Lives*, or teaching tools such as Yvette Krohn's 2010 *Thinking About Film: Morality*. Many writers and commentators tend to assume a Christian ethical framework when assessing morality in films, whether or not this is something deliberately foregrounded by the director. In western culture, 2000 years of Christian history is likely to have a residual, if sometimes subliminal effect on all media, especially when associated with a means of mass communication which needs to reflect the dominant culture in order to be successful commercially.

As film journalist K. Monk notes, 'the minutia of the moral choice is Boyle's hot spot and he's scratched at it in just about everything he's ever done...'.[1] Films such as *Indecent Proposal* (dir. Adrian Lyne 1993) put forward specific 'issues', in this case the morality of offering (or indeed accepting) a million dollars to sleep with someone else's spouse for one night. Boyle has an abiding preference for placing moral dilemmas at the heart of his narratives, but this is less to do with a passionate interest in

---

1   Monk, '*Slumdog Millionaire*: a modern Cinderella story,' 20 November 2008
www.canada.com/vancouversun/news/arts/story.html?id=7dfcbc32-4ab9-4388-8512-4fd2122b7e772

any given topic, than as a mechanism to explore character and to put dramatic constructs under pressure. His narratives focus on humans as fallible creatures who find themselves in situations of extreme pressure, often through their own actions.

Boyle's films do not descend into dry moral debates because of the energy with which the stories are told. He uses the protagonist as central to the moral quandary in question (and sometimes its chief apologist), which means we may be swept along by the narrative, rather than standing back in judgement on the characters. Pace, then, is key. When it is kept high, we may overlook behaviour that we might otherwise judge harshly; when it drops, such as in *The Beach*, we are left with little else to do than consider the morality of how characters behave, whatever they might say to excuse themselves.

Money

In *Shallow Grave*, three deeply unpleasant characters discover their new flatmate Hugo (Keith Allen) lying dead in his room, alongside a large suitcase of money. In the sequence that follows, Nina Simone's song 'My Baby Just Cares For Me' runs under several, apparently unconnected scenes. We see the empty house and a tracking shot up to the suitcase and then back from it; a cutaway of Hugo in death pose and, in between, snippets of Alex and Juliet at work, Alex eyeing up some girls in his office and Juliet reacting nonchalantly to Alex's reference in casual conversation back at the flat to 'a dead guy'. The sequence effectively conveys their lives as superficially unchanged, but with their thoughts dominated by the money and the dead body. The song seems to suggest that Hugo could be, in a sense, their romantic hero, whose money could take them away from their everyday drudgery.

Some days later, at dinner, Boyle juxtaposes the three characters, cutting between head-on shots as David declares he wants to 'secure' the money, whereas the other two encourage him to spend it. They try to distract him but its physical existence and how they obtained it remains, for David, an impediment to normality. After the second police visit to their flat, David realises that the police know, but the gap between suspicion and provable guilt means that the only thing that links them to the crime is possession of the money, making it more of a millstone than a blessing.

David seems the most 'normal' of the three flatmates: often he is shown in his suit, going to and from work, signalled by a number of sequences showing him walking to and from the coat-hooks by the door. The pressure on him to conform leads him to exhibit the greatest deviance when he breaks out of the moral confines of his life. Alex constantly harasses him, shouting abuse during a squash game, teasing him about a letter from his mother, mocking him about his 'discussion group' (about which we are never given details) and rejecting this group as a source of flatmates because 'they'll all be like him'. Christopher Eccleston's performance of a character willing to commit a crime in order to be accepted is highly reminiscent of his first film role as Derek Bentley in Peter Medak's *Let Him Have It* (1991) in which he plays an easily led 17-year-old, drawn into a life of crime and who ultimately pays with his life, hanged for shooting a policeman.

In discussion with his boss at work, David is told that accountants can be boring 'but by God, we get the job done,' followed by a backhanded compliment: 'that's why you fit in so well here'. There are some professions in which dullness and thoroughness are virtues. Despite being given an important client, effectively representing promotion, David looks round at his tank-top-wearing co-workers in the library and sees his future mapped out for him. By the time the camera pans back to the seat opposite, Juliet is sitting there, (although she may be a subjective vision) and the thought that has also been running through his head, of keeping the money and disposing of the body, is articulated as he declares, 'let's do it'.

There is situation comedy in the idea of shopping at a DIY store for the tools to cut up Hugo's body. For Alex this all has the jaunty charm of an adventure, during which he speaks too loudly and suggests that 'we just remove' hands, feet and teeth, glossing over exactly how this will be done, and more importantly, who will do it. The drawing of lots for who must do the grisly deed seems to belong to a more primitive era and carries the sense of Biblical punishment. It is telling that David, who draws the short straw, is in fact the only character with the mental toughness to dismember the body. Facing the visceral nature of mortality changes David's character. He becomes more withdrawn and his experience cuts him off from the others – a theme present in many classical studies of murder with consideration of guilt and redemption, such as Edgar Allan Poe's *The Tell-Tale Heart* (1843) or Dostoevsky's *Crime and Punishment* (1866). The protagonists in both these stories commit their crimes for money and become alienated from those around them. As with *Shallow Grave*, Poe's tale also features bodily dismemberment, hiding evidence under floorboards, and the stress of guilt leading to mental breakdown.

David is shown in a shallow pit, sawing Hugo's corpse just out of shot and then smashing out the teeth with a sickening crunch. In the following scene, there is a slow tracking shot into the bathroom but there is no human subject for the shot, just a pan left to the bloodied tools, soaking in the bath. For Alex and Juliet, the disposal of the body, which the three of them carry clumsily down the stairs, seems part of an adventure (including Alex noisily dropping a torch down the stairwell which miraculously provokes no reaction from their neighbours). David subsequently becomes more aggressive, threatening and bullying a man who approaches Juliet. It is not long after this that Juliet chooses to sleep with David, so perhaps she finds this protective pose attractive. For his part, he unquestioningly accepts her advances as it chimes with his fantasy, and he talks of 'us' to Alex as soon as he realises that the group dynamic has shifted and that he and Juliet now hold the balance of power. When he discovers Alex and Juliet rolling around amidst their luxury purchases, he does not appear jealous so much as angry at how they have risked attracting attention. He is very single-minded, focusing on consequences, angrily unplugging the TV, like a censorious parent. 'For you two to have a good time, we don't know the cost of that yet', he says.

David retreats to the loft, which becomes not just a hiding place, but a space that reflects his disturbed state of mind. He begins to sleep up there and, increasingly paranoid, he hides the money in the water-tank, tells his employers he is unwell, and spends his time worrying about what the other two are plotting. His physical actions become stranger, suddenly hanging down out of the loft hatch, or sitting flicking a torch on and off. This latter action conveys the sense that, after a transcendent experience, he has become more fascinated with his own body; in holding the torch under his face, he is constructed himself as a kind of bogeyman. His eccentric behaviour includes drilling holes in the ceiling, through which he spies from the loft, God-like, on the others, the light filtering through into the loft suggesting a Gothic Expressionist setting, like a mixture of *Edward Scissorhands* (dir. Tim Burton 1988) and *Hellraiser* (dir. Clive Barker 1987). We hear David's footsteps and the camera follows his apparent progress across the shared boundary state of floor/ceiling, with Alex below becoming aware of a hole appearing in the ceiling above him. In a neat touch, Alex is watching the final scene of Robin Hardy's *The Wicker Man* (1973), where Sergeant Howie (Edward Woodward) is about to be sacrificed, suggesting a parallel shift into uncontrolled, irrational destruction. David becomes more reclusive, eating less and seeming more animal-like, popping his head out from the hatch like an inverted meerkat and scurrying across the rafters like Kafka's Gregor Samsa in *Metamorphosis* (1919). He seems to have almost supernatural powers of perception, easily noticing Juliet hiding in the kitchen, though he does retain some humanity, self-censoring his voyeurism by looking away as Juliet dresses.

When Alex goes up into the loft, David is waiting for him below, holding a drill. Clearly unhinged, and in a nod to Abel Ferrara's 1979 *Driller Killer*, David marks Alex with a touch of his improvised weapon. The film is full of tight three-shots (Boyle motivates this by crushing them together in a Mini and later in the van when they take Hugo's body to the woods), but after they have been tracked down to their flat by the police, David drives confidently, while Juliet and Alex huddle together, clearly shaken. In facing down the police, David is framed alone in the middle of the sofa – he is now the one being interviewed while Detective Inspector McCall (Ken Stott) throws awkward questions at him.

Alex is a supremely cynical character, driven by a self-centredness that should be unattractive but is delivered by Ewan McGregor with such unabashed wit that he is actually quite likeable. Right from the start with his pointed questions in the interviews, Alex delivers the kind of trademark articulate dialogue associated with Ewan McGregor's early film roles for Boyle such as in *A Life Less Ordinary* and *Trainspotting*. After a shopping spree with Juliet, we see a grainy video-camera image of Alex: 'It's been a struggle but now our days of worry are over,' he says. 'The light at the end of the tunnel has expanded into a golden sunrise. At long last, nothing will ever be the same again.' His wit, however, only thinly conceals the casual cruelty in his character. When he is watching *The Wicker Man* it is not, as Page asserts, an example of 'ordinary people leading ordinary lives'. We see a character watching a scene of human sacrifice with no appreciable sign of horror or shock – indeed, *he is laughing*.[2] His drunken self-loathing at the dinner table, especially his approving, pig-like sniffing of Hugo's wad of cash, underlines his unpleasant nature.

His first reaction on finding Hugo's dead body is to rifle through the drawers in his room and it is he who finds the case under the bed. He justifies this to Juliet by asserting 'it's not every day I find a story in my own flat' but we do not see any subsequent evidence that he is interested in the 'story' – he is motivated solely by the money and is the first to suggest keeping it. Before drawing lots for who will dismember the body, Alex asks 'do you wanna play or not?' and this light-hearted (or superficial, depending on your point of view) attitude gives every indication that he is morally unconcerned by what they have done. For him, their worries are over. Discretion and subtlety are not Alex's forté and he is unnecessarily loud (at dinner, carrying the body and especially pushing the car into the quarry, after which he howls with delight). However, his lack of pretension is actually engaging and far from seeming loathsome, of the three he may be the most appealing. On being told that the proceeds from the charity dinner are for children, he loudly exclaims 'I hate children. I'd raise money to have the little fuckers put down'.

There is a frisson between Alex and Juliet. Alex's teasing about her mail makes Juliet emerge from the bathroom topless to retrieve it, just at the point that Alex quotes 'aroused and inflamed' from the letter. In a sequence evocative of Nic Roeg's *The Man Who Fell to Earth* (1976), we see Alex later drunkenly playing like a wayward rock-star with a toy crossbow and shooting a baby doll, inter-cut with remote control cars and a parade of ridiculous clothes. We have a montage of how bored both Juliet and Alex seem, needing constant stimulation from alcohol, excessive consumerism and sex. This wanton excess prompts Juliet to declare, 'I'm so happy, I could die' and a sexual relationship is implied here, albeit obliquely.

At the charity dinner, in a symbolic action, she and Alex indulge in a fierce spin on the dance-floor: Alex falls to the floor and Juliet puts her foot on his neck. In a reverse low-angle shot we see him looking back up at her and kissing her ankle, at which point she skips away. This vignette shows that she likes teasing men and being pursued by them (she had been flirtatious with Hugo, sitting next to him on the sofa and mirroring his body-posture), but has little concern for their feelings. Putting her foot on Alex's neck prefigures the moment when she will stab him, stepping on the knife to ensure he remains pinned to the floor.

When she coolly buys a ticket to Rio, her flippancy over the destination suggests it is unimportant, just that she plans to escape. At this stage we do not know whether she intends to take the money but at the very least, her departure could be seen as an emotional betrayal. In this context, her decision to sleep with David seems less to do with romantic feelings than a calculation to ensure her survival by siding with the individual she identifies as the alpha-male. Page cites the nature of Juliet as a criticism, specifically that she appears to echo those around her 'as if she is merely an extension of them' but this is precisely the point – she is a chameleon-like survivor, right up to the point of her final miscalculation.[3]

Boyle cross-cuts back to the two thugs tracking down the money, exacting increasingly violent retribution on those who withhold information from them. The violence is a reminder of the consequences of indulging in juvenile game-playing with people's lives: the flatmates cannot remain aloof from reality forever – it intrudes into their living-space first in the shape of Hugo and then his pursuers. We first see the thugs reflected in a cash-point screen, which runs with the blood of the man they attack. Later there is a red shot from beneath a basin into which they plunge the head of their next victim (foreshadowing the strong red backlighting of the two Gothic-style burial scenes). Then, in a parallel shot to the water-tank in the loft, hiding place of the money, there is a point-of-view shot up out of a freezer, the location of their following victim. The thugs track down Hugo's car, where Alex had dumped it in a flooded gravel pit, in a plot move which remains unexplained directly but uses the same notion of a secret buried underwater in a quarry that evokes George Eliot's use of stolen gold in *Silas Marner* (1861).

As in the closing frames of John Carpenter's *Halloween* (1978), Boyle uses slow tracking shots through the New Town flat in Edinburgh to suggest a presence within the domestic environment; the implication being that it is the everyday and domestic which is a source of terror, not some external monster. One such shot places Alex and Juliet on either side of the frame: the source of their problems, the door and what lies beyond it (the thugs who are about to enter and attack them) is in the middle. Boyle's elaborate shot composition thereby focuses the attention of the viewer on one particular part of the frame. The threat has been getting ever nearer and now the narrative speeds up as the door bursts in and violence is upon them, with Alex and Juliet savagely beaten. David, however, proves himself equal to the threat by dispatching the thugs with a repeated – almost comic – thud, followed by the rapid descent of two corpses down the loft ladder. Before, he was a reluctant participant in a grisly dismemberment but now he is a fully-fledged murderer. Later, Boyle has the camera rotate a full 360 degrees around the centre of the flat as if at a loss to find the characters, which are in a new position – Juliet and David are in bed together.

At the climax, multiple levels of betrayal are revealed with Alex trying to call the police, David making his way out apparently with the money, and Juliet calling coyly that he 'forgot' to wake her. Any empathy we might feel for David is sacrificed by the way he violently pushes Juliet

3   Page 2009 p.37.

and grabs her hair. The underlining animosity and selfishness of their individual natures and the group dynamic finally surfaces here as Juliet swings a toaster in David's face and then bites him, animal-like. Having shoved Juliet away, David pins Alex down and stabs him close to his heart with a knife, pinning him to the floor. Juliet stabs David in the throat but then, in a theatrical twist, she returns not to save Alex but literally to twist the knife further and tap it in with the heel of her shoe, while Alex stares up at her in disbelief.

The camera cuts between the flat, where Alex is still pinned to the floor and being photographed by forensic officers (in effect he has become a piece of evidence), and Juliet screaming in the car at the airport as the case is opened to reveal it is full of fake notes. She escapes the law but flies off penniless. It is unclear whether Alex dies laughing or survives to take advantage of the real money, revealed as we follow the drip of blood through the boards to its hiding place below. It could be seen as the ultimate irony if Alex does not benefit from his betrayal either. David's opening dialogue is shown as a red herring as he does not survive to tell the tale, thus breaking a basic narrative convention and strangely reminiscent of Eccleston's final appearance in *Cracker* (1994) ('To Be a Somebody'), in which, as DCI Bilborough, he is fatally stabbed but records 'the testimony of a dead man' before dying.

David's final words complete the frame device, his body now revealed at a mortuary. His closing words about friendship provide a fitting end to a bleak view of human nature as inherently corrupt, self-serving and duplicitous: 'Oh yes, I believe in friends. But if one day, you find that you just can't trust them anymore, well what then? What then?' The film closes with Andy Williams' upbeat song 'Happy Heart' over an earlier reprise of a moment of shared laughter. However, the music is ironic – the 'happy moment' was one based on extreme cruelty and in the belief that they could live aloof from the morality of the world, which the film has shown to be mistaken.

Drugs

In *Trainspotting*, we see the routine casuistry involved in petty crime to feed an expensive drug habit and the corrosive effect that has on Renton's moral compass as he has to decide whether to forsake his so-called 'friends' in order to rid himself of the life-sapping cycle of drug-addiction. The film takes no high-handed moral attitude to heroin and the central characters are presented as drug 'consumers', a parallel capitalist system with its own conventions and interdependencies. A prime reason that Renton, once he is clean, adapts so quickly to the world of estate agency is that it is little different from the world he has been inhabiting as an addict. In context, we also see other legal drugs – Begbie with alcohol and Renton's mother's with Valium. Whether legal or not, the purpose of all these substances not access to a higher plane of enlightenment, but oblivion; an escape from mindless work as symbolised in the list of consumer goods in Renton's opening ironic tirade.

This escape, reflected in the tropical backdrop to Spud's job interview or in the surreal pearl-dive of Renton into the toilet, is firmly illusory. The film has been criticised for offering a sense of voyeuristic tourism, allowing bourgeois viewers a brief visit to an alien subculture, before returning to their comfortable lives.[4] However, only an extremely selective viewing would see the film as advocating drug use. We see the inherent danger of infection (via a contaminated syringe in close-up), the personal consequences (with Spud either in prison or the gutter), the effects on the family (Renton's desperate family and the loss of Allison's baby), the risk of HIV (the tragic death of Tommy) and the sheer terror of Renton in withdrawal, not to mention the brief shot of Mother Superior (Peter Mullan) with his leg amputated.

However, Boyle is honest about the access to euphoric pleasures as well as the pain. At the end of Renton's opening monologue, he declares 'I chose not to choose Life. I chose something else,' underlining that this is a conscious decision to avoid conventionality via the oblivion of drugs. It is a very beguiling oblivion too, a kind of secular affirmation, as we see first Renton and then Spud, falling backwards, arms flung back in abandon, each with a broad, idiotic smile on his face. The more overtly sententious elements of Renton's voice-over are less convincing. 'Take the best orgasm you ever had. Multiply it by 1000 and you're still nowhere near it' seems closer to the hyperbole of Sick Boy, who is constantly prattling on about the supremacy of his cultural icons, like Sean Connery. As with Tommy later in the film, it is not enough to have the effects described, he wants to directly experience it, to really understand the appeal and the pull of the drug. As Renton says: 'and the reason? There are no reasons,' (consciously echoing The Boomtown Rats 1979 hit 'I Don't Like Mondays'). What we have is a dramatically engaging exploration of what William Burroughs termed 'the algebra of need'.[5]

4 See Michiko Kahutani cited by Callaghan in *New York Magazine*, 15 July 1996 p.39.
5 Burroughs 1992 p.163.

Our first introduction to the drug-taking environment, Mother Superior's flat, is via a slow ankle-height tracking shot, and the first person we see and hear there is Allison's baby. The visual dissonance between the tools of drug culture, the consequent lack of parental responsibility, and the innocence of a young baby, establishes from the outset a sense of inevitability. The child is glimpsed in shot on a further couple of occasions, crawling around in filth and squalor, and it is only a matter of time before it comes to a tragic end. When the scene does come, it is Allison's manic screaming that first breaks in upon Renton's dulled senses. Sick Boy's startled reaction in looking down into the cot is the first, and only, sign that he is the baby's father. In no scene up to this point in the film has Sick Boy shown any sense of responsibility for this child and now it is too late.

The most telling part of the death scene is not the direct image of a dead baby as the camera sidles round for a close-up through the bars of the cot (powerful though that is and extremely rare in film). It is Renton's inability to dredge up a semblance of human fellow feeling, so that when Sick Boy screams at him to 'fucking say something,' emotionally numbed by the drugs, he can only mumble the addict's mantra, 'I'm cooking up'. No-one speaks to the mother or even hugs her – they all share the addicts' inability to connect emotionally outside themselves. Renton gives the only help he can (some heroin) 'but only after me. That goes without saying'.

We see the process of getting 'clean' and Renton's easy familiarity with it (and implicitly the number of times he has already tried this). This is echoed in the routine way in which he describes what is necessary in comic, pseudo-military diction ('for this, you will need tomato soup, ten tins of…'). Nailing up boards across the door to his room seems extreme, but the subsequent image of the boards soon discarded on the floor vividly conveys the compulsion of an addict. Tommy attempts to bring the group out of their narrow, drug-related lives by dragging them out onto the Pentland Hills, but Renton reacts against this, stating ironically that he has 'made the healthy, informed, democratic decision to get back on heroin as soon as possible'. It is only at this point in the film where the reality, rather than the euphoria shown in the opening, starts to be emphasised: there is a montage of shots of petty crime, including Renton taking money from his own parents and the theft of a TV from an old people's home, and this underlines how being an addict is both 'a full-time business' and one that is completely devoid of morality. Renton's voice-over mentions further transgressive behaviour motivated by their habit, such as stealing drugs from cancer patients. Despite his intimate knowledge of heroin, Renton still supplies Tommy with his first hit.

Mother Superior, in the guise of a solicitous hotel manager, offers to ring for a taxi when Renton overdoses and the cutting initially suggests that the 'taxi' might in fact be the ambulance which we see racing through the city. He shows some concern for Renton, waiting with him for the taxi to arrive and putting money into his top pocket. The brutally mercenary actions of the driver, unceremoniously dragging him out of the cab on reaching the hospital, dumping him and driving away, make us think that even Mother Superior's concern might have been motivated by not wanting to lose a valued customer.

We see that drugs not only undermine relationships – familial, romantic and sexual – they actually replace them altogether. As Sick Boy notes: 'personality's what keeps relationships going over time and heroin's got great fucking personality'. After Renton, somewhat fortunately, avoids jail for persistent shoplifting, undertaken to fund his habit, the post-trial celebrations in the pub suggest that his parents are not really equal to the challenge presented by addiction, treating him just like a naughty boy, falling into a brief rendition of the plantation song 'Short'nin' Bread' with Renton designated by the lyrics as 'Mama's little baby'. There is still a sense of infantilism about Renton, in the train-patterned wallpaper in his room, and in the lack of dialogue as he is carried in like a baby, undressed and put to bed. Indeed, there is almost disbelief in his parents' tone as they complain, 'you lied to us, son. Your own mother and father'. As his parents watch television downstairs, they are betrayed again, as their son steals from their bedroom. However, they are also tougher than they first appear and despite his arrest, persistent re-offending and ultimately his overdose, do not give up on him. A three-shot in the taxi back from the hospital frames Renton as small and hunched between his parents who resolve to take him in hand. There is steel beneath their parental actions – this is tough love personified, locking the door and ignoring his screams.

Renton claims to his parents that he has something to do, which is revealed to be an AIDS test and then we see him in a pub/bingo hall, sitting zombified, his life hanging in the balance, juxtaposed with the fake cheerfulness of bingo-calls, which seem to speak directly to him – 'I'm alive, 35'. His disconnection with the outside world is underlined by the simple time-lapse effect of showing him motionless, surrounded by apparently frenetic action. In a cruel twist of fate Renton, who unwittingly was a drug addict in the middle of an AIDS epidemic, gets the all-clear while the hapless Tommy, new to drugs, is infected, facing a reduced lifespan, depression and suicidal urges.

Tommy is the truly tragic victim. Renton says that Tommy 'never told lies, he never took drugs and he never cheated on anyone' but the possession of virtue becomes a handicap when surrounded by a group of liars and cheats, and sooner or later will be exploited. Renton's ironic excess of energy is reflected in his desire to boot a ball around Tommy's small flat, while the ball, deflated and lifeless, is a closer approximation of the state of Tommy. The flat is a mirror image of Mother Superior's, a product of what Renton has made him. The life of a typical HIV-sufferer is made graphic by the graffiti daubed outside. 'PLAGUE' and 'JUNKY SCUM,' the latter with a helpful arrow, create an image that is almost medieval. The grisly nature of Tommy's death, alone and covered in filth, is conveyed in the slow track back from a kitten (the pathetic source of his death via toxoplasmosis), through a disgusting flat until the body that is revealed, is now a corpse, signalled by the cropped shots of Tommy's legs. Like Renton's overdose hallucination, we see a coffin descend and the parallel is clear – it could (and possibly should) have been him.

Although the film might be criticised for softening the edges of Welsh's novel, in terms of its dialect, sexual violence and the subsuming of Renton into the very society he purports to reject at the opening, it could be said that this is precisely the point. Having lost his indignation and anger, Renton seems seduced by Thatcherite capitalism, which replaces heroin addiction as a different kind of 'drug' but perhaps with only slightly less pernicious effects.

Despite its dark subject matter, as Andrew O'Hagan points out, 'the thing is mainly a comedy,' thereby softening the sense of moral transgression, possibly leading to the unease that some commentators feel.[6] The opening sequence sets the tone. From the outset, the film has a tremendous sense of kinetic energy as Renton jumps over a low angle camera – the film, as well as the main character, literally hits the ground running. The narrative begins in mid-chase and, via a reverse cut, we associate the voice-over with the leading runner who looks leaner, fitter and faster than his more comic side-kick. Renton not only personifies Iggy Pop's accompanying 'Lust For Life,' an anthem for youthful excess and exuberance, but of the low-lifes we are about to meet, he looks the fittest and most likely to survive. The supremely professional running style of Ewan McGregor here is also striking – his head is still while his

---

6 O'Hagan 1996 p.7.

arms pump, emphasising his skinny torso and his flapping jacket (reminiscent of Iggy Pop's own athletic frame on stage and in the packaging of his music). By contrast, Spud is laughable, trying to run with stolen items up his jumper, suggesting if he can outrun store detectives, then petty theft must really be easy.

Renton's articulate, first person voice-over is powerful right from the opening frames. As with most first-person address, it encourages us to share the point of view of the speaker, and implicitly find him more trustworthy. When allied to a literal point-of-view shot as he is chased and then a cheeky grin as he is running, it positions Renton as a highly engaging character. He stops when he runs into a car, staring right down the camera lens at the driver, and laughs. Like the slightly unhinged, manic laughter of Tyler Durden (Brad Pitt) as he is being beaten to a pulp in David Fincher's *Fight Club* (1999), and anticipating Ralston's similar reaction in *127 Hours* when he crashes his bike, he personifies an irrepressible force which is highly charismatic on screen. The voice-over reveals him to be a witty, articulate and perceptive character, given to philosophical turns of thought and able to view himself objectively. In the nightclub, he even talks about himself in the third person: 'young Renton noticed in the sexual sphere how as in all others, the successful segregated themselves from the failures'. This is the practical lesson he must learn – to break away from the failures, his friends with whom he has grown up. Despite professing that 'Mark Renton had fallen in love,' the speed with which he sleeps with Diane (Kelly Macdonald) and then rapidly dismisses her from his life (not just because he discovers that she a school-girl), suggests that a sexual conquest, a different kind of brief euphoric fix, is really what he is chasing.

The opening introduction to the group via a condensed montage of their footballing exploits is highly effective. The film opens with a high-octane rant by Renton, listing all the elements of what should make up a fulfilled, consumer-driven lifestyle. When he comes to the 'choose your friends' part of his opening monologue, we cut to a five-a-side posed photograph of the team before seeing each member in a defining action. Stylistically, it meshes well with the street chase, using forward and reverse tracking shots, interspersed with freeze-frames and on-screen captions to give us information directly. It establishes the five as a unit, all of them scruffily kitted out in contrast to the more professional-looking opposition. Using the visual conventions of a respectable sporting event, the freeze-frame and captions identify the team at the same time as making clear their lack of athleticism, interest or footballing ability.

Tommy's fair but dull play in a corner, Begbie's sadistic tackle, Sick Boy's tripping up his opponents (and subsequent protestation of innocence) and Spud's laughable star-jump as an attempted save, all economically position each one of the main characters. Sport is an excuse for violence, petulance and unsporting behaviour. Even Renton is not immune. Placed in a defensive wall, we see the ball fly straight at him via his point of view and his subsequent slow-motion fall parallels the shot of his ecstatic drug-related collapse at Mother Superior's flat in the next scene. Football feels like an exercise in cultural displacement, rather than an end in itself. Tommy finds watching a video of a football match more arousing while having sex with Lizzy (Pauline Lynch) than their own home-made sex tape; and in the club, Renton and Spud have to pretend to be talking about football when really they have been discussing Spud's lack of sex with Gail (Shirley Henderson). In turn, sex is surpassed by the euphoria of drugs – there is the sense of a hierarchy with the dictatorial 'need' of the junky as eclipsing all others.

Boyle creates absurdist situation comedy: Tommy and Lizzy discover their private sex tape has been returned by mistake to the video shop for general consumption; Sick Boy and Renton look as if they are preparing to fight a duel in the park, only to shoot a pitbull with a pellet; and Renton, seated at the family breakfast table after his conquest of Diane the night before, turns around to see her in the doorway, her school uniform revealing her age. None of these scenes carry a sense of moral judgement or outrage – in itself, a brave decision of Boyle's.

Spud's nocturnal exploits constitute a contrasting tale of embarrassment as he collapses drunk in bed, giving Gail, a girl whom he met at the club, the chance to inspect and then dismiss his rather unimpressive genitalia. The humour derives from the expression of incomprehension on Spud's face in the morning upon waking as he looks round an unfamiliar bedroom and then his gradual realisation as he looks below the sheets that he has soiled Gail's bed. Tight shots of Spud cowering by the door are juxtaposed with cutaways of plates of greasy fry-ups and Gail's family crowded around a small breakfast table. All this creates a sense of claustrophobia and panic which motivates Spud's subsequent fight with Gail's mother over who should wash the bedsheets. Situation comedy descends into slapstick as their tussle over the laundry leads to them both spraying the entire breakfast table with shit.

Sick Boy celebrates the 'ready wit' of Sean Connery, a quality that might equally be applied to many parts of this film, and much of which stems from the novel. He is a loser with a Sean Connery complex, full of laughable criminal schemes that are way beyond his actual capabilities. We are encouraged to laugh at his immaturity and his hubris. The way he prattles on about the relative merits of *Goldfinger* and *Dr No* taps into the same use of witty, quick-fire, but ultimately banal, dialogue used by directors like Quentin Tarantino in *Reservoir Dogs* (1992) and *Pulp Fiction* (1994). However, whereas Tarantino uses precise cultural, often filmic, references to offset extreme on-screen violence, there really is nothing but banality to the character of Sick Boy. The false compartment in his shoe does not reveal a weapon or something of global significance, just the means of injecting heroin. His childish delusions about his own sexual attractiveness extend to his theorising that Ursula Andress does not symbolise unattainability but the exact opposite. While setting up his *Day of the Jackal*-style hit in the park, Sick Boy recounts a long list of real-life examples to prove his theory about wasted potential – George Best, David Bowie, Lou Reed, Charlie Nicholas, David Niven, Malcolm McLaren and Elvis Presley. However, despite all his apparent bluster, the essence of his philosophy, with its distinct lack of sparkling originality ('at one point you've got it and then you lose it. And it's gone forever') is summarised and underlined by Renton's reply: 'so we all get old, we cannae hack it anymore and that's it?' Renton expresses the audience's surprise that there is not more substance to Sick Boy's façade. What makes his philosophising interesting and absurdly comic is not its content per se but the way he expresses it, applying the notion of the transitory nature of life to Sean Connery's acting career ('*The Name of the Rose* is merely a blip on an otherwise uninterrupted downward trajectory', he says).

Although Renton tells us that on seeing the dead baby, 'something died inside Sick Boy, was lost and never returned,' we do not really see any emotional connection for him to lose. This is particularly clear when he follows Renton to London. Renton appears to have grown and developed, accepting some responsibility for his actions as a semi-respectable tax-paying member of society, but Sick Boy's aspirations involve him becoming a pimp or a pusher. He immediately asks Renton if he wants to sell his passport and cannot believe Renton's outraged reaction to such an obviously good idea. The climactic drug deal (the plan to buy a consignment of drugs cheaply in Scotland and then make a large profit selling it in London) is Sick Boy's idea but he still expects Renton to put up the necessary £2,000 and also to try out the drugs, even though Renton is now clean. As Sick Boy's name suggests, there is

an enduring perversity about him all the way through the film – Renton
tells us that Sick Boy once came off drugs just to show him how easy it
was, 'thereby downgrading my own struggle'.

Paradise

Xan Brooks describes *The Beach* as 'tapping into the 90s rise in eco-
tourism' but actually we see very little responsibility being taken for any
action, whether personal, tribal or global.[7] A central problem with the
film is that there seems to be no fundamental philosophy behind the
community on the island: no difference between them and the drunken
hooligans that Richard (Leonardo DiCaprio) looks upon with disdain
on his trip to Kho Pha Ngan. When we follow the trio (Richard,
Françoise and Étienne) on their first introduction to the community,
Richard describes it as 'a lost world' but there is nothing quaint about it.
Sal is obsessive about destroying any map of the island, keeping
newcomers away – far from a sense of fellow-feeling, the so-called
community is based on a purely elitist imperative: they have found
paradise and are willing to fight to prevent others from sharing it.

The community appears to be self-sufficient through means that are
hardly explained, although hidden away in a visit to fetch rice (and in the
background of the shot) is Sal's deal with a hotelkeeper to sell some dope
she has brought. The group need regular runs to civilisation to bring back
luxury items they cannot live without: Boyle jump-cuts between
Richard's 'customers', each presenting him with a personal shopping list
(an addition from the book), which serves to underline their extreme
neediness. Beyond a short scene of Richard and Étienne cutting
bamboo, it is only the Scandinavian group of fishermen, who Richard
briefly joins, that shows any sustained work ethic. The vast majority
appear to do little useful work, spending the time playing football on the
beach and smoking dope.

When reality intrudes in the form of a shark attack in which Christo
(Staffan Kihlbom) is fatally injured, the community as a whole are
initially shocked and wallow in the ritual of grief, but quickly become
annoyed with Christo's groans. Led by Sal, they prevent help from being
called and callously dump him out in the forest to die, the speed of the
community's acquiescence to this revealing how detached they are from
any moral values. By the climax, we may actually feel quite grubby for
having spent so much time in their company. What we see is middle-class

---

7 Brooks in *Sight and Sound* 10:3, March 2000 p.40.

escapism − in cultural terms, the exact opposite of the heroin addicts in *Trainspotting*. It is not a dream that turns into a nightmare; it is the reality of that dream which was always a delusion. Richard's voice-over proudly declares 'there wasn't any ideology or any shit like that.' There is no spiritual core or meaning to *The Beach* (either the book or the film) − it is literally a lacuna, a beautiful setting that its inhabitants are content to contemplate only at a superficial level. Of all Boyle's films available on DVD, *The Beach* probably has the least substance on the audio commentary with lengthy pauses at times, where it seems there really is nothing to say.

The whole film feels like a romantic interlude in a James Bond story − a glamorous setting, an attractive young cast, and a narrative largely suspended for the indulging of sensual pleasure. There is the growing feeling that Daffy, who Richard comes to see as a visionary, was right to label them 'parasites' because, as a community, there is little that is attractive about them. Keaty's eccentric love of cricket does not compensate for a sense that we have stumbled onto the set of a reality TV show like *Survivor* or *I'm a Celebrity, Get Me Out of Here*, in which young people find themselves on a beautiful island without purposeful activity beyond childish games. There is no huge difference between the community and Jack's tribe in William Golding's *Lord of the Flies* (1954). Richard claims to have found his 'vocation…the pursuit of pleasure'. Like Jack, he shows himself to be a proficient hunter, dumping a heavy catch of fish in front of the cook, and later loses his identity under tribal paint. He is also, like Jack, chased for his life at the end but does not achieve the higher wisdom of Ralph. While lacking the complexity of Golding's narrative, *The Beach*, in both novel and film versions, presents an unwittingly inverted version of its central premise. In *Lord of the Flies,* the children stranded on the island act like adults, including a descent into sadistic brutality; in *The Beach*, adults act like children, the central character, Richard, most of all.

The final line of dialogue in Hodge's script (shown on the DVD as an alternative ending) has Richard talking about the fact that he is 'going to carry a lot of scars' but admitting that he 'likes the sound of it.'[8] This is not self-awareness − it is a further example of the self-absorbed, superficial character that we have seen up to this point. There is no sense that he has really learned anything from this experience or if he has, what that might be. There may not be the open depravity of Golding's novel

---

8 Hodge 2000 p.139.

but neither is there a Simon-figure who perceives a deeper meaning in the situation. Golding uses underwater phosphorescence of tiny plankton-like creatures as symbolic of the ascension of Simon's body into a spiritual realm, but for Boyle they are just the attractive backdrop for a sex scene between Richard and Françoise. Hodge's script includes the lines 'with every day that passed I felt closer to my surroundings, closer to this island, until I merged with it, hidden, camouflaged, invisible' but these words do not appear in the film and without it, the sequence of Richard losing his mind in the jungle actually seems no more deluded and self-involved than the rest of the plot.[9]

The film desperately tries to gather around itself the iconography of Francis Ford Coppola's 1979 *Apocalypse Now* (the protagonists crawling on their stomachs through the marijuana field, the ochre colour-wash of the scenes in the huts, and Richard rising up through a trap-door to surprise the farmers) but the analogies just seem empty and ridiculous. Before he arrives on the island, Richard recognises the irony of the backpacker myth (everyone seeking their own bit of paradise) and looks with contempt on the rows of spaced-out figures in the hostel sitting watching *Apocalypse Now*. The direct references to the film in this opening section work well as a symbol of American cultural imperialism and leisure packaging. The problem is that Richard's critical faculties then immediately vanish and he falls for exactly the same hedonistic attractions of the island.

The attempt to show a parallel between Richard's supposed breakdown and that of Martin Sheen in *Apocalypse Now* just seem ludicrous. This may be the intention: Boyle may be showing DiCaprio as willing to play a pathetic, deluded loser, but the effect seems more unwitting than this on the part of both star and director. When Richard breaks into the farmers' house we hear the sound of helicopter rotor blades, but whereas Sheen's character is in deadly earnest, murdering the demagogue Kurtz, here Richard only points a stolen gun at one of the men and makes the noise of shooting. Like the bandana he puts on while on patrol, Richard is attracted to the superficial paraphernalia of fighting but not its reality. Near the end of the film, he and Sal play Russian roulette with the farmers' leader in a scene evoking *The Deer Hunter* (dir. Michael Cimino 1978) but without a real war, such allusions seem hollow.

Boyle's film lacks anything approaching a 'heart of darkness'. In terms of a source of evil, Sal seems more like a deluded director of amateur

---

9 Hodge 2000 p.113.

dramatics than a demagogue. She may be shown reclining like a Roman Empress and have a nice line in sexual blackmail but Cleopatra, she definitely is not. The riflemen in the fields, despite shooting down the four new backpackers, are literally farmers, providing the community (indirectly) with the very drug they crave. They support their families and reject trespassers, upholding the deal they struck with Sal, which (from their point of view) she appears to have betrayed. The murder of the four backpackers is not excusable but it is at least understandable in terms of character motivation in ways which Richard's character is not. The group are not a screaming, face-painting lynch-mob as in Golding's narrative, but are the less interesting for it. Those who are shot are part of the capitalist tourist machine in which groups of individuals think they have the inherent right to go to a place halfway round the world and live there for free just because they want to.

The idea that there are a select few sensitive and caring backpackers who should be allowed entrance into paradise and a mass of boorish louts (often signalled as American) who must be excluded, is an arbitrary distinction unquestioned by any character in the film. When Sal meets the group to whom Richard gave a copy of the map, she patronisingly declares to Richard that they will be unable to do anything with it. They actually prove her wrong in constructing a raft (a far more intelligent idea than swimming to the island, especially after the presence of sharks is made clear) and by considering the journey rather more carefully than Richard, Françoise and Étienne had done. Richard and Sal's elitist attitudes are most obvious when they visit Kho Pha Ngan: there are several point-of-view shots from Richard, looking in horror at the antics of westerners in the bars and on the beaches. Garland's novel says 'everyone looked so strange to me that I couldn't believe I didn't look equally strange to them'.[10] It is exactly like Lemuel Gulliver designating his fellow men as 'yahoos' or brutish monsters on returning from his island adventures, imagining himself superior to the base behaviour he sees around him – a distinction which the reader there, and the viewer here, can see as highly subjective. Sal's community seems to be made up of spoilt, rich westerners, who give no sign that they have learnt anything from the experience other than giving up on *this particular* version of paradise. Nic Roeg's *Castaway* (1986) dramatises a voluntary marooning but focuses very explicitly on the battle for survival against the elements – something that *The Beach* glosses over completely. In Boyle's film, no-

10 Hodge 2000 p.171.

one appears to be hungry, become ill or dirty: the provision of clean water or sanitation are things that do not trouble the narrative. Even the scene in which a character has toothache is played for laughs, with the character able to drink and smoke after he has had the tooth pulled out. Whereas Chuck (Tom Hanks) in *Cast Away* (dir. Robert Zemekis 2000) knocks out a bad tooth with the blade of an ice skate, in Boyle's film, reality is softened by soporific substances.

As a satire of globalisation, or as a warning to the developed world not to pursue notions of paradise in other parts of the world, the film is only partially successful. Tourism only really seems like a form of warfare in Richard's egotistical idealisation of *Apocalypse Now*. He attempts to dismiss this narrative in the hostel as if he is superior to such western, manufactured culture but rather than reject it, he has actually internalised its drive to colonise. Richard recounts that what separates him from Bangkok is 'an eighteen-hour plane flight, three dumb movies, two plastic meals, six beers and no sleep'. In terms of privation, it hardly seems extreme. The progress through different means of transport (plane, train, ferry, small boat) suggests the difficulty in getting off the tourist trail. However, Richard, Françoise and Étienne make the fatal error (as illustrated by Alain De Botton's *The Art of Travel*), of assuming that they can find a form of paradise by spatially relocating themselves thousands of miles, forgetting that they bring themselves, the source of conflict and problems, with them ('I had inadvertently brought myself with me to the island,' says Richard on the voice-over).[11]

How to be good

In a sense, *Millions* can be seen as a more optimistic, child-centred version of the basic narrative premise of *Shallow Grave*, as we move from a Thatcherite universe to a Blairite, New Labour view of social justice. Perhaps reflecting the social phenomenon represented by the Random Acts of Kindness Foundation or novels like Nick Hornby's *How To Be Good* (2001), *Millions* questions the value and use of money. As Damian says at the beginning in relation to the pound, 'everyone says we're going to miss it'. Anthony has absorbed the adult mode of speaking about money, talking of houses as 'property' and mimicking the language of estate agents, describing the new house as 'surprisingly spacious' and with 'attractive views'. It is unclear how knowledgeable he actually is, as his justification to his brother Damian for keeping the money is that the

11 De Botton 2002 p.20.

government would take 40 percent, which he then goes on to explain is 'nearly all of it'. His worldliness contrasts with the innocence of Damian who takes a junk-mail letter, in which his mother is named as the winner of a prize draw, entirely at face value. Anthony uses their mother's death to get what he wants and teaches his brother to do the same – mention of their mother in the newsagent, in a neighbour's house and in the headteacher's office is enough to get them free sweets, biscuits and an escape from trouble.

Even Damian learns to lie: when the boys are visiting numerous banks in an attempt to change their millions into euros on the day of the currency changeover, he repeatedly claims he needs to go to the toilet, in order to get the cashiers to hurry up. This section of the film moves closer to narratives like *Brewster's Millions* (dir. Walter Hill 1985) in which characters have a fixed time to try and get rid of an unimaginable fortune, or *The Million Pound Note* (dir. Ronald Neame 1954), in which the value of a single note of huge denomination is at stake. The difference here is that although there are comic interludes (such as Anthony being carried into school like a hero on the back of a bicycle, surrounded by underlings all sporting sunglasses), much of Boyle's film and its central character are resolutely serious-minded.

The difficulty of what to do with the money is posed almost straight away – tellingly playing 'cash jenga' with the bundles of notes is more fun than spending them. A low-angle reverse shot shows the unreality of this money for them, as much a plaything as real. St Francis' advice to Damian, 'you could just help the poor,' proves to be more difficult than it seems. The jump-cuts of giving money to friends but swearing them all to secrecy, is amusing but also underlines their difficulty. The most obvious example of social benevolence for most of us is directly handing money to people in the street, so Damian tries a large donation to a seller of *The Big Issue*. However he soon discovers, as seen in the procession of homeless people across the road to Pizza Hut, that once acts of generosity become public, they are open to exploitation. Some of the so-called homeless admit they do not live round there but commute in by bus and even train. The speeded-up sequence of hands taking pieces of pizza literalises the notion of everyone wanting a slice of the financial pie. Anthony also calculates the thousands of meals it would take to distribute the money via such hospitality, so they rule out this strategy on practical grounds too.

The problem with giving to charity is later illustrated by the queue of people at their door in the middle of the night (originally a longer scene), all begging for money, all passionately believing in their particular cause. Deleted on the grounds of length, there was also originally a scene with a family at the Cunningham's door, desperately pleading for cash to stave off a VAT demand. Anthony answers the door and makes the family pretend to be carol singers to justify giving them some money (even though Dorothy unwittingly then gives them a bit of loose change as well). It may seem a minor scene but it is also an example of a request for money that might be viewed either as a culturally acceptable part of Christmas traditions, or a licence to demand money with menaces. Boyle has faced such dilemmas himself in 'doing the right thing' by seeking to recompense the children who starred in *Slumdog Millionaire* and facing vilification in certain sections of the press for not having done enough.

After approaching a number of neighbours, Damian bluntly asks one of the Latter Day Saints, 'are you poor?' underlining the relative nature of such terms. The man is initially taken aback by such a direct question but then goes on to explain that he lives without certain mod-cons such as dishwasher or microwave and manages to persuade himself (and Damian) that in a sense, yes he is poor. It may be morally comforting to think of oneself as relatively poor in the face of the corrupting reality of consumer goods. After subsequently being given money, the men do not spend it on religious activity (which their religious principles as Latter Day Saints would dictate) but on a binge of consumer goods. Anthony asks Damian if he has given money to anyone else, to which he replies 'not really,' at which point the neighbours cycle past loaded down with new purchases.

The slow-motion entrance to the school of Anthony and his hangers-on clearly evokes the iconic slow-motion walk-through in Tarantino's *Reservoir Dogs*, and Anthony seems to have initiated a gangster-like mini-economy fairly swiftly. A queue of children wishing to sell him things is headed by a boy claiming that a particular football game is 'the dog's bollocks'. We follow Anthony's dinner which is carried on a tray covered by a cloth and brought to his table, where three girls fawn over him, asking how much money he really has. Rivalries, jealousies, an imbalance in healthy peer-group relationships – the visible influence of money is unremittingly negative. The boy with the football game waves his money at the girls who just laugh at him, but not far beneath the banter is something quite unpleasant – a purely market-driven economy, driven by and pandering to our basest impulses.

The moral issue of whether it is acceptable to try and do good with money that you know to be criminally tainted is also raised. Ronnie justifies keeping the money by the fact that he works very hard, the house has just been broken into at Christmas, and if they gave the money to the police, it would ultimately be burned anyway. Damian, sticking to his principles, resolutely opposes him. It is the only point in the film where father and son are opposed and the only point at which Ronnie, who has been very even-tempered up to now, looks like he might lose his cool with his children.

The moral compass of Dorothy seems a little shaky. Anthony is openly hostile towards her, suggesting a protective reaction against someone seeking to supplant their recently departed mother. However, it is a little more complicated than that. Despite her job as a charity worker and her knowledge of the poor, Dorothy accepts the idea of keeping the money with surprising speed. The scene near the end, where along with their father and Anthony, she puts bundles of cash on the table, shows that all of them have been corrupted in some measure by the money. The joke she makes when Damian suggests giving the money to the poor (they would no longer be poor after that and would therefore have to give it back) seems a tactless and cheap excuse not to give to any charity and hardly in keeping with her day-job. The money is the narrative means of bringing the characters together, but the speed with which Dorothy and Ronnie wind up in bed together after converting the cash into euros is a little disconcerting (certainly for Damian who stumbles upon them).

The apparent driving force behind the narrative – stolen money – is really a narrative red herring or what Hitchcock called a 'McGuffin'. As Damian says, 'as it turns out, it wasn't about the money at all'. The scene in which he burns the pile of money feels a little like the KLF art installation from 1994 in which one million pounds was burned on the Scottish island of Jura (filmed as *Watch the K Foundation Burning a Million Quid*, dir. Alan Goodrick 1995) and raises some of the same ethical questions. Damian's declaration that money 'just makes everything worse' may be true, but one cannot help feeling that producing a pyre of notes evades the problem rather than solving it.

There are a number of typically Dickensian features in the narrative, such as the idealisation of a mother figure and a moral story in which evil is repelled and punished. The Christmas setting specifically evokes *A Christmas Carol* (1843) and what should be done with material wealth in order to live a morally useful life. In particular, the sudden appearance of a mysterious and threatening man, a robber, strongly evokes *Great Expectations* (1861). A naïve and innocent boy, who may not be an orphan like Dickens' Pip but who has lost a mother, comes into a mysterious inheritance and must fight off the advances of a menacing stranger who suddenly intrudes into the boy's world (by the railway tracks, in his room, at the shop where their mother used to work, and even in the school) as a convict on the run. Like the unnamed man, Dickens' Magwitch is guilty of stealing money from banks, is ironically the source of Pip's wealth without his knowledge, and forces the boy to do something for him. The shot of the robber's heavy hand dropping onto Damian's shoulder later and his face looming into threatening close-up, complements the casting of Christopher Fulford as the villain: his pronounced south-east accent only adds to the parallels with Magwitch. Like Dickens' villain, the robber evokes an ambiguous response – Damian asserts 'he's poor' and Anthony is unable to articulate in language Damian can understand the threat that the man could pose. He is never given a name and suggests the presence of lurking evil, not just by turning up unannounced but by his small black hat, serving as an alternative kind of halo.

Like Pip in the graveyard at the beginning of *Great Expectations*, Damian is drawn to places associated with his dead mother: the old house and Selfridges where she worked. In a deleted scene, Anthony dreams about breaking into his neighbour's house to get some money back, only for the robber to try and break in too, nightmarishly reaching through the blinds. In his novel, Cottrell Boyce also uses a Dickensian device of a physical defect being shorthand for moral evil, describing the robber as a man with a glass eye.[12] As in *Great Expectations*, Boyle dramatises a moral tale in which the pursuit of money is seen as less important than love, especially of one's family, and in which the possibility of redemption is always kept alive.

The value of human life

In *Sunshine*, the crew of the crippled spaceship Icarus II face a dilemma. Trey, the navigator, falls into a depressed state after his mathematical mistake in resetting the heat-shields, which leads to a fire and a severe depletion of oxygen levels. He is both responsible for this situation and part of a potential solution. Corazon, the biologist, whose name ironically means 'heart' in Spanish, puts forward the suggestion that there would be enough oxygen if there were three fewer crew members – Trey could therefore be killed. Although the moral question is later rendered moot by the discovery of Trey's body, an apparent suicide, the way that

12 Cottrell Boyce 2004 p.180.

scientist Capa expresses the choice they face is bluntly logical. 'What are you asking?' he says. 'That we weigh the life of one against the future of mankind? Kill him'. This feels like a pragmatic inversion of the sentimental, Hollywood logic behind films like *Schindler's List* (dir. Steven Spielberg 1993) which bears the tagline 'whoever saves one life, saves the world entire'.

Slumdog Millionaire is a love story rather than an exploration of morality, but it is explicitly structured around a moral question – can a beggar, a mere 'slumdog', who knows the answers to 15 quiz questions, be anything other than a cheat? Through the course of the film, we see demonstrated very clearly the possibility, however unlikely, that he is not cheating, and that life-experience brings a range of learning potential along with it. The morality of torture is only lightly touched upon (although highly relevant in the global fight against terrorism and controversies over so-called 'extraordinary rendition'). The use of torture in Indian police stations is presented as unremarkable, but possibly by the end the inspector may have re-evaluated how useful a method it is for extracting the truth. This lies outside the scope of the film however, which is primarily apolitical and Boyle opted to film but ultimately delete scenes which would have humanised the inspector further, such as his act of ripping up the police file on Jamal. Jamal's life-story, as told through the course of answering the quiz questions, suggests that it is possible to be both poor and virtuous, unlike Salim who chooses a life of crime.

127 Hours is not so much about a moral choice as about one man's drive to survive in spite of his revulsion for what he needs to do. In theory, social taboos about disfigurement and self-harm may play a role here but since he is alone, hallucinating and close to death, it is the battle with his own mental processes which remains uppermost. The moral choices under consideration here are of the kind associated with willpower – could we have done the same in Ralston's position? On the one hand, it can be seen as an amazing story of one man's will to live; on the other, it might seem as if an irresponsible individual leading an aimless existence has gained subsequent fame and fortune from what really was a self-inflicted injury. It is both a story of triumph over adversity, and desperation over self-indulgence. The narrative of *127 Hours* is close to the blind egocentrism of *The Beach* in the way it portrays young thrill-seekers given to casual drug-taking, who use the natural world/environment for their own hedonistic pleasure. The protagonists in both films are yearning for significance in their lives but seek this through the pursuit of contrived thrills, such as speed and danger. As with David Fincher's *The Social Network* (2010), it is tempting to see this as part of a self-aggrandisement on the part of the characters and possibly a diminution of the creativity of the directors concerned. It would be easy to be judgemental about Ralston's behaviour – not being sufficiently equipped for the terrain, carrying no effective means of communication, failing to tell anyone of his whereabouts – especially given his general confident manner which verges on arrogance. However, whereas in *The Beach*, Boyle fails to make Richard's unattractive character sympathetic, the provision of an inner life for Ralston, combined with James Franco's performance, help to overcome these theoretical handicaps.

By giving him visions of acquaintances and family with whom he has failed to have an emotionally close relationship, (visions of 'Christmas Past', so to speak), he is offered a Scrooge-like chance of redemption. When he screams 'I need help' he is finally acknowledging his need to connect with a world that he had, until now, largely ignored or at least taken for granted.

Conclusion

The extent to which films offer moral redemption for their protagonists and thereby the possibility of narrative closure, differs over time and between genres. In terms of classical Hollywood films, especially in genres like romantic comedy, narrative closure symbolised by marriage is a defining element and *A Life Less Ordinary* does provide that. Typical of a Bollywood ending, *Slumdog Millionaire* offers a joyous version of this, symbolised by Jamal and Latika coming together, the lyrical refrain of 'Victory!' ('Jai Ho!'), the exuberance of the final dance routine and perhaps – often missed in all this – the winning of the money as a sign of divine will. Other genres, such as horror, especially after George Romero's *Night of the Living Dead* (1968), conventionally end on a bleak note in which evil is rarely completely vanquished. Particularly after Brian De Palma's shock ending in *Carrie* (1976), the sudden re-animation of the source of threat has become almost a genre staple in itself. Boyle's *28 Days Later* refutes this. There is certainly plenty of horror in his vision of an infected Britain but the hero and heroine do survive and there seems to be life elsewhere (symbolised by a shot of a plane passing overhead).

The way that Boyle offers repeated hope at the close of his narratives is unusual in contemporary Hollywood. *Millions*, as a family/children's film, closes with family harmony, a new candidate as a replacement mother/wife (Dorothy) and a solution to water provision in Africa (which, although expressed as a fantasy sequence in which the Cunninghams somehow miraculously travel to Africa and help distribute water, could literally be made real by viewers donating generously). Renton escapes drug addiction in *Trainspotting* by showing enough moral fibre and brutality to abandon his friends, and Alex in *Shallow Grave* survives by being more Machiavellian than his less attractive flatmates. In contemporary science fiction, closure is usually achieved by spectacular conflict (think of the ever-increasing size of the armies in the *Star Wars* franchise) whereas *Sunshine* looks back to the personal, psychological and philosophical tone of *Solaris*. *Sunshine* ends with a huge explosion. Capa sets off the bomb and time appears to be extended as he reaches out to an oncoming wall of flame, inviting his own destruction, which will mean a reanimated sun and the survival of our species. Boyle presents the moment in personal terms, rather than in conventional spectacle, as Capa experiences an epiphany at the birth of a new star.

There is an underlying morality to most of Boyle's narratives. Killers meet a grisly end (David in *Shallow Grave*), murderous entities are destroyed (Pinbacker in *Sunshine*) and criminals are punished (the gangster Maman dies at the end of *Slumdog Millionaire*). If you live by the sword, or in most cases the gun, then that is how you meet your premature end. Violence is judged within the narrative – the ridiculously violent Begbie is cheated at the end of *Trainspotting*. Money does not bring happiness but divides friends (*Shallow Grave*) or corrupts youth (*Millions*) and an apparently idyllic setting does not ensure harmony (*The Beach*).

However, the engaging rogue and the charming thief are also indulged by Boyle. Renton steals the money from his supposed friends in *Trainspotting* but is allowed to get away with it, possibly on the grounds of being slightly less despicable than the addicts he associates with. Alex lies stabbed at the end of *Shallow Grave* but the implication is that he will survive and is the only one who knows the whereabouts of the money hidden beneath the floorboards.

Boyle also seems to feel a sense of moral responsibility in his own role as filmmaker, doubling up his crew on *The Beach* with Thai equivalents in part to avoid local problems, but also to give valuable work experience to the indigenous film industry. His attempts to restore the beach used (Maya Bay, part of the Phi Phi Islands National Park) to its original state, leaving a deposit with the Thai government as a show of good faith, went largely unappreciated by the media, which reported many stories of damage to the environment around the central beach setting. Critics such as Toby Miller contradict Boyle's account of the care taken over the beach, recording that a superficial makeover of the area was undone by the monsoon rains the following year.[13] More recently, Boyle's trust fund set up to pay for the schooling of several child actors from *Slumdog Millionaire* was overshadowed at times by stories of family conflict and house clearance, with relatives claiming they were being thrown out of their houses and arguments over exactly who the legal guardians were of all the children. Thus his principles also create problems for him. His decision to employ a Thai crew on *The Beach* also had the unfortunate consequence of pushing up the budget, meaning he had to opt for a bigger-name star, Leonardo DiCaprio, to recoup the investment, which indirectly led to the fracture of relationship with Ewan McGregor, who felt he had been promised the part.

Clearly, to some degree film-makers should be held responsible for the state of the shooting environment and the welfare of those involved in production, and should show sensitivity to issues portrayed in their work. However, it is highly debatable to what extent Boyle himself should be held responsible for the actions of others. Film history is littered with similar cases, such as Leni Riefenstahl's use of children of Sinti and Roma background in the filming of *Tiefland* (released 1954 but filmed in 1940), some of whom (it is alleged) later died in concentration camps. Riefenstahl is an immensely controversial figure for many reasons and is not necessarily blameless in this instance or in others. The point here is that the imputed responsibility of filmmakers to those around them is not a new issue and can have lifelong creative and personal consequences when the media adopt a hostile position. In a sense, *The Beach* is a useful metaphor for the filmmaking process, a cinematic version of the scientific principle (often erroneously termed the Heisenberg Principle), in which the act of observing actually changes that which is being observed. Even if viewers are intended to be critical of the island community, shooting a film about such a beautiful setting will inevitably encourage others to come, making it an inherently invasive, corrupting process.

13 Miller 2002 p.145.

CHAPTER SIX

· RELIGION ·

'Art and Religion are the two roads by which men
escape from circumstance to ecstasy'

Clive Bell[1]

There has been something of an explosion in writing about religion and
film over the last decade or so with texts falling into two basic categories
– collections of case studies analysing films with overtly religious content
(such as Pamela Grace's *The Religious Film*, 2009) or studies using film as
examples of ethical questions (such as Bryan P. Stone's *Faith and Film:
Theological Themes at the Cinema*, 2000 and Joseph Kupfer's *Visions of
Virtue in Popular Film*, 1999). What has been largely missing is the
consideration of how religious subjects can be used as part of creative
filmic choices. Boyle's work has been overlooked in this context perhaps
because the films most relevant to this question, *Sunshine* and *Millions*,
are also among his least known. This chapter will consider his use of
religious imagery, overtly religious concepts (such as the portrayal of
angels in *A Life Less Ordinary* and saints in *Millions*) and the extent to
which the endings of Boyle's films attempt to offer an element of
consolation to the viewer.

Paul Schrader's seminal work *Transcendental Style in Film* (1972),
although specifically about Yasujiro Ozu, Robert Bresson and Carl
Theodor Dreyer, describes how film and religion both seek to bring
viewers 'as close to the ineffable, invisible and unknowable as words,
images and ideas can.'[2] Some elements of this have been touched upon
in Chapter Three on performance, where I used the term hyper-realism
to suggest how Boyle conveys a sense of experience beyond the self, of
gaining access to a different realm of apprehension which might be
deemed spiritual. Boyle is certainly interested in moral dilemmas to
reflect character conflict, but sometimes goes a stage further and addresses
religious issues directly. In media interviews he is fond of telling how a
priest, Father Conway, persuaded him as an adolescent that perhaps he
was not best suited for a life in the priesthood. Having been raised as a

---

1   Clive Bell, cited in Schrader 1972 p.7.
2   Schrader 1972 p.8.

Catholic, this was a difficult decision for Boyle, especially since his mother, to whom he was very close, wanted him to pursue a vocation. Boyle demonstrates an enduring interest in spirituality in his films and shows how, in a largely secular age, individuals still express a need for transcendence, for something beyond the self. However, despite his strict religious upbringing, direct images of Catholic sin and redemption do not figure in his films as they do in the films of Martin Scorsese whose work Boyle openly admires. For example, in *Goodfellas*, Scorsese shows us a freeze-frame of narrator Henry Hill (Christopher Serrone, at this point of the film), in a crucifix pose framed by a dramatic explosion, the pose indicating that, despite being 'trained' as a gangster, he still retains some potential for moral redemption.

In some of Boyle's early television work, we see scepticism about organised religion or at least the ways in which it can be perverted. *Elephant* (1989), which Boyle produced and Alan Clarke directed, is a shockingly brutal depiction of the mindless cycle of sectarian killings in Belfast during 'The Troubles' in Northern Ireland. There are lengthy tracking shots approaching each victim, taking us through a range of different settings – interior and exterior, personal and professional, public and more personal – but what makes them particularly powerful is the fact that we are following the progress of the *killer*. This makes us complicit in the act, especially since such tracking shots are generally used in film to generate excitement. We are denied any commentary, any point of identification with the characters we see, and after each murder the camera dwells on the physical reality of the body – the repulsive result of sectarian violence and 'the elephant' of the title (that which is usually ignored).

The sheer repetition of the murders is critical. Like the opening three sex scenes in David Cronenberg's *Crash* (1996), the repetition is the meaning. Whereas Cronenberg is dramatising a world of emotional and sexual numbness where characters are engaged in bizarre and perverse acts to try and stimulate themselves in an affectless universe, so here in *Elephant*, the effect of watching one senseless murder after another, performed in the name of religion, makes the viewer acutely aware of how Christianity has been perverted. It is also quite a strange viewing experience: after the first couple of executions, we know, or feel we know, what will happen but continue to watch anyway, just in case there is any variation of the pattern or if anyone escapes. The narrative is relentless in its brutality and we are denied the conventional signs of action movies (close-ups or driving music to heighten the drama). The killings are mostly shown in long shot and decidedly undramatic, filmed mostly in a single take. The killer approaches, fires his gun and walks away. There is no context provided for the act, no cause-and-effect relationships created, and therefore the stark and barbaric act of killing is allowed to stand cinematically as a literally senseless act.

Mr Wroe's Virgins (BBC 1993) dramatises the way religion creates and perpetuates the cult of one particular tyrannical individual. Boyle's series, based on a real religious order established during the Industrial Revolution and on Jane Rogers' 1991 novel of the same name, creates a powerful evocation of a claustrophobic perversion of religious belief akin to Arthur Miller's *The Crucible*. We may not be in the realm of witch-hunts but religion is nevertheless used as a means to enforce a distinctly male form of power. The series is structured so that the story is told from the points of view of four women living in the group. It requires particularly powerful performances from all four female narrators: Hannah (Kerry Fox), Leah (Minnie Driver), Joanna (Lia Williams) and Martha (Kathy Burke), but perhaps especially the latter, as she was closely associated up to this point with her comedic TV work with Harry Enfield. Boyle coaxes some truly stunning performances from his cast and these possibly helped to offset objections from some quarters over the series' portrayal of sexuality, including rare full-frontal nudity.

Even in a film like *Trainspotting*, where an association with religion does not automatically come to mind, there is a natural recourse to iconography that has a spiritual echo in its extremely secular parody. The very first shot of Renton after the opening scene during which he has been pursued by security guards, shows him standing waif-like before falling back in ecstasy, arms outstretched as if crucified in an image of narcotic transcendence. Unlike the image mentioned earlier from *Goodfellas*, which is a long-shot held in freeze-frame, Boyle uses a bird's eye view and the character falls in slow-motion, which is slightly less intrusive stylistically. Renton's drug-dealer, Swanney, carries the ironic name Mother Superior, not on account of any spiritual comfort on offer, but due to the length of his 'habit'. Such verbal wit seeks to obscure the desperation behind addictive behaviour. It would be an overstatement to see the toilet-diving scene as a kind of baptism but it does show that Renton still has the capacity to think in images that are pure and beautiful.

Angels

Religious iconography and the whole nature of divine intervention is a key part of *A Life Less Ordinary*, which structures its narrative around a pair of angels. Their mission is to contrive a successful romantic relationship, a seemingly impossible job in an era that sees the formation of enduring emotional ties as under threat. The use of angels is a narrative device that has been used before, notably in Wim Wenders' *Wings of Desire* (1987), which does not fall into any neat generic category. What Boyle adds is a multi-generic element (see Chapter Two) and an underlying brutality in the tonal mix of the film.

A Life Less Ordinary opens with a black screen and the sound of a comedy routine, based on the concept of Original Sin and Eve's temptation of Adam, establishing the two dominant themes of the film – the battle of the sexes and female culpability. The screen fades to white and the main opening sequence features Heaven as a police station, with everyone in white, shown in high contrast to exclude all other colours. The scene reanimates the cliché of an overrun station – St Peter is a harassed desk sergeant busy processing prisoners, a scantily clad prostitute (a sinner) is being interviewed and an angry boss, the archangel Gabriel (Dan Hedaya), is berating the performance of a pair of angel detectives, O'Reilly (Holly Hunter) and Jackson (Delroy Lindo). The dialogue is close to a playful parody of film noir at times, such as in O'Reilly's declaration to Gabriel: 'strip the flattery, where's the beef?' The chaos of the scene is softened by dissolves between shots and a soundtrack featuring Diana Ross. Edwin Page asserts that the film subverts 'our expectations as to normal angel behaviour,' as if that is a given, and states that the film would have been better without the frame story: in fact it is central to the meaning of the film.[3] The basic metaphor works well, with Gabriel decrying the failure-rate in relationships. He talks of 'pressure from above' (meaning from God) to achieve 'results' and is therefore introducing 'new incentives for leading operatives' in which failure to bring about romantic success will be punished by an inability to return to Heaven. With a minor echo of Shakespearean tragedy, the angels will bring Robert as low as possible, strip him of any pretensions he might have, remove his job, his girlfriend and all his possessions, then manipulate circumstances to allow love to triumph.

After Robert has 'kidnapped' Celine, we cut back to the pair of angels, now inhabiting what looks like a converted basement/garage. O'Reilly is reading the same romance book as the protagonists, suggesting it was planted deliberately in the cabin. In a sense, the presence of these characters is a distancing device, performing the function of a Greek chorus, commenting on the action and reminding us that we are watching a contrived fiction. However, these particular supernatural beings are also part of the earthly narrative and are humanised too, blurring the distinction between human and non-human. They look no different from mortals, having adopted suitable apparel, and as yet have not shown any supernatural powers. Furthermore, Jackson is moaning about life on earth and wishing Robert and Celine would hurry up and fall in love so they can go home. As a chorus, he is describing the progress of a romantic film narrative and so his role is aligned with a disgruntled (probably male) viewer of the film, who knows that usually once the lead characters fall in love, the narrative ends and they can leave the cinema.

Later the angels approach Celine's father, offering to rescue Celine and kill Robert, effectively acting as earthly bounty hunters. Holly Hunter's tailored tweed jacket, scarf and red hat seem to echo Cameron Diaz's retro-noirish look. This outfit, complete with boots, produces a combination of air stewardess style and Russian military uniform. Her action in rubbing a gloved hand down her body as she speaks evokes the previous scene where she appears to be touching her breast in a sexually gratifying way while reading in bed. It also brings to mind her role in David Cronenberg's *Crash* (1996) a year earlier, in finding mortal life in all its forms seductive and even arousing.

Boyle frames the first money-drop like a Sergio Leone western, in open countryside with cars on the edges of the frame, the scene accompanied by the sound of a tolling bell. As Robert approaches the car, which should contain the money, tension is raised via inter-cut, handheld forward and reverse tracking shots. He opens the car boot, which initially is shot from inside looking out so we can see his reaction, before Boyle cuts to the reverse angle and we see the source of his fear – a bomb. He stops it with a second to go, but the 'money' is revealed as only bag of carrots. The extent of the angels' power, in that they can directly interact with the real world, is clarified as the car is then raked with gunfire, problematising the romantic comedy genre. We assume Naville, or perhaps the police, are firing at Robert, but then we see the shooter is actually O'Reilly, armed with a high-powered rifle and telescopic sights. Jackson, lying next to her, compliments her on her shooting. Robert then pursues the fleeing angels in a car chase but O'Reilly subsequently escapes, commandeering a vehicle by posing as a hitchhiker and during the ride she seems to enjoy flirting with the young driver.

'Jeopardy, Jackson, jeopardy. It always works' says O'Reilly, but there is very little genuine jeopardy in the film, even when the lives of the romantic couple are supposedly threatened. Jackson, in his role as bounty hunter, captures Robert, who cries and bleats while digging his own grave (hardly standard romantic comedy material) but we never get the sense that any real pain will be suffered. After all, the entire premise of the plot, of the angels and of Boyle, is to bring these two together. Accordingly, Celine escapes and rescues Robert, dealing Jackson a blow with a shovel, sending him into the grave instead. Jackson complains like a disgruntled employee about an apparent lack of divine direction, saying that 'I don't think even He knows what's going on down here'. The upbeat REM track 'Leave' reflects this generic confusion and jars badly here, suggesting adventure and escapist fantasy rather than the film's exploration of the sustainability of love in the modern world, as well as actually obscuring some of the dialogue.

The plot becomes a series of episodes with little sense of development in character, relationships or even location. Certainly from the time the protagonists reach the cabin, many scenes could be shown in virtually any order. The consequence of this is that the film loses momentum and direction from mid-point on. Celine and Robert hit O'Reilly with a truck and although she is dragged along behind the truck, she then climbs up the bonnet, like the apparently indestructible T-1000 in *Terminator 2* (dir. James Cameron 1991), shifting the film once more into a cartoonish realm. Celine and Robert roll out of the truck like James Dean in *Rebel without a Cause* (dir. Nicholas Ray 1955) and we see it fly off the road with O'Reilly still pinned to the front of the vehicle, and crash with a sickening thud against a rock. Such sequences do not sit easily at all within the romantic comedy genre.

We cut back to the angels with Jackson sitting at a table-tennis table, trying to compose a love letter to draw the couple back together. O'Reilly is hobbling around (as a result of her supposed injuries from the truck), seeking to inspire Jackson by creating a clichéd romantic ambiance – music, pictures, even a small flower in a vase on the table. It is only through the revelation of personal experience, his own writing to a young girl, that Jackson accesses the 'romantic soul' that O'Reilly never knew he had. The music, Elvis Presley's 'Always on My Mind,' bleeds into the following scene as we cut to a shot from inside the mailbox. Celine's mother picks up the post and delivers it to her daughter, along with a cynical warning about men. A dramatic romantic climax is set up:

Robert is working at a bar as a cleaner and Celine approaches by car. The angels are positioned on a nearby hillside, huddling under a plastic shelter, surrounded by sophisticated surveillance equipment, in a stake-out parody. We see events from their perspective, partially obscured by the distance and aurally distorted before cutting to a more privileged view inside. Celine starts to make a romantic declaration but easy closure is denied by Robert's admission that he did not write the poem she received. She storms off and the bar owner, Al (Tony Shalhoub), maps out Robert's future, bringing him to his senses: 'she will be going to some heaven for glamorous pussy,' he says 'and you'll be cleaning the floor of a diner in hell'.

After all their machinations fail, the angels kidnap the pair, reprising Robert's earlier role. Again, however, there is an uncertainty about the tone of this final sequence and the sudden transformation of Mayhew from Celine's former phlegmatic butler to Naville's hired killer, seems unconvincing. Verbal wit is undercut by the brutality of Mayhew, who shoots the angels dead in a trap at the cabin, so that Naville will not have to pay them. We cut to a scene in Heaven, where the case seems to have galvanised the entire staff who press up against the window of Gabriel's office, hoping he can find some way to save the earthly couple. Back on earth, Robert is in the cabin searching for Naville's money in the crawl-space under the floorboards, while being pursued by Mayhew with an axe. Celine shoots Mayhew and Naville, but the bullet passes through Robert. Although he appears to be hit, with a hole made in his heart, the staff in Heaven cheer and the earlier animation of a beating heart emphasises that somehow this is an emotional bullet and the two are finally united.

Originally, John Hodge's script ended with a scene of God playing basketball. The role was written for one of Hodge's own personal gods, Sean Connery, but when he turned it down, the scene was cut. In retrospect, this seems a pity. Even with a different actor, the action of scoring a basket at the exact moment that the power of Celine's love supposedly magically heals Robert's heart (and God's accompanying line, 'I still haven't lost my touch') would be an effective repudiation to Gabriel's fears that God is not fully in control of events.

Paradise re-gained?

The Beach could be seen as a secularisation of a spiritual quest – the search for an earthly paradise, an unspoilt location untouched by the transgressions of humankind. Ironically, those who find the mythical island bring their flawed selves with them and spiritual concerns soon seem lost in a repetitive round of empty hedonism, in which the prime motive seems to be defending their secret place, as if it somehow reflects their own virtue (when they themselves have no right to be on the island). The sheer beauty of the island is conveyed by aerial shots during Daffy's initial description of the place, and when the trio eventually walk up to the eponymous beach, via inter-cut forward and reverse tracking shots, we are invited to contemplate images of unspoilt ineffable beauty. In response to their first view of the bay, Richard sits down, Étienne flips a somersault and Moby's anthem 'Porcelain' invites us to experience a moment of ambient 1990s spirituality, while the song's title suggests the vulnerability of the setting. The community gather on the beach at night to release fire-balloons (small structures, each containing a single candle), supposedly suggesting a farewell to previous lives and this motivates further high-angle shots of the island enhanced by computer-generated imagery as the balloons soar away. Such sequences evoke elements of wider eastern culture which we really only glimpse in the film. The film is dominated by western idealisation of what is seen as exotic, represented by escapist, adventure fantasies like the James Bond franchise. As in *Thunderball* (dir. Terence Young 1965), there are shots later of a spectacular underwater cave where they unload provisions, lit by a single light source via hole in the roof, and the beach scene may also remind viewers of the climactic section of *The Man With The Golden Gun* (dir. Guy Hamilton 1974) where Bond's plane is destroyed.

The status of the island as a paradise is ambiguous when any original thought or action which disrupts the status quo is marginalised and ignored by the group. Garland touches upon the fascist undertones of this situation in the novel, when Richard expresses to Étienne a wish to restart everyday life just like the perfection of the island: Étienne replies that such thoughts are 'the same as everybody's.'[4]

Hope eternal

In *28 Days Later*, as in *The War Game*, Peter Watkins' 1965 vision of a Britain immediately after a nuclear conflict, organised religion seems to offer no real hope. Jim opens the doors of a building, his figure shot in high angle past a huge cross, designating the setting as a church. Inside, there is graffiti on the stairwell, revealed piecemeal as Jim ascends the stairs, ('repent the end is fucking nigh') and in the nave, Jim comes across a full congregation who appear to be at prayer but are actually dead. The

4 Garland 1996 p.134.

slow pan, unconventionally right to left, reflects a world out of kilter. Ironically, his 'hello' does elicit a response, but not one that he wants: several figures spring up and chase him, the closest being a priest who, rather than offering help, staggers towards him, blindly clawing and forcing Jim to hit him.

The images of Mark, Selena and Jim making their way out of London, walking along railway tracks, is accompanied by a choirboy singing 'Abide With Me,' linking secular football–terrace chants with an unspoken need for spiritual help and protection. Later, they are accompanied by Gabriel Fauré's 'In Paradisum,' suggesting a spiritual journey and, although there is some irony in this, there is also beauty in the peace of walking along a railway line with absolutely no other human presence. The Biblical allusion on a postcard that Jim finds at his parents' house, is from the Book of Nahum. Nahum was a prophet who predicted the destruction of the great city of Nineveh, capital of the Assyrian empire, as a punishment for the great wickedness of its inhabitants. Its inclusion here suggests the element of divine punishment for mortal sin, although there seems little coherent attempt to present this view overtly in the film. Major West's radio broadcast, inviting survivors to the army base, talks of 'salvation' but despite promising an answer to infection, in reality only offers sadistic killing and the luring of women for sexual exploitation.

The night-time escape from Major West's base is secured as Hannah crashes the cab through the gates and Selena and Jim are thrown forward, held in freeze-frame – this shot being one potential ending that Boyle considered. The actual coda, shot in daylight with sweeping aerial shots of open countryside, is much more optimistic. We see Jim waking, reminding us of the opening of the film, but here he is with Selena and Hannah in a country cottage, presumably somewhere in the Lake District. The 'Help' banner that they have made and laid out on the ground outside is spotted by a passing jet pilot, suggesting the survival of other pockets of humanity. Although we see a couple of infected individuals, they look too starved to do much more damage, and the film closes with a close-up of Jim, a faint smile playing across his face. An inverted flash-cut of the pilot's point-of-view forewarns us of the help that is on the way but could also be read more negatively – the slightly obscured message ('Hel-'), suggesting the 'Hell' that the survivors will

---

5   There are in our existence spots of time/That with distinct pre-eminence retain/A renovating virtue... (Wordsworth, The Prelude, Book 12. Ll. 208-218)

face. Like the Latin spoken in *Millions*, here the pilot speaks a non-English language (Finnish) without subtitles and the whole sequence is shot in 35mm, which gives the coda a fresher, more optimistic feel.

In his lengthy poem, *The Prelude* (1805), William Wordsworth wrote about sudden moments of experience which are particularly intense and which hold spiritual value. He termed these 'spots of time' and in Boyle's films we find similar, often critically neglected, episodes.[5]

In *28 Days Later* Frank, who seems at first to be a stereotypically brash cabbie, stops the car at the ruins of a monastery. The scene is a brief, peaceful interlude and it is Frank who is most contemplative, refusing the mind–numbing Valium offered by Jim and noticing the beauty of a group of horses. Page calls the horse a 'symbol of liberty' but the scene can also be read as symbolising hope of a potentially idyllic future: for Frank in particular, who calls the others over to share the vision and even blows the animals a kiss, it is the hope that humanity, including his daughter, will survive.

The use of horses here evokes a number of literary and cinematic sources, as well as connotations of Biblical apocalypse. Ted Hughes' short story 'The Rain Horse' (1967), Edwin Muir's poem 'The Horses' (1956), and even D.H. Lawrence's use of Ursula Brangwen's encounter with the anarchic, archetypal horses in *The Rainbow* (1915), all portray an urban-dweller's encounter with the animals, suggesting an unknowable, frightening and elemental power as well as a sense of freedom. For Lawrence this is primarily sexual, but for Hughes and also for Muir (whose poem is an optimistic description of returning to nature after surviving an apocalypse), this freedom is primarily artistic. With luck, and perhaps divine grace, the characters have reason to hope.

In cult film *The Swimmer* (dir. Frank Perry 1968), protagonist Ned Merrill (Burt Lancaster) experiences a transcendent vision of a horse running free, reflecting the frustrations and limitations in the hero's own life, the vision superimposed over a bravura close-up of his eyeball. More recently, the eponymous hero of *Michael Clayton* (dir. Tony Gilroy 2007) is inexplicably drawn to a field of horses – an action that miraculously saves his life as his car, left behind him at the roadside, explodes. Director and screenwriter Andrei Tarkovsky, with whose work Boyle is familiar, also used horses in a number of his films, most particularly at the close of *Andrei Rublev* (1966), his biopic of the fifteenth century Russian icon painter, to symbolise hope and freedom of creative thought.[6]

---

6 Tarkovsky on *Andrei Rublev*: 'I'd like to point out the film ends with an image of horses in rain. It is

As Selena and Jim walk around the ruins, there is a huge tree that occupies the centre of the frame, strongly suggestive of the Biblical tree of knowledge in connection with Selena's dialogue about the predictable nature of all future creativity. At this point, Selena assumes she knows what Jim is thinking and expresses the bleak idea that art can only ever be replayed now, not newly created (suggesting she has not responded to the images of the horses in quite the positive light that Frank apprehends them).

In the open air, next to the ruins, Jim suddenly wakes to find himself alone and sees a vision of sheep all running together. The distorted nature of the image and the fact that he has taken Valium to help him sleep, should signal to us that this is a dream sequence, but a few seconds later Boyle uses the same music and some of the same shots in another sequence, also showing running sheep, so that we are unsure for a moment if this will become a double-dream device. It is a slightly odd sequence but its purpose, beyond injecting a little fear into a calm episode that threatens to slide into sentimentality, is to underline Jim's fear as Everyman, of being in such a world, left to follow the crowd (as well as a possible allusion to the Biblical Gaderene swine who, possessed by devils, run blindly off a cliff to their death).

Along with Frank's contemplation of the horses, there are other transcendent moments, often forgotten in the context of action and chase sequences. In the cab, we see Jim put his arm out of the window, angling his hand like a bird's wing – an action no longer dangerous on an open and empty road and almost childlike in its indulgence of uninhibited sensual pleasure. Later, in fleeing from the murderous soldiers, Jim falls over but in looking up, sees a plane and its tell-tale vapour trails. Such images suggest that there is life (and thereby hope) elsewhere. Like the other examples here, a moment of contemplation brings tranquillity and thoughts of something higher. Without using a voice-over or a cut to a literal image of what Jim is thinking at this point, we cannot 'know' for sure that Jim is contemplating something of higher spiritual significance but the slower pace, lack of music and shots of him looking upwards that have no specific narrative purpose, might suggest this.

a symbolic image as horse for me is a synonym of life. When I'm looking at a horse I have a feeling I'm in direct contact with the essence of life itself. Perhaps it's because horse is a very beautiful animal, friendly to man. The presence of horses in the last, final scene means that life itself was the source of all of Rublev's art.' Tarkovsky interview by Ciment and Schnitzer in *Positif* 109, October 1969 pp.1–13.

The ineffable

In *Sunshine* the scene where the captain of Icarus II, Kaneda, gathers the crew in the observation room to watch Mercury passing in front of the sun, is one of the film's visual highlights but it is debatable exactly what are we being invited to contemplate. Viewers may receive this scene as a tribute to the work of God, the ability of science to bring humans close to such bodies, or simply as the skill of filmmakers in manufacturing such a spectacle. It seems more likely that in such scenes, where forward narrative momentum is deliberately paused, when we are invited merely to contemplate an image that it is there for its own sake, it is the spectacle that we are drawn by rather than its spiritual connotations. Boyle tried the scene originally with juxtaposed voiceovers but this would have given it a human focus, with observers looking inwards, rather than outwards at something beyond themselves. The scene requires no commentary as the screen contrasts the immensity of the sun with the tiny, almost fragile, sight of Mercury. It is a rare example of where the film tries to capture the spatial relationship of the sun to the planets and it also reflects one of the key pleasures of science fiction in matters of scale. Original viewers of the first (in the sense of first-made) *Star Wars* film (dir. George Lucas 1977) often recall the striking sense of almost-crushing claustrophobia as a huge space cruiser appears from the top right of the frame, an effect made almost routine in subsequent episodes and largely robbed of this power viewed in a domestic context on video or DVD.

Another contemplative moment occurs at the end of the film after Capa's battle with Pinbacker. The ambiguous disappearance from the scene allows Capa a moment of Hollywood serenity in the split-second before the bomb goes off and he is engulfed by flames. Granted, there are questions about the precise operation of time in such a situation, but Capa experiences this as an extended moment. A billionth of a second is stretched out, allowing him (and us) to experience what he has talked of earlier – the beauty and miraculous nature of creation in destruction. Capa is the only one who can activate the bomb, so effectively the continuance of the human race relies on him alone. He is granted the God-like power of reanimating a star and in that moment he raises his hand in a gesture of welcome and acceptance to the greater power of nature (echoing the pose used by NASA in sending communications beyond earth in search of alien life). To the accompaniment of John Murphy's swelling orchestral score, Capa, giving a faint smile, fades slowly to white. The reality of what would happen to his body (far closer to his repeated, screaming nightmare about falling into the molten heart of the sun) is therefore replaced with an uplifting vision. It is open to question whether this constitutes a reconciliation between the forces of Science personified by Capa, the earth's premier physicist, shown on the right hand side of the frame, and the forces of elemental nature on the left, possibly representing Religion. What is more certain is that it is the spectacular nature of the image on which we are encourage to dwell, in the slowing down of narrative time. On the DVD commentary, Boyle states that 'out of all this chaos and carnage, out of all this horror and fear…out of all this indescribable energy and force, comes something very, very beautiful.'

Some of Boyle's contemplative episodes are less effective, such as in *The Beach* where Françoise and Richard gaze up into a starry sky. The narrative wider notion that they are looking up at an alter ego somewhere in the cosmos who is looking back at them, is undercut here by the juxtaposition of grander metaphysics, of dreaming of a world 'where anything you want to happen, does happen' with Richard's very obvious, more prosaic designs on Françoise. The pretentiousness of the dialogue is punctured by Françoise's crushing comment 'that's just the kind of pretentious bullshit Americans always say to French girls' in order to seduce them, but this is exactly the point. Richard thinks he is being original when he is mouthing the same thoughts, in the same language, as countless others before him.

Saints

Millions opens with a scene of Damian reading a book called *The Six O'Clock Saints*, a 1940s compilation of tales of martyrdom, torture and gruesome death. On the DVD, Boyce recalls it was supposedly Martin Scorsese's favourite book and the inspiration behind *Raging Bull* (1980) and *Mean Streets* (1973). At various points in the film, saints appear to Damian, a fact that he accepts as completely normal and in line with his strong Catholic faith. In telling the narrative through the point of view of a small boy (a highly unusual boy certainly) Boyle presents such fantastical events alongside the everyday with no fictive markers that would allow us to distance ourselves and to mark these visions as delusional. For Damian, and for us, these figures exist in the real world (signified ultimately by the act of St Joseph in stepping forward and speaking Damian's line in the nativity play). Boyle's saints, despite their appearance and clothing which clearly place them as emanating from a different era, seem very approachable and all use contemporary colloquial dialogue, apart from St Nicholas who speaks Latin in which Damian can apparently miraculously converse.

Frank Cottrell Boyce's novel *Millions* (2004), published to coincide with the release of the film, spells out more strongly Damian's fixation with saints, his fascination with mortification and his possible progress up the 'ladder of virtue' for every good deed performed, all of which make him seem a social outcast.[7] Along with his attention to microscopic detail and his struggle with metaphorical language (such as the 'better place' to which his mother has supposedly gone), he seems close to the Asperger Syndrome sufferer Christopher, hero of Mark Haddon's *The Curious Incident of The Dog in the Night-Time* (2003). Damian's behaviour in the novel is more extreme than in the film (including beating himself with holly) and results in his being psychologically assessed. The toning down of this in the film is probably designed to make Damian a more empathetic central character – he is, after all, the source of the narrative and we need to find him engaging and quirky rather than just plain weird.

In the film, the first apparition, St Clare, sits and chats in Damian's 'box-house' while blowing smoke-rings and claiming to be the 'patron saint of television' because she sends visions to those who need them. Damian asks about Heaven and whether you are allowed to smoke there, to which she replies that you are allowed to do what you like, even smoke – it is back on earth where it is harder to be good. Catholic traditions are updated and secularised: St Clare describes Heaven as 'bloody infinite'. St Francis of Assisi appears after Damian has released some doves from the top of a hill, and the appearance of 'the Ugandan martyrs of 1881' brings the notion of sainthood slightly closer to the modern era, as well as opening it out to involve the developing world. At several points in the narrative (such as after the sudden first appearance of the money and when the boys are on the run after the nativity play), Damian looks up to see clouds racing, in fast-forward, across the sky, sometimes accompanied by heavenly choirs as a symbol of divine presence.

St Peter (Alun Armstrong) casts himself as a Geordie security expert, a kind of spiritual bouncer, and the patron saint of keys. The character was not in Cottrell Boyce's original script, but was added to his novelisation: it worked so well that it was included in the film. When Damian expresses his disappointment that the arrival of the money was

7 Cottrell Boyce 2004 pp.20-24.

not a miracle, but the fruits of a robbery, St Peter comes up with a purely secular explanation of Christ's feeding of the 5,000, 'loaves and fishes' miracle (that each member of Christ's audience on that occasion brought a little food with them and so the miracle is one of human hospitality rather than divine intervention). Saints appear almost like social workers, offering advice and help when called upon to do so – St Peter promises 'I'll have a word upstairs. See if I can get someone on your case more permanent.'

Saints help Damian throughout the narrative: in the nativity play, St Joseph says Damian's lines and later helps Damian by closing the back door to the Cunningham home, thereby trapping the unnamed robber as he is trying burgle the house, looking for 'his' stolen money. The man, who is both train-robber and burglar, remains unnamed throughout and functions as the personification of evil. This might seem simplistic but, as Damian reminds us, it is his story and his view of moral absolutes is clear-cut. The shot of St Joseph pulling the nativity play donkey along the landing of Cunninghams' house, unseen by the police who arrive to arrest the burglar, underlines the impression that the saints represent a gently benign spiritual presence.

Both Cottrell Boyce and Boyle pay tribute to production designer Mark Tildesley for the little touches that help realise their vision. These range from the rail of shirts bought by the acquisitive Latter Day Saints (themselves a literal manifestation of 'sainthood' in the everyday world, to Damian's eyes at least), who are shown to be very open to materialistic corruption, to the male saints which are given the look of El Greco paintings via the use of top lighting as well as the computer-generated addition of halos that appear to 'bounce' a little when the saints move.

Cut from the final version of the film was a scene in which Damian talks to one of the porcelain figurines of saints in his room of his old house. He is aware that he should not be there but seems to need some kind of spiritual connection with his dead mother, Maureen.

Also deleted on the basis of length, there was further footage up in the loft of his former home, where Damian is suddenly surrounded by all the saints he has seen up to this point, all praying for him. Damian's hiccups, which would have given away his hiding-place, disappear and the person who climbs into the loft is his father, rather than the robber Damian had been expecting. These events are therefore all shown to be the result of prayer. The idea of a fluid shift between the 'real' adult world and the fantastical world of a child's imagination, which is more open to what might be possible, works well here. It also adds to the sense of Damian as a rather strange and atypical young boy. As the saints have come to Damian, who expresses a consistently moral point of view throughout, it might suggest that he himself is a saint – his mother claims at the end that the miracle she has produced is him. He seems to be guided, like the shepherds at the nativity, to his old home by a star which bathes him in an unreal glow.

The coda of the finished film, a dream-like bringing of clean drinking water to Africa, might seem sententious, but the fact that the film has been constructed around Damian's viewpoint and his desire to do some good with the money, makes this coda both straightforward and true. The need and the potential solution, are both simple.

The Sun God

Sunshine is an implicitly religious film as it considers man's place in the cosmos. The sun literally has the power to blind if looked at directly, a power attributed to deities in primitive societies. More precisely, *Sunshine* features a battle between the crew of Icarus II, who are prepared to sacrifice themselves for the continuance of the human species, and the captain of Icarus I who sees it as man's destiny to be vanquished by the power of the sun. Thus Capa, as chief physicist, is the Christ-like saviour of humankind, and Pinbacker a destroyer of worlds on a par with God. As in *The Beach*, which Garland also wrote, characters travel away from what is familiar, but in apparently alien surroundings they discover truths about their inner nature.

The film ends with the success of the mission to reignite the sun, albeit at the cost of the lives of everyone on board Icarus II, and this suggests that Boyle has a fundamentally optimistic view of human destiny (especially in the hands of scientists). The notion of science being the solution to problems, rather than the source of them, is rare in the science fiction genre of the last 50 years, which has tended to focus on the destructive capacity of inventions or discoveries that spin out of control. Implicit in the narrative of *Sunshine* is the issue of the use of nuclear weapons: the sun is a mass of explosive potential, repeatedly showing more destructive power than we can possibly imagine. In order to allow human survival, the protagonists must deliver the most deadly destructive device they have in order to 'kick-start' the sun's own explosive nature.

In terms of religious meaning, there is an interesting collision of perspectives between Garland and Boyle. Garland describes *Sunshine* as 'a film about atheism' in which 'the sun is God-like, but not God. Not a conscious being. Not a divine architect.'[8] For him, to see the presence of the divine here is to make 'an awestruck category error when confronted with our small place within the vast and neutral scheme of things.'[9] However, Boyle himself sees the situation slightly differently and according to Garland at least, 'he believed that the crew actually were meeting God.'[10]

There are several scenes in the film in which characters express a sense of overwhelming wonder, akin to religious awe. This is first seen in psychological officer Searle, who undergoes ever-stronger bouts of exposure to the sun's rays in the observation lounge. Gradually, like Pinbacker before him, he becomes obsessed by the notion of giving himself up to this unimaginable power. Searle's sacrificial death on the abandoned Icarus I, allowing Capa, Harvey and Mace to have a chance of survival, is therefore (for Searle) the logical outcome. At the climax, Capa shares some of Searle's sense of awe, although he remains true to his mission and delivers the bomb.

The sun, as source of light and heat to all life-forms on earth, represents very literally the giver of life for us all, leading not surprisingly to its status as an object of worship in primitive human societies. For D.H. Lawrence the sun represented a savage power which humankind should view with respect and almost mystic dread. It was beyond his imagination that humans could dare to try and impose their will on such a force of Otherness. Pinbacker's philosophy blends this sense of Lawrentian awe with a Nietzschean view of 'becoming,' of flux as superior to permanence, something that is alluded to in I Am Klute's closing song, 'Avenue of Hope' over the credits, with the repeated lyrics of 'we wait to see just what we will become'. It may be tempting to see Pinbacker as representing Religion and Capa representing Science but the film is not so schematic. Much of Pinbacker's dialogue seems less that of a mystic and closer to the ravings of a madman, who has somehow survived alone on Icarus I.

Page attempts to see Pinbacker as a real figure, reading him as 'symbolic of terrorists'. But Pinbacker cannot be real: his irradiated body, from lengthy exposure to the sun, could not have survived for seven years and he performs apparently impossible movements in the climactic fight with Capa and Cassie.[11] Page later shifts ground to portray him as a

---

8 Garland 2007 p.vii.
9 Garland 2007 p.vii.
10 Garland 2007 p.vii.
11 Page 2009 p.180.

representative of Jung's 'collective unconscious' but without theoretical underpinning, this argument is unconvincing.

Searle spends progressively more time in the observation room, exposing himself to dangerously high doses of sunlight, and starts to peel skin off his face, visually linking him to the appearance of Pinbacker. Searle's early dialogue, about the significance and meaning of light in which 'it becomes you' seems similar to some of Pinbacker's ranting, and Searle's fate in self-immolation is sun-worship taken to its logical extreme. Searle's final words to Capa while helping him into the only space-suit (saying 'we're only stardust' and snapping the helmet shut before he can reply) evoke *2001*. In taking the decision to stay on Icarus I, Searle appears, like the captain, to be making a heroic sacrifice but it could be that he has already been seduced by Pinbacker's acquiescence to the inevitable (and possibly God-driven) destruction of the earth by the sun. He is an acolyte of Pinbacker and, though he never meets him, he comes to resemble him physically and to embrace the fate that Pinbacker advocates for them all. It is ironic that it should be the psychology officer who is first to submit to the lure of the sun's psychological effects. Searle touches the arm of one of the incinerated crew, who are huddled together like victims of the bombs at Hiroshima or the volcano at Vesuvius; frozen as if in a moment of epiphany. The arm shatters in slow motion at precisely the moment that Pinbacker uncouples the craft, suggesting a certain passing of the torch to his spiritual heir.

The flash-cuts of Pinbacker, in contrast to those of the rest of the Icarus I crew, use outline only, are blurred and are coloured orange, a colour almost completely denied to internal shots of the ship. The style of the flash-cuts is also different in that they do not occupy the whole frame but only the left-hand side, juxtaposed with a side-on shot of Capa. Capa has not met Pinbacker, nor seen his final transmitted message, in which he describes spending more and more time watching the sun, so these flash-cuts only make sense as a vision, an apprehension of the problem he has posed to the computer which has talked of a fifth crew member. As the most intelligent scientist humanity has to send on such a mission, one assumes that Capa is a genius, and perhaps has a higher level of emotional, even spiritual, apprehension too. The earlier flash-cuts are given to us, the viewer (there is no indication that Mace, Harvey and Searle see them) but here Capa shares our privileged view.

After the on-board computer has told Capa about the presence of an unknown life-form in the observation room, he races to the scene but has to shield his eyes to try and make out a figure apparently lying recumbent on the floor. Like the flash-cuts of Pinbacker, the figure is only shown in silhouette, is cropped and could even be the source of the blinding light. Pinbacker combines humanoid and alien features (the distorted voice and otherworldly content of his speeches, although spoken in English). His status as human, and his prime motive (to kill the entire crew) becomes more apparent at the moment he lashes out at Capa. However, Boyle's choice of visualising Pinbacker in this way has consequences. At this point, the narrative changes in terms of pace and generic references, shifting more explicitly towards horror. With an unknown entity wishing him dead, Capa no longer has time for philosophical debate. This is now a fight for survival against a literally shadowy opponent, whom it is difficult to view in a spiritual or religious light when he is fulfilling the role of a monster.

Despite Boyle's protestations on the DVD extras about the continued philosophical battle between Pinbacker and Capa in this final section, we are indisputably now in a slasher narrative. Once they face each other standing on the bomb, Pinbacker declares 'for seven years, I spoke with God. He called me to take us all to heaven,' but this seems more like religious mania than access to a higher truth. While pursuing Capa and Cassie, Pinbacker's burnt appearance, his snarling teeth (seen by Capa through the airlock window), distorted voice, use of a knife as a weapon, apparent superhuman strength (he picks up Capa one-handed) and ability to appear at will (where is he supposed to be hiding when he appears behind Capa who is standing on the giant bomb itself?), all strongly evoke the appearance of Wes Craven's slasher icon Freddy Krueger. His human characteristics are strongly compromised – in the confrontation on the bomb, Cassie rips pieces of flesh from him, so that he looks like an anatomical model. As a 'monster' not only are Pinbacker's exact capabilities unclear, but he changes methodology from a silent stalk-and slash-killer in hunting down Corazon and Trey, to a figure who talks and then – for no apparent reason other than for cinematic spectacle – throws his victims around (his method of trying to kill Capa).

Pinbacker forfeits audience sympathy at the point when he brutally stabs Corazon in the back at a moment of hope, when she finds a small shoot amidst the ashes of the oxygen garden. If Pinbacker's motives are unclear, then this act (shown from an overhead point-of-view) definitely determines his role as force of evil in the narrative. There is not only a callousness here but a strangely sadistic element so that the dead woman is subsequently positioned in a yoga pose of peace, for no apparent reason other than to mock her (and possibly our) optimism. In stalking Cassie, Pinbacker smashes his hand through a glass wall, and, as when Jim is grabbed by an infected man at the climax of *28 Days Later*, this strongly evokes the movement of Roy Batty (Rutger Hauer) in *Blade Runner*. The difference here is that whereas in *28 Days Later* a woman has to judge the sanity of an attacker, here Cassie grabs Pinbacker's arm and drags it onto the broken glass (the precise action of the similarly named Cathy, in Emily Bronte's 1847 *Wuthering Heights* towards a ghost who breaks into her bedroom). Thus a standard girl-in-jeopardy scenario is given a slight twist with a literary allusion.

Science is something of a 'get-out clause' for Boyle (or perhaps for an impossible plot situation). The huge forces of close proximity to the sun would supposedly distort the physics of time and space as we currently understand them. However the editing of the fight on the bomb, using freeze-frames and distorted images, is not coherent. We do not know exactly what Pinbacker can do: he has demonstrated apparently superhuman powers, so the point-of-view of the camera racing down the side of the bomb could be him jumping down. The exact fate of Pinbacker is unclear too. A planned scene, which was only partially shot, would have shown him eviscerated but that really would have made the transformation into horror complete. On the DVD, Boyle talks of Pinbacker as representing a kind of 'extreme fundamentalism' in which it is better for science to submit to a greater power, whether that be God, fate or destiny, rather than striving to improve matters. This sounds strangely like the therapeutic nihilism favoured by Joseph Conrad, that the cure is worse than the disease, and that problems should often be allowed to work themselves out without human intervention.

The name Icarus, glimpsed on the spacecraft just as it turns, perhaps suggests that it is hubris to imagine we can usurp the God-like power of creating new stars, although in the myth, Icarus' father tells him exactly how to use his wings, in which case it might also be read as a comment on the responsible use of science. However the denouement of the film, while making clear the human sacrifice required, also suggests that science can, and perhaps should, accept such challenges. The crew all die but the earth has a second chance, literally a new dawn, as a re-invigorated sun casts its rays across a snowscape. Actually shot in Stockholm, but with the iconic Sydney Opera House in the background (suggesting how far temperatures have dropped), the coda repeats Capa's dialogue from his earlier message on voice-over. This reminds us of the success criteria of the mission, an understated slight brightening of the sky, representing the continued survival of humanity, as we see a mother and children, presumably his family, playing in the snow.

The film ends with a sudden burst of Underworld's 'Peggy Sussed' (fusing 1970s glam-rock and electronica), which is arguably a dissonant way to end the film. As the credits roll, the music suddenly shifts to I Am Klute's 'Avenue of Hope' which musically and lyrically complements the film much better. Accompanying the music and the credits is a 'retrospective trailer' of key images on the left of the frame. It is a reminder of the journey that we have been on, fictionally and cinematically, in the preceding two hours as well as a nice way to keep people in their seats and see how many people played a part in the production.

The film does not provide the viewer with the instant gratification, associated with science fiction which, post-*Star Wars* especially, have been seen as adventures in space. As Boyle notes, 'the interesting thing is that the more commercial sci-fi films, like *Event Horizon* or *Alien*, tend to go for Hell in space. But maybe it's more ambitious to aim for Heaven'.[13] After the credits, the final sound heard is the distress signal from Icarus I, a mixture of whale-call and rusty hinge – either persistent and aggravating, or consoling and otherworldly, depending on your point of view.

Conclusion

A religious sensibility permeates Boyle's work, from overt religious concepts to the need he feels, particularly at the close of his narratives, to offer his audiences a repository of hope. Even in the bleakness of Trainspotting, hard drugs, casual sex, football and music offer portals to imaginative release. Murray Smith feels the film 'depicts poverty realistically, but in a way that encompasses possibilities of escape as well as stories of entrapment.'[14] Boyle seems to shy away from completely nihilistic endings – not always a problem-free option. Renton in *Trainspotting*, Alex in *Shallow Grave*, Robert and Celine in *A Life Less Ordinary*, all close their stories with a sense of pleasure. Through their experiences, being slightly more virtuous than those around them and relying on their own quick-wittedness, they have survived and come out ahead.

13 Danny Boyle cited by Kermode in *The Observer*, 25 March 2007.
14 Murray Smith cited in Petrie 2004 p.103.

Richard in *The Beach* is more problematic as he appears to gain little self-knowledge through the course of his experiences and remains unapologetic about his immorality. He still seems to be drawn to the blind hedonism of the myth of the beach, and his memories are sentimentalised in the group photo he presumably sends to others. Jim and Selena survive in *28 Days Later* via a mixture of luck and necessary brutality, although as with most apocalyptic narratives the underlying question of how a benevolent God could inflict such suffering remains unanswered. *Sunshine* overtly addresses matters of spirituality and represents Boyle's strongest statement on the potential positive influence of science, not so much in opposition to the notion of religion but as its complement, since human knowledge can be seen as God-given. In *Slumdog Millionaire*, knowledge of religion provides an answer to one of the questions (about the god Krishna), but organised religion is not generally seen as a force for social cohesion. It leads directly to the death of the boys' mother and is shown more as a reflection of tribal divisions, a label put on people by circumstances of family or birth, and little to do with the conscious embracing of philosophical ideas.

Like *The Beach*, *127 Hours* presents us with a central character whose spiritual dimension is largely dormant and whose empty life is underscored by the increasingly extreme means used to add thrills to it. Ralston's ability to withstand great physical and mental anguish could be seen as a tribute to the human spirit (and thereby to any deity attributed with its creation). However, the pain is self-inflicted, a direct result of hubris, and leads only to introspection of a narrowly personal variety. In neither film is any appeal for spiritual help seen as a meaningful activity in times of need. Like the children of the slums in *Slumdog Millionaire*, characters survive by the speed of their wits, their ability to outrun those who would hurt them and a fair degree of luck, rather than by recourse to prayer.

Ralston's offer to be a 'guide' to the girls he befriends suggests that he possesses special knowledge, almost like a priest interceding for his laity. His dismissal of 'the guide book' and his statement 'but I know a better way,' seems arrogant, especially in retrospect. Yet viewers may respond more positively to Ralston than to Richard, not only due to Boyle's use of flashbacks to humanise the trapped man, but also because the real Aron Ralston was trying to achieve something positive both prior to the incident (to break a lone climbing record in Colorado) and afterwards (he now earns his living as a motivational speaker). Indeed, his survival could be seen as something of a miracle, an example of divine intervention in which human hubris is punished, the subject undergoes a process of purgatory and through the extraordinary exercise of willpower (also God-given, some would say), he overcomes apparently insurmountable odds. The water that suffuses the early part of the film may not directly represent a force of baptism but it does convey the notion of taking the basics of life very much for granted. Boyle sees Ralston's ultimate survival less in terms of individualism than being driven by a greater awareness of how he is connected to those who love him. As Boyle notes, 'my take on Aron's story is that there's something wider and bigger that sustains us in the end.'[15]

15 Raphael in *Times Magazine*, 28 August 2010 p.23.

· CONCLUSION ·

'A heart of lightness...rather than darkness'
Boyle on the DVD commentary for *Sunshine*

As the film-star character Neelima Kumari says in *Q&A*, the book on which *Slumdog Millionaire* was based: 'a great artist is not one who merely fits into a genre, but one who defines a genre.'[1] The easier it is to categorise a Boyle film, the less accomplished the finished film seems to be. It is perhaps harder in this respect for a film like *Sunshine* to stand out. Science fiction (particularly when set in outer space) is an inherently derivative genre, as few of us have any experience of the environment shown on screen except with reference to other films. In trying to update screwball conventions, *A Life Less Ordinary* falls between several genres, while the flaws of *The Beach* derive in large part from Garland's novel and from Boyle's attempt to emulate *Apocalypse Now*. Boyle's first few films and his more recent output demonstrate a narrative pace and depth of characterisation that is missing from the mid-career films scripted by Alex Garland. *The Beach*, *28 Days Later* and *Sunshine* are all interesting but derive their fullest meaning in juxtaposition with Boyle's other films. *Trainspotting*, *Millions* (not so much 'a children's film' as an intelligent film featuring children) and *Slumdog Millionaire* transcend generic boundaries through their innovative use of original source material, their high-quality scripts, and their fusion of theatrical and filmic ambition – showcasing charismatic, engaging peformances in a variety of gritty realism and fantastical, 'impossible' sequences.

In the Introduction, I wondered whether David Fincher could have made *Slumdog Millionaire*. Such is Fincher's technical perfectionism that it is sometimes difficult for him to work effectively with actors who are not able to take technical direction – he needs to work with experienced professionals. Boyle's background is different. Like Fincher, he did not go to film school, but neither did he enter the film world through the parallel world of pop videos, the portal of choice for a growing band of indie rebels who have become mainstream directors (including Michel Gondry, Gore Verbinski and Spike Jonze). Compared to Fincher's tally of over 50 videos for a range of artists from Michael Jackson to Nine Inch Nails, Boyle has not directed a single one. However, a large number of

1 Swarup 2006 p.249.

his films feature musical 'numbers,' most obviously the song and dance fantasy in *A Life Less Ordinary*, the chase sequence in *Trainspotting*, the dance routine of *Slumdog*, the opening of *127 Hours* and even the final credit sequence of *Sunshine*, where distinctive music accompanies striking, rapidly edited visuals. Only *Strumpet* features a narrative about the music business and acts as a cautionary tale, showing the abasement of natural talent and spontaneity through music company packaging and media marketing.

Boyle and Fincher are both interested in the ways in which thought can be shown on screen but Boyle's approach is far more dynamic and disruptive of the continuity of the narrative. In both *Slumdog Millionaire* and *Benjamin Button* thought and memory are portrayed in distinctly cinematic terms: for example, in *Slumdog*, Jamal's memory of the Bollywood star Amitabh Bachchan is conveyed through a montage of defining heroic images, and in *Benjamin Button*, we have slower-paced editing, a voice-over commentary to create coherence and a series of flashbacks placed in precise chronological order. However, unlike *Button*, which is set in New Orleans and takes a panoramic view of American history from the Jazz Age of the 1920s through to the present day, *Slumdog* signals the end of each flashback by cutting back to the TV studio, thus acting as a reminder of contemporary media. In *Slumdog's* opening sequence in the TV studio, we see a split-screen effect, not demarcated by a rigid line as favoured by directors like Brian De Palma, but by the distinctive outline of Jamal's large ears in close-up. Boyle's challenge is to show his character thinking, and rather than do this, as Laurence Olivier did for his 'to be or not to be' soliloquy in *Hamlet* (1944) with the camera tracking towards his forehead, Boyle uses a mixture of rapid editing, eye-line matches and dialogue links. For example, the speech about his name, which begins in the torture scene, is effectively completed in Jamal's opening answers in the TV studio.

Boyle often opts for apparently simple solutions to the problem of representing movement, favouring shots that might seem theatrical in their occupation of real time and space, rather than a post-production dependence on CGI effects. In *Millions*, the way Boyle shows Damian's walk through the house is the polar opposite of a scene in David Fincher's *Panic Room* where, in a three-minute sequence, the camera passes around the interior of the house, through objects such as banisters and the handle on a coffee pot, that would be physically impossible. In *Millions*, we simply pass slowly via a crane-shot over the walls (and again later in *Slumdog* over the top of the cubicles in Pila Street, where individual prostitutes ply their trade, illustrating the set for what it is – an effect that is simple but still works). Rather than Fincher's elaborate computer-generated sequence, which appears to offer us a clear sense of the geography of a house but actually gives us the opposite in a pursuit of a technically perfect, fluid long take, Boyle's slow track over the rooms also suggests a God-like presence watching over the house, possibly even the spirit of the mother, the 'St Maureen' that Damian keeps asking about.[2]

Accepting his BAFTA for *Slumdog Millionaire*, Boyle quoted David Lean's maxim about making a film's ambition clear in the first five minutes. With the possible exception of *The Beach*, all of Boyle's films do this – think of the headlong tracking shots of *Shallow Grave*, *Trainspotting* and *Slumdog*, the deserted city in *28 Days Later* and the epic scale of *Sunshine*. Boyle's films have a powerful sense of forward momentum and appear to revel in the energy of their central characters.

Boyle's protagonists may be flawed and at times delusional but they are also figures of hope and redemption. The basic premise of Edwin Page's book on Boyle argues that his protagonists are 'ordinary' folk, but this study would suggest that exactly the opposite is true. In *Sunshine*, Capa is literally the world's best physicist and earth's last hope of survival. The trio of roles played by Ewan McGregor as Alex (*Shallow Grave*), Robert (*A Life Less Ordinary*) and Renton (*Trainspotting*) are all distinguished by exceptional wit and resourcefulness. Richard in *The Beach* is a complete fantasist given to bouts of self-delusion in which he sees himself as a commanding hero despite the fact that his behaviour shows him to be the exact opposite. No-one else in the film behaves like him.

Damian in *Millions* is far from ordinary, possessing the ability to see saints and having a strongly moral element to his faith. His generosity to others, especially in one so young, is highly unusual. It is the singularity of Jim that is stressed from the opening of *28 Days Later*, wandering the streets of London alone. It may be pure chance that allows him to survive initially, but he goes on to show a greater concern for others (in his care for Selena) than we see displayed by other characters, alongside the ability to be brutal when necessary (as with the infected child he must kill in the café). The very fact that he survives marks him as exceptional. Ralston performs the apparently impossible in *127 Hours*: it is hardly ordinary to survive alone for five days and then cut off one's own arm. It is precisely the extraordinary nature of this true story that makes it fascinating.

2   See Browning 2010.

The only character who does partially match Page's description is Jamal in *Slumdog*. He is ordinary in terms of where and how he lives, what he dreams about (film-stars and TV shows) and even how he reacts to what happens to him. He is a very unheroic hero forced to sit for much of the film, being quizzed either in a police station or a TV studio. However even here, what makes the film so powerful are not the everyday elements but the elevation of the premise from extremely unlikely social realism to the status of myth. In his single-minded pursuit of Latika, his shyness around her, his lack of interest in the money, it is his extraordinary nature that the film constantly underlines. If we can recognise ourselves in him, it is because he represents a better version of ourselves. Like the term 'ordinary,' Page does not really define 'hero,' stating that Hollywood heroes are necessarily 'muscular or macho', but outside the genre of action or gangster movies (neither touched upon by Boyle), this is not necessarily so. If heroism is seen as engaging in acts that are morally selfless, then Boyle's films are full of heroes: Robert risks his life to 'take a bullet' for Celine in *A Life Less Ordinary*, Jim acts heroically to save Selena from sexual imprisonment in *28 Days Later*, and if the final close-up of Capa in *Sunshine*, saving humankind by his battle to deliver the bomb, is not heroic, then it is hard to see what is.

At the same time, there is a contradictory impulse in Boyle's films, a tendency to include a Kurtz-like figure, a symbol of the human potential for evil, deriving from Joseph Conrad's *Heart of Darkness* (1899) by way of Francis Ford Coppola's *Apocalypse Now* (1979), who seeks to establish a community that is apparently based on a shared vision but is actually dominated by the will of a single egomaniac. Major West in *28 Days Later*, Sal in *The Beach*, Pinbacker in *Sunshine*, even the eponymous hero in *Mr Wroe's Virgins*, all seem to follow this pattern. In *Sunshine*, Pinbacker's video transmission and the focus on his manic eyes in a face masked with static, evokes Martin Sheen rising from the swamp in *Apocalypse Now*. Similarly in *28 Days Later* the red colour-wash used to convey the point of view of the Infected and the focus on their eyes as a key indicator of ill-health recall Coppola's close-ups of Sheen and Marlon Brando. However, it seems Boyle cannot bring himself to fully endorse this striving for a sense of the demonic: all his films offer the possibility of redemption. The use of I Am Klute's 'Avenue of Hope' over *Sunshine*'s end-credits has a melancholic wistfulness but also suggests the possibility of transcendence, which lies at the heart of Boyle's film aesthetic. *28 Days Later* was shot with two possible endings, one in which Jim is spotted by a reconnaissance plane and another, more pessimistic one, in which Jim dies. Even in the case of this second ending (shown in US theatres in response to viewers looking for the generic norm of a downbeat ending), his death still provokes tears of hope, rather than despair, from Selena.

In *Trainspotting*, over and above the ironic references like Swanney's nickname as 'Mother Superior,' the conscious choice of hard drugs could be said to represent a desire for some kind of transcendent, higher state of consciousness, akin to spiritual revelation. In this, the paraphernalia around drugs become the ritualistic tools of an alternative religion, the codes of behaviour it promotes constitute a kind of anti-faith, and episodes like Renton's overdose become a kind of resurrection. The purging of Renton, first in his own short-lived DIY attempt and then later at the behest of his parents, both have an element of religious ceremony about them. The buying of certain foods, the nailing oneself in, smacks of a mixture of Lenten, self-imposed privation: Lou Reed's lyrics 'you're gonna reap what you sow' (echoing Galatians chapter 6 verse 7) would suggest a judgemental Old Testament God, but more prevalent in the film is a more forgiving, flexible spirituality.

Boyle's approach is very much actor-focused. He rarely makes storyboards except when required by complex technical set-ups, unlike Fincher who composes whole sequences using pre-visualisation software. In the commentary for *Sunshine*, Boyle refers to actors as 'mini-directors,' who need to be overruled at times but who often provide the source of the best ideas. In terms of preparing the cast, he states 'everything's done for the actors as much as you can, especially something as technical as this…so everything's as real as possible'. During the filming of *Sunshine*, because many shots required the use of blue-screen technology, Boyle used a light-source like a disco glitterball so that the actors had some frame of reference to focus upon. This is particularly important in the 'Mercury-observation scene' as there are ensemble shots with multiple eye-lines, which in theory are all following the same object. His attention to detail *in performance* can be seen in casting athletes as the Infected in *28 Days Later* as he felt they would move differently to 'normal' people, or using actors rather than cheaper, non-professionals, as extras as the audience for Richard's shark story in *The Beach*, so that their reaction would be more animated.

Children, and their potential energy and chaos, seem central to Boyle. Even in a film like *Trainspotting*, where children do not figure at all (apart from the baby), there is a childishness to Renton and Spud, in the sense of a joyous energy and an openness to new experiences, even surreal ones at times. On the DVD extras for *Millions*, Boyle notes that the oft-quoted witticism about never working with children or animals was coined by actor W.C. Fields, who may well have been afraid of being upstaged. Certainly, the legal constraints governing the hours and locations that children can work can create logistical headaches: in *Millions* stand-ins had to be used for locations next to the railway track and for scenes filmed at night.

The three-shot in *Millions* in which the two boys sit with their father in front of the money for the first time is a good example of how Boyle tends to prefer to retain the integrity of the shot. He does not cut to close-ups and reaction shots and this could be said to hark back to his theatrical roots and a feeling that audiences know when they are being emotionally manipulated by editing. This is also reinforced by the use of the photograph at the end of *The Beach*, *Sunshine*'s closing montage and *Slumdog*'s dance sequence and closing credits, which all feel like cinematic versions of curtain calls.

Boyle's special effects do not always draw attention to themselves, like the portrayal of weightlessness in *Sunshine*, which took him an agonisingly long time to film. However *28 Days Later* shows a struggle between the dramatic integrity of a situation and the commercial thirst for spectacle. The petrol station explosion is not strictly necessary to the narrative: although it allows for a nice colour contrast, with orange fire placed in the middle of the frame surrounded by grey, it does have the look of a spectacular special effect for its own sake, particularly because it is shown from multiple viewpoints and in slow-motion. Perhaps the real special effect in Boyle's films are his actors and the performances he coaxes out of them. From his experience at the RSC and later in television with the BBC, Boyle's great strength is not so much what the camera is doing but what the actors are doing. On the DVD commentary for *Sunshine*, Boyle expresses an almost emotional attachment to the physical material of film (what used to be termed 'celluloid'), which he feels conveys a warmth that allows audiences to connect with an actor's performance in a way which digital production does not.

As in the theatre, Boyle prefers to work with a small crew and with an established 'company' of familiar faces. He seems more open to a genuinely collaborative process than many directors and likes to keep writers involved in the production process. Boyle is happy to adapt from novel to film quite freely but when a script is written, he tends to adhere to it. When he cuts material, he usually removes whole scenes rather than tinkering with individual lines too much, reflecting perhaps a respect for the lines-as-written, which may have its roots in his theatrical background. Although Boyle claimed no credit for the script of *Millions*, he and Cottrell Boyce worked on it for around a year, with the result that the only material that survived the re-writing process completely unscathed was the robbery sequence.

Boyle's tried and tested collaborators include John Murphy (music), Chris Gill (editor), Mark Tildesley (production design), John Hodge and Alex Garland (writers) and in the last decade particularly, Anthony Dod Mantle (cinematography) and Fox Searchlight (production company). This might make him look slightly 'cliquey,' but films take so many years of preparation − often it is incredible that films get made at all − that it is not surprising that when he finds individuals who make the impossible possible, he wants to work with them again. It is something of a movie cliché that directors remake their first film over and over, but in Boyle's directing choices one might see an attempt to rediscover the 'innocence' of his first directing experience. Certainly *Shallow Grave* casts a shadow over later work, but that is no bad thing. The producer-writer team (Andrew Macdonald and John Hodge), the leading men (Chris Eccleston and Ewan McGregor) and even narrative features, such as a suicide and a scene with a vote (*Sunshine*), the discovery of a mystery bag of cash (*Millions*) and the use of game shows (*Slumdog Millionaire*) − all reappear elsewhere.

The kind of stories to which Boyle is drawn tells us much about him as a filmmaker. He certainly seems attracted to unlikely-sounding projects. On the face of it, *Slumdog Millionaire*, a film about a TV quiz show, does not sound like the stuff of riveting cinema. However, therein lies the challenge and this is a key element in Boyle's selection of projects. He seems to pursue a sense of the impossible, to paint himself into corners from which only his creativity can rescue him. In *Trainspotting*, Renton deliberately rips off Begbie because he knows it is only by making a return impossible that he can escape his old life: there is a similar sense of 'burning bridges' as Boyle moves from one film project to the next. There seems to be a conscious desire to choose films that create the edginess of his first film, *Shallow Grave*, a sense of not quite knowing how he will get out of it. When he is asked in interviews about any of his films during production, he will often reply 'I don't know'. This restlessness with which he imbues his productions is reflected in the forward-drive of his narratives and in his attitude: he will even change seats between rounds of promotional interviews to create a sense of freshness in his responses.

This restless attraction to unpredictability, almost a courting of risk, is reflected in the way in which he makes films. In *Strumpet*, there is a great shot with the camera strapped beneath a van, giving a sense of headlong motion but also reflecting Boyle's guerrilla-style aesthetic. Rejecting the bloated budgets and crews of *The Beach*, embracing film-making that is fast, open to changing circumstances and based on small budgets, modest-sized crews and light-weight digital technology, this is closer to his dynamic and cinematic sense of vision. In such shots, he affirms not just the vitality of the lives he portrays but cinema's creative potential in representing it.

Linked to this is a sense of disbelief in the life he is leading, that his successes are in some ways undeserved. Certainly in interviews he still blushes at compliments, batting them away with an element of schoolboy shyness. Along with several other directors, including David Cronenberg, he was offered *Alien Resurrection* (ultimately directed by Jean Pierre Jeunet in 1997) but claims he rejected the opportunity because it was a franchise and the distinctive nature of each project seems important to him, but adding a little cheekily that he only turned it down 'after we got to meet Sigourney and Winona.'[3] It is as if he is engaged in a never-ending pursuit of the impossible, to recreate the conditions of uncertainty from his very first experience at directing.

Like many successful theatre directors, Boyle displays prodigious stamina and endless enthusiasm, driving projects forward by willpower alone. It seems ridiculous in retrospect that until Fox Searchlight stepped in, *Slumdog* could have been without a distribution deal, but Boyle did not give up. In his own approach to filmmaking as well as the films themselves, Danny Boyle is an inspirational character to those around him. Like the endings of all his films, where he is determined in his own words to 'give the audience something,' his hours of painstaking preparation, his shooting style on set, his relationships with actors, even his manner in the tiresome grind of promoting a film, are all dominated by a strong sense of faith, a belief perhaps not necessarily religious in nature, but a belief in himself and the integrity of the story he wants to tell.

Managing to eschew both cloying sentimentality and cynical pessimism, Boyle's narratives are full of choices that are braver from a commercial and emotional perspective than they might at first seem. At one extreme, much of the humour in *Shallow Grave* and *A Life Less*

---

3   Danny Boyle cited by Callaghan in *New York Magazine*, 15 July 1996 p.39.

Ordinary is brutal and often not particularly engaging, but the more dominant impression, through films like *Trainspotting* and *Slumdog*, is that vitality wins out over cynicism, especially in the latter where love really does conquer all. *Millions*, with its quirky child hero, addresses passionate religious belief directly and non-judgmentally and *Sunshine's* consideration of humanity's place in the cosmos leads to a final heroic act of self-sacrifice. It is possible to read *The Beach* as symbolic of man's attempt to re-appropriate paradise, but the film's weakness is that its characters really only speak to themselves, and fail to look outside their narrow lives to see how self-indulgent they really are.

Boyle's dominant subject matter is people and the forces that bind them together – friendship (*Shallow Grave* and Trainspotting), hedonism (*The Beach*), religious faith (*Millions*), survival (*28 Days Later* and *127 Hours*) and love (*A Life Less Ordinary* and *Slumdog Millionaire*). At the close of all his films, with the exception of *The Beach*, there is a sense of transcendence, of lives being enriched rather than impoverished and a re-affirmed belief in human integrity. Iggy Pop's iconic 'Lust for Life' not only helped complement Boyle's breakthrough success with *Trainspotting*, it also represents his cinematic mantra.

BIBLIOGRAPHY

Books and articles cited

Blandford, Steven, *Film, Drama and the Break-Up of Britain* (Bristol: Intellect Books, 2007).

Boyle, Danny, at http://www.cilliansite.com/production-notes/28-days-later-prod-notes.pdf

—————, 'Mumbai Rising', *Sight and Sound* vol. 12 no. 2, February 2009, p.42.

—————, 'Into the heart of the sun', *The Guardian*, 6 April 2007, p.16.

Brooks, Xan, 'The Beach', *Sight and Sound* vol. 10 no. 3, March 2000, pp.39-40.

Callaghan, Maureen, 'The Scottish Invasion', *New York Magazine*, 15 July 1996, p.39.

Carroll, Noel, *The Philosophy of Horror or Paradoxes of the Heart* (New York: Routledge, 1990).

Cottrell Boyce, Frank, *Millions* (London: Macmillan Children's Books, 2004).

Browning, Mark, *Stephen King on the Big Screen* (Bristol: Intellect Books, 2009).

—————, *David Fincher: Films That Scar* (Santa Barbara, CA: ABC-CLIO, 2010).

—————, *Wes Anderson: Why His Movies Matter* (Santa Barbara, CA: ABC-CLIO, 2011).

Cavell, Stanley, *Pursuits of Happiness: The Hollywood Comedy of Remarriage* (Cambridge, Mass: Harvard University Press, 1981).

De Botton, Alain, *The Art of Travel* (London: Penguin, 2003; first published by Hamish Hamilton, 2002).

Finney, Angus, *The State of European Cinema* (New York: Cassell, 1996).

Forster, E.M., *Room with a View* (London: Penguin, 1908).

Garland, Alex, *The Beach* (London: Penguin, 1997; first published by Viking, 1996).

—————, *Sunshine* (London: Faber & Faber, 2007).

Gehring, Wes, *Screwball Comedy: Defining a Film Genre* (Muncie, Ind.: Ball State University Press, 1983).

Genette, Gérard, *Palimpsests: Literature in the Second Degree* (Lincoln: University of Nebraska Press, 1997).

Hodge, John, *The Beach* (London: Faber and Faber, 2000).

Kelly, Richard, *The Name of this Book is Dogme95* (London: Faber & Faber, 2000).

Kemp, Philip, 'Trainspotting', *Sight and Sound* vol. 6 no. 3, March 1996, pp.52-53.

Kermode, Mark, '28 Days Later', *Sight and Sound* vol. 12 no. 12, December 2002, pp.59-60.

—————, '2007: a scorching new space odyssey', *The Observer*, 25 March, 2007, http://www.guardian.co.uk/film/2007/mar/25/sciencefictionspecial.features

McFarlane, Brian, *Novel to Film: An Introduction to the Theory of Adaptation* (Oxford: Oxford University Press, 1996).

Miller, Toby, *Cultural Policy*, (Core Cultural Theorists, 39) (Thousand Oaks, CA: Sage Publications, 2002).

Mitchell, W.J.T. (ed.),: *On Narrative* (Chicago: University of Chicago Press, 1981).

Moore, Harry (ed.), *D.H. Lawrence, Collected Letters, Volume I* (London: Heinemann, 1962).

Morace, Robert A., *Irvine Welsh's Trainspotting: A Reader's Guide* (New York: Continuum, 2001).

Mulhall, Stephen (ed.), *The Cavell Reader* (Hoboken, NJ: Blackwell, 1996).

Murray, Robin L., Joseph K. Heumann, *Ecology and Popular Film: Cinema on the Edge* (New York: State University of New York Press, 2009).

Neale, Steve, *Genre* (London: BFI, 1980).

O'Hagan, Andrew, 'The Boys Are Back in Town', *Sight and Sound* vol. 6 no. 2, February 1996, p.7.

Page, Edwin, *Ordinary Heroes: the Films of Danny Boyle* (London: Empiricus Books, 2009).

Petrie, Duncan J., *Contemporary Scottish Fictions: Film, Television and the Novel* (Edinburgh: Edinburgh University Press, 2004).

Raphael, Amy, *Danny Boyle: In His Own Words* (London: Faber & Faber, 2011).

Sarris, Andrew, 'The Sex Comedy Without Sex', *American Film*, 3:5 (1978).

Schrader, Paul, *Transcendental Style in Film* (Berkeley: University of California Press, 1972).

Sobchack, Thomas and Vivian C. Sobchack, *An Introduction to Film* (Boston: Little, Brown, 1980).

Smith, Murray, *Trainspotting* (London, 2002).

Stam, Robert and Alessandra Raengo (eds), *Literature and Film: A Guide to the Theory and Practice of Adaptation* (Malden: Blackwell, 2005).

Stollery, Martin, *Trainspotting* (London: York Press, 2001).

Street, Sarah, *British National Cinema* (London: Routledge, 1997).

Swarup, Vikas, *Q&A* (London: Swan Books, 2006).

Terashima, Nobuyoshi, *HyperReality: Paradigm for the Third Millennium* (New York: Routledge, 2001).

Welsh, Irvine, *Trainspotting* (London: Vintage, 2004; first published by Secker & Warburg, 1993).

Williams, Linda, *Hard Core: Power, Pleasure and 'The Frenzy of the Visible'* (Berkeley: University of California Press, 1989).

Wright, Will, *Six-guns and Society: A Structural Study of the Western* (Berkeley: University of California Press, 1977).

Žižek, Slavoj, *The Fright of Real Tears: Krzysztof Kieślowski Between Theory and Post-Theory* (London: BFI, 2001).

FILMOGRAPHY

Shallow Grave (1994)
Channel Four Films. Director Danny Boyle; scriptwriter John Hodge; cinematography Brian Tufano; music Simon Boswell; distributor Film4 and PolyGram Filmed Entertainment. Running time: 89 minutes. Cast includes Alex (Ewan McGregor), David (Christopher Eccleston), Kery Fox (Julia) and Keith Allen (Hugo).

In an elegant Edinburgh townhouse, Alex, David and Julia lead lives of selfish pleasure until they find their new flatmate, Hugo, dead in his room along with a suitcase full of cash. They keep the money and dispose of Hugo's body, but both the police and the criminal owners of the money are on their trail. The resulting tensions force the three main characters to decide what kind of people they really are and whether their relationship is one of close friendship or rivalry.

*Trainspotting (*1996)
Channel Four Films and Figment Films. Director Danny Boyle; scriptwriter John Hodge; cinematography Brian Tufano; music various artists; distributor Film4 and PolyGram Filmed Entertainment. Running time: 90 minutes. Cast includes Ewan McGregor (Renton), Jonny Lee Miller (Sick Boy), Robert Carlyle (Begbie), Ewen Bremner (Spud), Kelly Macdonald (Diane) and Kevin McKidd (Tommy).

Renton is one of a group of heroin addicts in Edinburgh in the 1990s. His everyday life is dominated by a life of petty crime and increasingly desperate lies to allow him to gain his next hit. He struggles to maintain any kind of meaningful relationship and despite attempts to get clean, repeatedly fails to do so. Finally, he realises it is only by breaking away from his friends (the clueless Spud, the innocent Tommy, the amoral but entertaining Sick Boy and even the psychotic Begbie) that he can hope for a normal life. Sick Boy's plan of a drug deal in London presents Renton with a stark choice – his friends or the possibility of making it to 30 years of age. Will he 'choose life'?

A Life Less Ordinary (1997)
Film4 and Figment Films. Director Danny Boyle; scriptwriter John Hodge; cinematography Brian Tufano; music supervisor Randall Poster; distributor PolyGram Filmed Entertainment. Running time: 99 minutes. Cast includes Ewan McGregor (Robert), Cameron Diaz (Celine), Holly Hunter (O'Reilly), Delroy Lindo (Jackson) and Ian Holm (Naville).

In Heaven, the angel Gabriel decides to test whether true love is possible in the modern world by giving angels O'Reilly and Jackson an apparently impossible task: to make a romantic relationship work. In modern-day California, they set their sights on Robert, a cleaner, and Celine, the spoiled daughter of Robert's boss, Mr Naville. Robert's grand plan of kidnapping Celine and demanding a ransom starts to unravel as it becomes clear that Robert is a terrible kidnapper and that Celine knows far more about violent crime than he does. Naville unwittingly employs O'Reilly and Jackson as bounty hunters to track down his daughter.

The Beach (2000)

Twentieth Century-Fox. Director Danny Boyle; scriptwriter John Hodge; cinematography Darius Khondji; music Angelo Badalamenti; distributor Twentieth Century-Fox. Running time: 119 minutes. Cast includes Leonardo DiCaprio (Richard), Virginie Ledoyen (Françoise), Guillaume Canet (Étienne), Robert Carlyle (Daffy) and Tilda Swinton (Sal).

Richard is looking for the ultimate backpacking experience. In a Thailand hostel, he is approached by Daffy who tells him about a mythic beach, unparalleled in beauty. Richard persuades fellow travellers Françoise and Étienne to go with him to the island, which they find is populated by an alternative community led by the dictatorial and manipulative Sal. Richard betrays his fledgling relationship with Françoise by sleeping with Sal and finds that the isolation of patrolling the island begins to affect his sanity. When another backpacking group try to reach the island using a map given to them by Richard, the stability of the community is threatened.

Vacuuming Completely Nude in Paradise (2001)

BBC TV in association with BBC Worldwide Americas Inc. Director Danny Boyle; scriptwriter Jim Cartwright; cinematography Anthony Dod Mantle; music John Murphy. Running time: 75 minutes. Cast includes Timothy Spall (Tommy Rag), Michael Begley (Pete) and Katy Cavanagh (Sheila).

Tommy Rag is an odious, corrupt, fast-talking and completely unprincipled vacuum cleaner salesman, who is forced to take on a trainee, Pete, and show him the tricks of the trade (of which there are plenty). Pete sees close up how Tommy swindles vulnerable people out of their last penny and what Tommy is prepared to do to win the coveted Golden Vac, awarded every year at a prestigious ceremony in Blackpool. This year, Tommy resorts to even more underhand tactics than usual to win.

Strumpet (2001)

BBC TV in association with BBC Worldwide Americas Inc. Director Danny Boyle; scriptwriter Jim Cartwright; cinematography Anthony Dod Mantle; music John Murphy. Running time: 72 minutes. Cast includes Christopher Eccleston (Strayman), Genna G (Strumpet) and Stephen Walters (Knockoff).

Strumpet is an iterant musician in an unnamed northern town in modern-day England, who befriends Strayman, an enigmatic poet known for writing on any available surface. Together the two record a single, which takes the charts by storm and under the tutelage of aspiring manager, Knockoff, they head for a live performance on *Top of the Pops*. A life of fame and fortune beckons but Strayman's uncompromising approach is not quite what the London-based record executives are expecting.

28 Days Later (2002)

Twentieth Century-Fox. Director Danny Boyle; scriptwriter Alex Garland; cinematography Anthony Dod Mantle; music John Murphy; distributor Fox Searchlight. Running time: 108 minutes. Cast includes Cillian Murphy (Jim), Naomie Harris (Selena), Christopher Eccleston (Major West), Hannah (Megan Burns) and Brendan Gleeson (Frank).

Jim wakes from a coma in a London hospital to find the city apparently deserted. He soon discovers that the country has been abandoned after animal rights activists, in freeing some chimps used for experimentation, set loose a disease called Rage that changes sufferers into homicidal maniacs. He befriends fellow survivors Selena, Frank and Hannah, and the group set off for apparent safety in an army base set up near Manchester. However, the leader of the base, Major West, is not all that he appears to be and sanctuary is the very last thing he is offering.

Millions (2004)

Twentieth Century-Fox. Director Danny Boyle; scriptwriter Frank Cottrell Boyce; cinematography Anthony Dod Mantle; music John Murphy; distributor Fox Searchlight. Running time: 95 minutes. Cast includes Alex Etel (Damian), Lewis McGibbon (Anthony), James Nesbitt (Ronnie), Daisy Donovan (Dorothy).

Damian and Anthony Cunningham are two boys living ordinary lives in a modern town in northern England until Damian finds a bag of money, mysteriously left by the railway that backs onto their garden. He takes this as a gift from God and tries to use the money to do good but soon finds this is more difficult than he expects. When his father Ronnie and new girlfriend Dorothy find out, they join the boys in a race to convert the money into euros: the country is changing to the new currency in a few days' time and the sterling notes will be worthless. Then the man who stole the money from a mail train appears and the brothers' problems really begin.

Sunshine (2007)

Twentieth Century-Fox. Director Danny Boyle; scriptwriter Alex Garland; cinematography Alwin Küchler; music John Murphy and Underworld; distributor Fox Searchlight. Running time: 127 minutes. Cast includes Rose Byrne (Cassie), Cliff Curtis (Searle), Chris Evans (Mace), Troy Garity (Harvey), Cillian Murphy (Capa), Hiroyuki Sanada (Kaneda), Benedict Wong (Trey) and Michelle Yeoh (Corazon).

In the near future, the earth is suffering from a dying sun. In a last-ditch effort to re-animate it, the spacecraft Icarus II sets out, carrying a massive bomb to drop onto the sun and hopefully restart its chemical reactions. Disaster soon strikes as a mathematical error leads to an error with vital heat shields and the crew lose their captain, Kaneda, as he seeks to repair the damage. Chief physicist Capa must then decide if they should divert from their main mission to answer a distress beacon apparently emanating from Icarus I, which disappeared in space some 16 years earlier under mysterious circumstances.

Slumdog Millionaire (2008)

Twentieth Century-Fox. Director Danny Boyle; scriptwriter Simon Beaufoy; cinematography Anthony Dod Mantle; music A.R. Rahman; distributor Fox Searchlight and Pathé Pictures. Running time: 115 minutes. Cast includes Dev Patel, (Jamal), Madhur Mittal (Salim), Freida Pinto (Latika), Anil Kapoor (Prem), Irrfan Khan (Inspector).

Jamal, a humble call-centre worker in Mumbai, reaches the final stage of *Who Wants to be a Millionaire?* However, just before the final question, he is arrested on suspicion of fraud. How can a child born into extreme poverty, a 'slumdog', know all the answers? Under interrogation, including torture, Jamal explains how and in doing so, he tells the story of his life - how he became estranged from his criminal brother Salim and separated from the love of his life, Latika.

127 Hours (2010)

Twentieth Century-Fox. Director Danny Boyle; scriptwriters Danny Boyle and Simon Beaufoy; cinematography Anthony Dod Mantle and Enrique Chediak; music A.R. Rahman; distributor Fox Searchlight and Pathé Pictures. Running time: 93 minutes. Cast includes James Franco (Aron Ralston), Kate Mara (Kristi) and Amber Tamblyn (Megan), Treat Williams (Aron's father), Lizzy Caplan (Sonja).

Aron Ralston is a young thrill-seeker, drawn to extreme sports and living a life of carefree hedonistic pleasure until one day a hike in Utah goes horribly wrong and he becomes trapped in a crevice with a huge boulder pinning down one arm. He survives for several days through a mixture of luck and ingenuity but slowly realises that he can only survive by taking the most drastic action imaginable.

INDEX OF NAMES

INDEX OF FILMS

HAVERING SIXTH FORM
COLLEGE LIBRARY

This book is due for return on or before the last date shown below.